Economics and Prestige
in a Maya Community

Economics and Prestige in a Maya Community

The Religious Cargo System in Zinacantan

Frank Cancian

Stanford University Press
Stanford, California

Stanford University Press
Stanford, California
© 1965 by the Board of Trustees of the
Leland Stanford Junior University
Printed in the United States of America
Original edition 1965
Reprinted 1969

To Franzi

Foreword

This book is the first of several that will result from work sponsored by the Harvard Chiapas Project. The Project was initiated in 1957 and will continue in the decades to come to study a variety of ethnographic and social anthropological problems in the Highland Maya area of the Tzotzil and Tzeltal Indians of Southern Mexico. These Indian communities in the high, pine-covered mountains of central Chiapas constitute one of the most interesting surviving pockets of American Indian culture in the New World, and hence provide a field site of major importance for the development and testing of new methods for ethnographic description and for the analysis of the processes of change. The recent work with the Tzotzil and Tzeltal has already been productive in providing hypotheses of interest to archaeologists for interpreting ancient Maya patterns, in supplying field situations in which young ethnographers and linguists could develop new methods for the elicitation and analysis of data, and in giving us a series of successive and cumulative readings on the trends of social and cultural change as these Indian societies begin to adapt more and more to the modern world.

Professor Cancian's penetrating study of the religious hierarchy in Zinacantan is a most appropriate first volume because it superbly demonstrates the contributions to basic ethnography and to anthropological method and theory that are possible in a long-range project. Since 1957, each year has brought increasingly closer rapport with our Indian informants and increasing precision in our understanding of the complex life of Zinacantan. The project has been based not upon "re-visits" but rather upon "continuous field study" by at least one observer since 1957. Add to this the methodological and theoretical sophistication with which Professor Cancian handles his field data, and the result reaches a level of precision and a sharpness of focus that has been all too rare in Middle American ethnological studies.

Professor Cancian provides us with an intensive ethnographic study of a crucial institution of contemporary Middle American Indian communities. This institution is variously labeled the "civil-religious hierarchy," the "cargo system," the "ceremonial ladder," etc. But whatever it is called, it constitutes one of the keys to understanding the social, religious, and economic system of the Indian *municipios*. His description of this cargo system, based on 18 months of interviewing and observation, is the most detailed and most systematic that has appeared.

But Professor Cancian does more than describe the cargo system. He goes on to analyze it, skillfully using statistical methods, demographic models, and a brilliant treatment of functional theory to test hypotheses and to demonstrate how the cargo system functions in Zinacanteco life. The results of this analysis will be of interest and significance not only to social scientists concerned with developing new concepts and methods, but also to economic planners and to policy-makers involved in the problems of communities of this type in the underdeveloped regions of the world.

Finally, Professor Cancian has been courageous enough to set down some predictions as to what will happen as the growing population outstrips the number of available positions in the cargo system and the increasing surplus wealth of the Zinacantecos can no longer be effectively exchanged for prestige in this ceremonial ladder. He predicts that the importance of the cargo system as the social institution through which the community is integrated will be destroyed. While I find his data impressive and his argument persuasive, I do not entirely agree with his predictions, and we have a spirited discussion on this issue whenever we meet. I think it possible either that the community will undergo some kinds of fission which will ultimately lead to the development of additional cargo systems or that the present cargos may become restricted to an emerging economic elite. The strength of a long-range project of the type we are operating in Chiapas is that we shall be able, a decade or two hence, to check and see whose predictions were correct and thereby test our data, methods, and theories against events in the "real world" of the Zinacantecos as they adapt to modern trends and conditions.

Professor Cancian's volume will shortly be followed by a general ethnography entitled *Zinacantan: A Maya Community in the Highlands of Chiapas,* which I am writing, and by three additional specialized monographs (now in thesis form) that will substantially supplement our knowledge of religion in the community: Robert M. Laughlin on Zinacantan mythology, John D. Early, S.J., on Zinacantan ritual life, and Daniel B. Silver on Shamanism in Zinacantan. In the meantime, the interested reader who knows Spanish may find additional information in Evon Z. Vogt (editor), *Ensayos Sobre Zinacantan,* Colección de Antropología Social, Instituto Nacional Indigenista, Mexico, 1965.

Evon Z. Vogt

June 1, 1965

Acknowledgments

The data on which this study is based were gathered in Zinacantan, a township of Tzotzil-speaking Maya Indians in the Mexican state of Chiapas. Between August 1960 and August 1962, 18 months were spent in the field. The research was done as part of the Harvard Chiapas Project, which is directed by Professor Evon Z. Vogt, and the first year of fieldwork was supported by funds from Grant MH-2100 made to the project by the National Institute of Mental Health (NIMH). The project is sponsored by the Laboratory of Social Relations and the Peabody Museum of American Archaeology and Ethnology at Harvard University, and by the Instituto Nacional Indigenista in Mexico. During the remainder of the fieldwork, and during the period of writing an earlier version that was submitted to the Department of Social Relations, Harvard University, as a doctoral dissertation, I was supported by NIMH Pre-doctoral Fellowship MPH-17,719. Further analysis of data and part of the rewriting into the present form were supported by NIMH Small Grant MH-08261. A grant from the Milton Fund of Harvard University made possible a short field trip in the summer of 1964.

Among the many residents of San Cristobal Las Casas, Chiapas, to whom I am grateful for friendship and help during the field period, I would like especially to thank the late Franz Blom, Gertrude Duby de Blom, and Leopoldo Velasco Robles and his family.

My debt to Zinacanteco informants can be seen again and again in the pages that follow. Domingo de la Torre, Manuel Perez con Dios, Juan Vasquez Shulhol, Pedro Perez con Dios, Antonia Gonzales, and their families were principally responsible for making work and social life in Zinacantan pleasant as well as productive.

Besides the usual debts, I owe a special one to Professor Vogt and the others who worked in Zinacantan on the Harvard Chiapas Project. Their work on other aspects of Zinacantan society and culture made it possible for me to focus on a limited topic with good conscience, and their knowledge made it possible for me to learn more about Zinacantan more quickly than would otherwise have been possible. I am particularly grateful to Nick and Lore Colby, George and Jane Collier, Robert and Mimi Laughlin, and Manuel and Carmen Zabala Cubillos, and thankful for the opportunity to have been associated with the project approach to intensive ethnography. Many fellow anthropologists from the University of Chicago and Stanford University who worked in the area were also helpful.

Bo Anderson, T. O. Beidelman, Francesca Cancian, Dr. Laughlin, Professor Vogt, and Robert Holloway of the Stanford University Press read all or part of the manuscript, and the book has been improved in the many places where I accepted their advice.

Since 1959, when he first interested me in the research reported here, Professor Vogt has assisted me, intellectually and practically, in bringing it to completion. I deeply appreciate his continuing interest, and hope that the product justifies his effort. My wife, Francesca, who worked on an independent project in Zinacantan, has given my work an incalculable amount of time and intellectual energy, and has contributed immensely to whatever clarity this presentation may have.

F. C.

Contents

Tables and Illustrations

FIGURES

MAPS

Eight pages of photographs follow p. 110.

Economics and Prestige
in a Maya Community

Two ritual kinsmen
(compadres) exchange words:

Look, compadre, you don't
have to talk to me in that tone.
I passed a cargo, too, you know.

That cargo, compadre, my wife
could pass that cargo!

One
Introduction

This is a study of the cargo system in the township[G] of Zinacantán, Chiapas, Mexico. The cargos are religious offices occupied on a rotating basis by the men of the community. That is, the office-holders serve for a year and then return to their roles in everyday life, leaving the office to another man. The incumbents receive no pay for their year of service. Rather they spend substantial amounts of money sponsoring religious celebrations for the saints of the Catholic church.

As in many communities in the Maya area (Nash 1958), the cargos in Zinacantan are arranged in a hierarchy so that a man may occupy a number of offices in a specified order. In Zinacantan a man may serve in any one of 34 cargos at the lowest level, if he has not had previous experience. After "resting" a number of years and clearing away his debts, he may pass on to one of the 12 offices of the second level. Then there are six offices on the third level, and two on the fourth and final level of the hierarchy. Almost all Zinacantecos participate at the first level; but clearly, for sheer lack of space if for no other reason, few of these men ever reach the top level.

[G] In an attempt to keep my exposition as uncluttered as possible, I have used English glosses for most Spanish and Tzotzil words. This seems desirable inasmuch as I am trying to describe and analyze a social system, not make an ethnographic dictionary. The glosses are identified at their first occurrence by the superscript letter G, and Spanish and Tzotzil equivalents for them are given in the Glossary, pp. 225–26. The following Spanish and Tzotzil terms do occur in the text: names of civil and religious positions, which are used as proper names; a few agricultural terms, which are defined as they occur in the text; and *cargo, Ladino,* and *moletik.* Spanish words are accented on first occurrence only.

The degree and manner of a man's participation in the hierarchy is the major factor in determining his place in the community. As Manning Nash has pointed out, "the hierarchy is virtually the entire social structure of the Indian municipio. At the most general level of social integration this structure does [for] Indians what kinship does for African societies, and what the social class system does for Ladino societies" (1958: 68).

I have three purposes in writing this book: (1) to make an ethnographic record of the cargo system in Zinacantan; (2) to analyze the community-wide social structure of Zinacantan as it can be seen in the cargo system; and (3) to give support to a number of methodological and metatheoretical points by illustrating their value as tools for understanding the cargo system in Zinacantan.[1] The first two purposes are rather straightforward and need no further discussion here. Any monograph that did not accomplish the first, and to some degree the second, would be deficient.

The concern with method and metatheory may be divided into two principal areas: (1) the employment of extensive samples of individual behavior in making generalizations about social structure; and (2) the demonstration, through the functional analysis of change, of the validity of synchronic functional analysis.

Wherever possible the present study tries to generalize about social structure on the basis of extensive samples of individual behavior. Thus, it produces a record that carries information about exceptions to its own generalizations. While I have concentrated on what Zinacantecos do, I have tried not to forget the fact that knowing what the subject of study thinks is an indispensable aid in figuring out what he is doing; I am as often concerned with what is particularly important to Zinacantecos as I am with what is displayed in their behavior as I see it.

The use of extensive samples of individual behavior may be con-

---

[1] I use the term "metatheory" to refer to the examination of the logical implications and consistency of theories and concept systems. This examination does not include evaluation of their power in handling empirical materials; but since the ultimate aim is improved ability to handle empirical materials, the theories and concept systems selected for metatheoretical examination are ones that hold promise of practical utility.

trasted with two other approaches to the study of social structure:
(1) the approach that generalizes about social structure on the
basis of intensive analysis of a few "crucial" cases, and therefore
carries little information about the actual proportion of the population that follows any particular pattern; and (2) the approach
that generalizes about social structure on the basis of information
about norms, and therefore carries virtually no information about
what people actually do. Many anthropologists are able to argue
convincingly that the proper goal of a field study is the production
of a report showing how the native system makes coherent sense
as a way of looking at the world and a way of living. I cannot object to this goal, but I think that the usual way of attaining it leaves
too much to the imagination of the anthropologist. The more
powerful his intellect and imagination, the more likely the anthropologist is to use this power to create coherence, whatever the
actual situation. Careful attention to extensive samples of behavior
may help avoid these dangers.

Too much and not enough have already been written about
functional analysis. My excuse for adding Chapter 13 to this literature of ambiguous status is that the detailed case described in this
book throws some light on the problems of such analysis. The
chapter is offered as a working paper developed in the course of
my thinking about the analysis of this case, not as a polished
piece of metatheoretical writing.

Plan of the Book

The book may be divided into four parts: background for the
study (Chapters 2 and 3); a description of the cargoholders and
their activities (Chapters 4 through 6); a synchronic analysis of
the cargo system as the basis for the community-wide social structure of Zinacantan (Chapters 7 through 12); a diachronic analysis
of the same (Chapters 14 through 16). Chapter 13 is the logical
link between the last two parts. Though at some points I have in-
tentionally sacrificed rapid development of the argument in order
to record ethnographic detail that is only marginally relevant to
the present study, each part rests on what has preceded it. The

appendixes include a description of the field procedures, selected detailed examples of ethnographic materials, and summaries of data and procedures used in the analysis of social and economic stratification.

Zinacantan and Zinacantecos are characterized briefly in Chapter 2. Chapter 3 brings the focus upon public life in Zinacantan and delimits the sector of public life that is the cargo system. With this background the description of fieldwork (Appendix A) may be read by those interested in the conditions under which the study was done.

The complex elaboration of formal roles and ritual activities in the cargo system (Chapters 4 through 6) will probably be as much of a burden to the reader as it is to the uninitiated observer. In the end, however, the effort put into unraveling the complexity is handsomely repaid. Each cargo and each auxiliary role has explicitly defined responsibilities and a consistent set of duties. And, differing amounts of talent and differing degrees of wealth are required to play each of the roles. Thus, the cargo system includes a well-defined variety that becomes, for the anthropologist as well as for the native, a way of distinguishing and classifying individuals.

The third part comes to the heart of the matter. The cargo system is viewed as a system in which money is exchanged for personal prestige. Since the expenditure of economic resources in the cargo system is the key to differentiating the individuals who serve in it, the third part begins with a discussion of corn farming, the means of livelihood of almost all Zinacantecos (Chapter 7).

Comparison of the typical earnings described in Chapter 7 and the expenses of cargos described in Chapter 8 immediately supports the proposition that the more expensive cargos are open only to the rich, and consequently performance in the cargo system is a measure of a man's economic success. With this proposition in mind, a scale of relative costs of all cargos on each level is constructed. Economic factors, however, do not always determine the amount of prestige that accrues to a man because of his service in a cargo. A few cargos, principally because of their traditional authority, bring prestige out of proportion to the required expenditures. Another scale, representing the Zinacanteco's view of the relative prestige rank of cargos, is constructed.

Chapter 9 digresses slightly to review the manner in which Zinacantecos perceive and meet the economic problems involved in passing cargos. It is demonstrated that rich persons do participate fully in the cargo system, as the norms of the society demand. It is also shown that a kin group has a distinct advantage in meeting the organizational problems that confront every cargoholder. This latter advantage results in greater participation by members of larger families.

In Chapter 10 it is demonstrated, taking cargo performance as an index, that Zinacantan society is stratified in terms of both wealth and prestige. This stratification is seen both in the participation of individuals during their lifetimes, and in the participation of sons and their fathers over generations. Finally, it is demonstrated that the selection of marriage partners follows the same patterns.

Chapter 11 examines the data on the proportion of Zinacantecos who participate in the cargo system, and the consequences which this participation has for the definition of the boundary of the Zinacanteco community.

In Chapter 12 the integrative functions or consequences of the cargo system for the community are reviewed, and a difference between my interpretation of the important consequences and that normally made by Middle Americanists is discussed.

Chapter 13 is a metatheoretical discussion that attempts to unravel the problems of scientifically testing any functional analysis of a single society. The solution proposed demands the use of the equilibrium model and the study of the society in question over time.

In Chapter 14, population growth is seen as a disequilibrating force that will eventually bring about the destruction of the integrative consequences of the cargo system in Zinacantan. Chapter 15 reviews the history of the cargo system and shows that the equilibrating forces that have countered the effect of population growth are rapidly reaching the limits of their capacity for compensation. It is concluded that the importance of the cargo system as the basis for social stratification and integration of the society is now declining, and it is predicted that the decline will continue more rapidly in the future.

No other specific predictions for the future are made, for the factors that will determine the future are too complex to be evaluated in this study. However, Chapter 16 argues that the direction of future change will probably be determined by the manner in which economic surpluses that cannot be absorbed by the cargo system are handled.

The ethnographic present of this study is 1962. A very short field trip was made in the summer of 1964, and this and other communications with Zinacantan since 1962 are occasionally used as the basis for additional comments. These references to later periods are all indicated as they occur.

Names have been assigned to informants so that no two persons are designated by the same name. Some of the names are fictitious, but all uses of the same name designate the same person.

Two

Zinacantan and the Zinacantecos

Zinacantan is a township of some 7,650 Tzotzil-speaking Indians and a handful of Spanish-speaking *Ladinos*.[1] It lies on both sides of the Pan American Highway just west of the city of San Cristóbal Las Casas in the highlands of the state of Chiapas. The township is a political subdivision introduced by the Spanish colonial government, but it coincides almost exactly with the clearly defined linguistic and cultural community of the Zinacantecos.

Besides the use of Mayan languages (Tzotzil and Tzeltal), the characteristic that most clearly distinguishes the Indians of the region from the Ladinos, or Mexicans, is their dress. Among the approximately 150,000 Indians of the highland area that use San Cristobal as a market center, there are about a dozen distinctive non-European costumes, each worn by all the members of a different "tribal" group. The groups are endogamous, and there is a tendency toward economic specialization by township. The closest neighbors of the Zinacantecos are the Chamulas (Pozas 1959), who have similar, but readily distinguishable, language and customs. They wear a completely different type of clothing and concentrate less on corn (maize) farming and more on other economic enterprises. Other groups in the area are even more strongly distinguished from the Zinacantecos and from each other. In their own view Zinacan-

[1] The population figure is from 1960 census reports. Ladinos are persons who wear European clothes and speak Spanish as their principal language (although their ancestors may be Indians). A forthcoming monograph by Evon Z. Vogt, *Zinacantan: A Maya Community in the Highlands of Chiapas,* will provide fuller ethnographic background than is offered in this chapter.

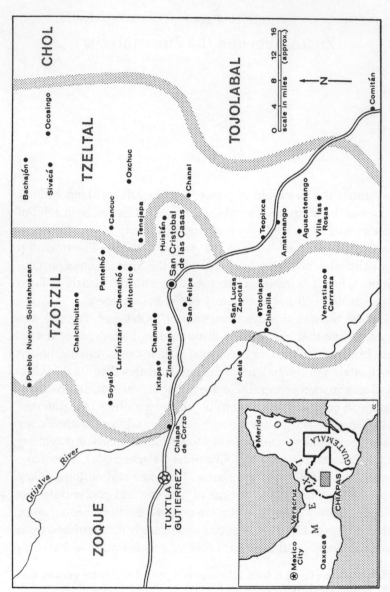

Map 1. Central Chiapas.

8

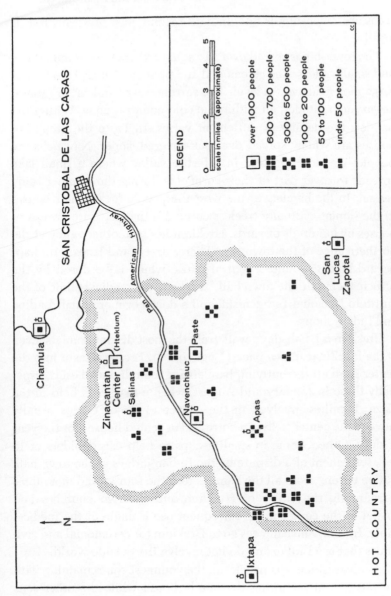

Map 2. The township of Zinacantan.

9

tecos are Zinacantecos first, Indians second, and Mexicans last, if at all.

The township is spread over 117 square kilometers of mountains and small valleys. The ceremonial and political center, Hteklum, is 2,152 meters above sea level. The surrounding hamlets^a are found at varying altitudes, all within the cold-country^a zone. Within the hamlets the density of settlement varies. In Paste the groups of houses are widely spread over oak-covered slopes. Navenchauc's people live close together in a fertile valley where a small lake spreads to cover part of their cornfields during the summer rainy season. In the hamlets to the west the people locate their houses in the sloping, virtually treeless cornfields that separate groups of houses by hundreds of yards. Hteklum lies in another valley at the northern edge of the township. There, streets and lanes form haphazard blocks around a central plaza, which is bordered by the principal church, the town hall,^a a school, the medical clinic of the Instituto Nacional Indigenista, and a dozen or more small Ladino and Indian shops.

Hteklum is a half-day's walk from the most distant hamlets, even at the fast Zinacanteco pace (Vogt 1961a). People stream into the center from all the outlying hamlets for the religious fiestas, especially those in January and August, when a market is held in the plaza. Families involved in the service of major cargos usually move to the center to live in borrowed or rented houses for the year of duty. Others come in small groups to help cargoholders or to seek settlement of a dispute by the Indian judges at the town hall. Native curers^a from all the hamlets tour the four sacred mountains surrounding the valley of Hteklum and the two churches and chapel in the center itself. Infrequent use is made of the medical clinic. In sum, Zinacantecos go to Hteklum for ceremonial and civil affairs that are Indian and do not involve the outside world.

Ideally, residence is patrilocal, the youngest son remaining with the father and inheriting the family house while the other sons build houses nearby on family land. Where space permits, the ideal is usually carried out. In Paste, for instance, 81 per cent of the

nuclear families (couples and their unmarried children) live patri-
locally, 17 per cent matrilocally (uxorilocally), and only a bit more
than 2 per cent, or six of the 246 families, have purchased land located away from the parents of both of the spouses.

The houses are one room with wattle and daub walls and high-
peaked thatch roofs, or adobe walls and tile roofs (a recent development). A variety of intermediate types is found, and in the
warmer western parts of the township house walls often consist
solely of rows of vertical planks.

Corn tortillas, beans, and a variety of greens are the staples of
the diet, meat and fowl being commonly eaten only on ceremonial
occasions.

In characterizing the relationship of Zinacantan and its people
to the Ladino world, and especially to the market city of San Cristobal and its 23,500 inhabitants, it is useful to divide the peasant
society's partial dependence on the larger society (semi-auton-
omy) into economic, political, and cultural components (Fallers
1961).

Zinacantecos are most clearly peasants in the economic sense.
They are dependent on buying and selling transactions that can
only be carried on in Ladino cities, especially San Cristobal. There
they sell their corn and beans and such small items as chili pep-
pers, coffee, eggs, flowers, and produce. There they buy the cotton
thread from which clothes are woven, axes for chopping wood and
clearing fields, and many other items in frequent use.

Corn is the most important cash crop as well as the staple food.
Most of the farming on a commercial scale is done in the lowland
valley of the Grijalva River, which is in a hot-country[a] zone outside of Zinacantan. There Zinacantecos rent land from Ladinos
(Stauder 1961). In selling their corn crops they flood into San Cristobal. Beans, also an important cash crop for some Zinacantecos,
are more often sold in the hot-country town of Chiapa de Corzo.
Flowers, which in recent years have become an important source
of cash for a limited number of people, are principally sold in the
state capital of Tuxtla Gutiérrez, which is located in hot country

on the far side of the Grijalva River (Bunnin 1963). Virtually all Zinacantecos sell some corn, and a limited number also participate in other types of trading activity (Zabala 1961a).

In recent years wage work on Chiapas's constantly expanding and improving system of roads has been a source of income for many young men. However, road work does not provide full-time employment, and in any case the traditional emphasis on corn farming seems to keep other occupations from taking more than a minor share of the Zinacanteco male's time.

In the political sense, too, the Zinacantecos are peasants to some extent. For matters of internal justice they have adapted the Mexican system of civil government to their own purposes. Most disputes between Zinacantecos are settled in the Hteklum town hall in a distinctly Indian fashion, but serious crimes, such as murder, must be referred to high Ladino officials in San Cristobal. Also, in the continuing struggle for more farming land, and in cases of conflict between important political leaders of Zinacantan, Ladino law and officials play an important part.

The continuing viability of the Zinacantan community is the best evidence that the Zinacantecos are not peasants in the cultural sense. The elements of the higher culture that are "incorporated" (Vogt 1961b) into Zinacantan culture are so well embedded that they have been completely separated from their sources. In religion, for example, the elements taken from Catholicism have been thoroughly reworked into Indian ritual patterns, and the priest who visits Hteklum one or two times a month is allowed to fit into these patterns.

Nor has formal education changed substantially the language skills of Zinacantecos. The number of one- and two-room schools in the township increased to eight in 1960, but very few Zinacantecos can speak Spanish. A liberal estimate of the proportion of men who speak more Spanish than necessary for the most basic economic transactions might be 20 per cent. Of the women who have learned Spanish while working in San Cristobal as maids, only a few are now permanent residents of Zinacantan. Most relations with Ladinos are little more than trade requires, and mistrust colors many of them.

Though such acceptance may now be on the increase, very few Zinacantecos have accepted the standards of the Ladino world, which mark them as stupid Indians. For the most part, they find it easy to define Zinacantan as the center of the world and the Zinacantan way of life as at least as good as the Ladino one (van den Berghe and Colby 1961: 71). Though they are quick to adopt from the Ladino world material objects that satisfy a need dictated by their own culture, they are equally quick to reject those that do not suit them.

Women, for instance, had no trouble understanding my wife's interest in learning to weave on a backstrap loom: they thought this technique for producing obviously superior cloth was going to make her a fortune when she returned to her homeland.

Nor did an aged Zinacanteco curer find it hard to employ the advantages of an anthropologist's Land Rover in making his rounds. Walking the trails from his home in Navenchauc to the sacred mountains around Hteklum had become too difficult for his old legs, but the Land Rover solved that. On one occasion, when leaving the valley of Hteklum by car after a tiring circuit of the mountains on foot, he proved that his ability to adapt had few limits. The last cross to be visited was located near the road. When we arrived he had me stop the car, took one look at the downpour, ordered a young assistant out into the rain to light the necessary candles at the base of the cross, and did his praying from the front seat of the Land Rover.

Three
Public Life in Zinacantan

This chapter briefly describes the range of roles that Zinacantecos may play in public as opposed to family life, and delimits the sector within this range that the remainder of the study will focus on. The processes of recruitment for participation in public life will also receive limited discussion, as will the idea of "career" in public life; these two topics will be important in the later chapters, which treat the religious hierarchy in detail. Public life may be divided into three relatively well-defined sectors: (1) the native curers; (2) the civil government;[a] (3) the religious hierarchy.

Native Curers

The native curers are primarily concerned with maintaining good relations with the deities and with curing any sickness that is diagnosed as resulting from an offense to these deities or from witchcraft. Their activities usually involve prayer and the offering of candles at the home of the patient and at the sacred mountains surrounding Hteklum (Vogt 1961a). A few of the curers also prescribe herbs and practice bonesetting.

Curers perform both public and private ceremonies. A public ceremony may be for the entire township, in which case representatives of each hamlet participate; or it may be for a hamlet or smaller subdivision of the township, in which case all the curers of that subdivision participate (Vogt 1964). These public ceremonies are performed at regular intervals and also during epidemics. The scheduled ceremonies seem to be the most frequent. For all public ceremonies the curers themselves make door-to-door rounds to collect the money needed to purchase food, drink, and candles.

Similarly, private ceremonies may be divided into those performed for emergencies and those performed for general pacification of the deities. However, in the case of private ceremonies, the emergency type seems to be by far the most frequent. These are performed when someone is sick. Few families can bear the expense of a ceremony if it is not absolutely necessary, though the need for general placating ceremonies for an individual is often discussed. The expenses of the private ceremony are borne by the patient and his family. They include the purchase of large quantities of candles offered at home and on the ceremonial round of the sacred mountains, and liquor served to the assembled group. In addition, a ceremony of moderate to large size requires a number of chickens for meals, sacrifice to the deities, and gifts for the curer. These chickens as well as other items of food may be either taken from the family's supplies or purchased. In an emergency, chickens may be borrowed, to be returned in kind when the lender has a similar need, if not before.

Except for the numerous special meals and the gifts of consumables (meat and liquor), the curer receives no material compen-

TABLE 1

The Three Sectors of Public Life in Zinacantan

Sector	Term	Expenses or Remuneration	Percentage of Adult Men Participating
Curers . . . . life 100–150 persons[a]	life	paid in goods	5–10%
Civil Officials . . . . 3 years 1 Presidente Municipal, 1 Síndico, 6 Regidores (civil),[b] and 4 Alcaldes Jueces	3 years	no significant pay or expenses	5–10%
Religious Cargos . . . . . . 1 year 55 cargos, on 4 levels[c]	1 year	substantial expenses	70–90%

[a] Ranked by length of service.
[b] In 1962 for the first time.
[c] See Chapter 4. The figure 55 includes 8 Mayores, who function in the civil government as well as in the religious cargo system.

sation for his efforts. Curers are never paid in money. However, native midwives and bonesetters, who combine other skills with praying, are paid in cash as well as with gifts and meals.

The curers are organized in a systematic hierarchy based on length of service. Vogt (1965) has discussed this organization in some detail. This ranking of curers is always recognized in interaction between curers, but the frequency with which a curer is asked to perform private ceremonies depends more upon his reputation for success than upon his rank.

The curer's role is public, for it is recognized and brings prestige in the community. However, curers are marginal public figures in comparison with the civil and religious officials, who are involved in community efforts and operate almost entirely in the ceremonial center.

Another crucial distinction between curers and the civil and religious officials involves length of service. The curer is a curer for life, once he has made his debut (recruitment is discussed below). He lives an ordinary life, serving specifically as a curer whenever a patient or the community chooses to call for his help. The other officials serve for specific terms: the religious officials for one year and the major civil officials for three.

Civil Government

The officers of the civil government are principally concerned with public works, the administration of justice, and the relations of the community and its members with the Ladino world outside. Zinacantan is an independent political entity under Mexican law, and the organization of the civil government is dictated by that law. Certain important adjustments are made in order to allow the requirements of law to fit the traditions of community service in Zinacantan; but, as it faces the outside world, the civil government is like any other one established under the laws of the state.

The formal arrangement of civil offices has changed considerably in Zinacantan since the turn of the century, and especially in the last ten years. I will first describe the present situation and then review the most important changes.

As of January 1, 1962, all townships in Chiapas were made equal with respect to the formal organization of their municipal governments. The law requires that a township be administered by a Presidente, a Sindico, six Regidores, and three alternate Regidores. In addition, each township is required to have an Alcalde Juez (municipal judge) and an alternate to him.[1]

The Presidente is the principal authority in the township (much like a mayor in the United States) and the representative of the township in dealings with the larger governmental system. In Zinacantan the Sindico is more of a vice-president or alternate to the Presidente than an officer in charge of the "social welfare" of the community, as intended by the lawmakers. In a Ladino town the Regidores are heads of the various municipal subcommittees. In Zinacantan, however, they do not yet have very specifically established responsibilities, for 1962 was the first year in which they served. Finally, two men are formally appointed as judges. All these men serve three-year terms, as required by state law.

In addition, there are eight Mayores. They serve as general policemen and messengers for the civil officials and for religious officials who sit in the town hall. The Mayores were part of the governmental system before the establishment of the civil government in its modern form around the turn of the century. The offices remain one-year posts, and, unlike other civil offices, count for progress in the hierarchy of religious cargos. For this reason, they are discussed at greater length in later chapters.

The law requires that all officials be paid, but this requirement is overlooked in Zinacantan. All officials serve in the traditional Maya way, without pay, except for the Presidente, who has a small income from liquor taxes collected from local stores. From time to time small fines or other special fees are collected and divided among the civil officials, but the monthly total of such income for an individual official is not likely to reach the amount he could

---

[1] This organization is stipulated in the Leyes del Estado de Chiapas (1959). When these laws were published Zinacantan was a third-class township, but the modifications put into effect in 1962 made all townships of Chiapas first-class ones.

make in a single day working as a laborer in someone's cornfield. Thus, office-holding is a community service, for although the civil officials are not required to spend any money, they do contribute their time without remuneration.

The tradition of half-time active occupancy of office is also maintained. The officials serve two weeks at a time, alternating in a fixed pattern. For example, four Mayores serve while the other four are free to engage in private activities. After two weeks the first group becomes free while the second group of four serves its turn. In the case of the higher officials this pattern is not held to rigidly, but it is the expressed norm. The Presidente is the single exception: he is expected to be on duty every day.

In the case of the judges (Alcaldes Jueces), another kind of adjustment of the law to the traditional system has been made. Officially, one man can handle any case, but the custom of officials in Zinacantan is to talk out the difficulties and disputes among many people; all civil officials present at the town hall, and especially the Presidente, contribute their opinions to the settlement of disputes. Apparently because of this custom, the civil authorities in Zinacantan include four judges instead of the legally prescribed two. They are usually referred to as first, second, third, and fourth judges, or as first and second judges and first and second alternates. By custom, the first and the third alternate in serving two-week shifts with the second and the fourth, so that one judge who is officially recognized by outside authority is present should there be a case requiring referral to San Cristobal. Apart from their ranking from first to fourth, litigants make no distinction between them.

Besides these officials who serve in the ceremonial center, there are young men appointed to act as government representatives to each hamlet. They collect money for public expenditures and deposit it with the officials in Hteklum, and carry messages and announcements back to the hamlets. Most of the hamlets have two of these representatives, but some of the smaller hamlets have only one. They serve terms of one year, and are called Principales.

A number of committees, both permanent and temporary, require the occasional service of many men. Almost all the hamlets have permanent education committees, which are responsible for seeing that children attend school and for guarding the schoolhouse. Another committee, which controls the land given to the community under the national land reform program, is a very powerful independent institution in Zinacantan (see Edel 1962). The most common types of temporary committees are those appointed to collect funds and direct activities for fiestas and public works.

Attached to this civil government is a Secretario Municipal, or town clerk. He is responsible for keeping records and preparing the papers required by the Indian officials. In Zinacantan, as in most of the Indian townships of Chiapas, he is a Ladino.[2] He is hired and paid by the township, a special monthly contribution for his salary being made by each household. The Secretario is hired by the civil officials with the help of the state's department of Indian affairs. Ladino Secretarios have traditionally been very powerful figures in Indian communities in Chiapas, but the Ladino who has served in Zinacantan since 1956 has a seemingly sincere desire to do his job and avoid direct intervention in the internal political affairs of the township. The extent to which he is the local eyes and ears of the Ladino side in issues that involve the relation of Zinacantan to the Mexican world outside is hard to estimate.

As noted above, until 1962 the townships of Chiapas were divided into three classes. As a township of the third class, Zinacantan was required to have only a Presidente, a Sindico, two Regidores and two alternates, and a judge and his alternate. Under the same laws the term of service was two years instead of three.

All the offices were filled as they are now, with one important exception: the four Regidores of the religious hierarchy were nominally appointed to fill the offices of Regidores and alternate Regidores required by state law. They served their one-year terms

---

[2] For two years, 1954–55, Zinacantan had a native Indian as Secretario Municipal, but the conflict created by having a native in the position was too great and he was forced to resign.

as religious officials and were seldom required to attend to any civil function. Their appointments as religious officials were made entirely according to the standards of the religious hierarchy, and their appointments as civil officials were simply accepted by the other civil officials and made legal through papers drawn up by the Secretario.

In 1960, a political crisis in the community precipitated a situation that, in combination with the new laws of 1962, ended the convenient fiction under which the religious Regidores were able to fill the required civil posts. The Presidente was impeached in October 1960, after a long political fight. Under the law, the First Regidor became Presidente for the fourteen months left in the term of the impeached Presidente. This First Regidor, of course, was a religious official who had intended to serve in a religious position for the calendar year 1960 only. Moreover, he was a man who could not speak Spanish and did not have much talent or inclination for settling the disputes brought before the civil officials.[3] The Sindico was therefore accepted as the de facto Presidente, but the former religious Regidor was required to settle law cases and be present on many occasions of contact with Ladino officials in San Cristobal. By the end of the year 1961, both the man and the government of Zinacantan had suffered greatly from the situation. As I interpret it, this situation and the new laws of 1962 were responsible for the total compliance with the provisions calling for the appointment of six civil Regidores.

Before 1952, all offices of the civil government in Zinacantan were served for terms of one year. All available information indicates that this situation had existed since 1899, when the first Presidente and civil government were installed. Before that date Zinacantan was not officially a township, and was controlled by an official appointed by outside powers. Authority for settlement of disputes in the native population was apparently vested in the officials

---

[3] This was an unfortunate coincidence. The first Regidores in 1957 and 1958 were past Presidentes who could have handled the situation, and the Regidores in 1961 and 1962 were also men who could have served as civil officials, though they had never been chosen as Presidente in the past.

that have since become religious Regidores with no civil authority.[4]

Over this formal organization lies a political power structure that has also changed over the years. Little is known about the situation before the turn of the century and up until the 1920's, but it can be guessed with some assurance that the political powers of the Ladino world had a much firmer and more direct control over the appointment and election of officials in Zinacantan than they do now. Within the community, according to informants, there has been a series of political leaders. Most reports indicate that there were usually two or three men who held great political power in the community. These were usually men who could speak Spanish and manipulate the Ladino world as well as maintain the respect of Zinacantecos. In the late 1930's there seem to have been three such individuals at one time. Two are now dead and the third is often seen in the role of elder statesman when Ladino officials appear in Zinacantan on business.

Through the 1930's and especially in the early 1940's the national land-reform program of Mexico was making great changes in Zinacantan. The township and its people were eligible for much new land under the reform laws. The man who led the community in its demands for land emerged as a solitary political power in that period and maintained his hold on the community until very recently (Edel 1962). Until the incident which resulted in the impeachment of the Presidente in 1960, that old leader was a politi-

---

[4] These statements are based on the reports of my oldest informants. They also indicated that some of the judges appointed just after the turn of the century were Ladinos, for the Ladino population of Zinacantan was greater then than it is now (see Carey 1962). I set the date of the establishment of Zinacantan as a township and the installation of the first Presidente at 1899 on the basis of the following information: Amid the heap of documents left in the town hall after the confusion of the revolution in the 1920's are comparable documents for 1898 and 1900. The first refers to an Agente Municipal, the type of official who presides over a large subdivision of less than township status. The second refers to a Presidente Municipal. In addition, the chapel in Zinacantan center is dated 1899 and bears the name of a man who is said to have been the first Presidente of Zinacantan. There is no other information on Zinacantan, but this change in government and its date are consistent with other changes in state laws just before the turn of the century. I am grateful to Professor Prudencio Moscoso Pastrana of San Cristobal for the sources and interpretations on which this last statement is based.

cal boss in the full sense of the word. The impeached Presidente
became the center of an opposition group that caused the leader to
be jailed early in 1962. He was free within a few months, but his
hold on the community was shaken. He is an older man and his
probable successors do not seem fully capable of replacing him. It
is difficult to predict how the political situation in Zinacantan will
develop.

Religious Hierarchy

The cargos that are the principal concern of this study are, with
one minor exception, all religious positions.[5] That is, they are offices
devoted to the performance of ritual connected with the Catholic
Church. The system in Zinacantan is not the typical civil-religious
hierarchy found in the Maya area. As Manning Nash has described
it for the Guatemalan communities (1958), the civil-religious hierarchy involves alternation between civil and religious offices as the
individual climbs up the ladder that leads to the highest office in
the community. In fact, the distinction between civil and religious
office is only a conceptual one made by anthropologists: "Indians
tend to think of them as one system" (Nash 1958: 67). However,
Zinacantecos make a very sharp distinction between the civil offices
that have been discussed above and the religious cargos, and the
anthropologist cannot help but follow their lead.

None of the offices of the civil government in Zinacantan count
for progress up the ladder of religious cargos. In indirect ways
there is some small degree of interaction between the civil sector
of public life and the religious hierarchy. Most of this interaction
seems to have a negative tone, however. Service in civil cargos requires an investment of time that delays the progress a man might
make toward accumulating the financial resources necessary to
participate in the religious hierarchy. Because of this, one former
Presidente went so far as to call his two-year term in civil office a
"waste of time." Also, the political-power situation in Zinacantan

---

[5] The exception is the Mayores who were discussed above. The offices have
civil functions in large part, but are considered cargos because they count for
progress in the religious hierarchy.

sometimes affects participation in the hierarchy. Some who were anticipating cargos suddenly found themselves crossed off the waiting lists because a political enemy had been able to influence the keepers of the lists. I know of only two cases of this, and one of them is not absolutely certain, but the threat of political complications has certainly kept a number of men from coming to the ceremonial center to serve religious cargos.

Before the turn of the century, it seems, the hierarchy was closer to the typical Maya civil-religious pattern.[6] The Mayor positions that are principally civil in nature were served as a first cargo by some. Then, whether he had passed Mayor or not, a man began his religious service with a "Mayordomo" cargo of the present first level.[7] He passed on to an Alférez cargo on the second level, and finally to a principally civil third cargo as Regidor and a fourth cargo as Alcalde Viejo.[8]

Today, the man who has passed four religious cargos is considered an elder,[6] but this status does not give him the privileges often given to elders in other Maya communities. All elders in Zinacantan are exempted from payment of tax levies of any kind, but they have no formal political or religious power, and there is no organized group of elders. All elders are respected for their service, and almost all are sought out for advice on the performance of ritual. Since the economic and managerial skills required to accumulate the money necessary to pass four cargos are great, elders tend to be more capable people than those who do not achieve their status.

[6] For discussion of the part of this difference that may be the result of different actions of national governments in Mexico and Guatemala, see Cancian (n.d.).

[7] "Mayordomo" is used to refer in general to the several types of religious cargos on the first level. They are described in detail in Chapter 4.

[8] The names of the cargos in the hierarchy indicate that the origin of the system in its present form is definitely post-Conquest, but the extent to which its structure is a blending of pre-Hispanic elements and the organization imposed by the Spaniards is not known. "Mayordomo" clearly indicates origin as a religious cargo, while "Regidor" and "Alcalde" indicate civil cargos. Zabala (1961b: 150) says that the Alfereces had civil functions at one time. Other aspects of the problem of the origin of the system are discussed in Cancian (1964), Carrasco (1961), and Foster (1960).

This picture of the cargo system just before the turn of the century is based on the statements of older informants who reported statements by their fathers.

Thus they hold political and ecnomic power out of proportion to their numbers, but this seems to be more a simple concomitant of, rather than a result of, their service.

Recruitment for Positions in Public Life

The manner in which a person is differentiated from all other people in his community and placed in a specific role can be very complex. This is especially true in a society such as Zinacantan, where kinship does not give substantial clues to the placement of a person in the community-wide social structure. Here I will try to describe only the most obvious and basic procedures by which an individual is recruited for a position in public life.

Curers recruit themselves in a manner unique in the realm of public life. They learn of their calling in a series of dreams in which they see the native deities who live inside the mountains. Once they have had such dreams, they report to a senior curer for their interpretation. The interpretation reveals whether the dreamer should become a curer. It is believed that a person who is called and does not become a curer will die.

Because the civil officials are responsible for representing the community in relations with the Ladino government, they need facility in Spanish. Most of them speak some Spanish, though an examination of the incumbents over the past few years indicates that this is crucial only for the top officials—Presidente, Sindico, first Regidor, and first Alcalde Juez. As the administrators of justice in the community, they must command the respect of those who come to them for settlements. They do so mainly by their ability to make appropriate comments and present a reasonable perspective when a case is brought before them.

Under Mexican law all these officials are elected by popular vote. Like the manner of service in office, this requirement is adjusted to local conditions. As specified by law, there is a nominating meeting before the election. Before, during, and after this meeting, candidates are discussed and groups are formed in support of candidates. For weeks there is talk about who will be chosen. Finally, on election day, it seems that only the supporters of the candidates who will win appear, for by that time the matter is settled. The opposition does not take the trouble to vote for its candidates.

In fact, the candidates of the political boss mentioned above have been elected for a number of years. However, the opposition is always active. This activity reached a peak in 1952, when about half a dozen younger relatives of the major opposition leaders appeared at the town hall carrying guns and demanding that the Presidente be unseated. Their protest did not carry, but opposition leaders are always talking of similar moves that will remove the incumbents with whom they are dissatisfied.

Most of the important civic decisions are made by the political boss and his close associates, while the civil officials settle disputes and carry on the official contacts with the Ladino government. Thus, though authority usually increases with age in Zinacantan, the civil officials may be relatively young and unimportant men. It is not uncommon to have a Presidente in his late 20's. Of the six Presidentes who served between 1952 and 1963, four were younger than 30 when they entered office.

Since a substantial portion of this study is devoted to the factors that are important in the recruitment of religious officials, I describe only the most basic formal rules here. Formally, all cargoholders are appointed by the six *moletik* (the four Regidores and the two Alcaldes Viejos), who are responsible for seeing that all positions are filled and that the required ritual is carried out. They communicate their appointments to the individuals some months in advance so that they may make the necessary preparations for entering a cargo. This has been the system of recruitment for religious offices as long as the oldest informants can remember. The moletik supported by the community have the power necessary to coerce individuals who are reluctant to undertake the expense and obligation of a cargo. An appointee who is able to resist the persuasion of six old and respected men, and who is willing to endure the mark that refusal may leave on him in the eyes of the community, may appeal an appointment to Ladino officials in San Cristobal. They will issue an order stating that it is illegal to force a person to serve a religious cargo, and the appointee will be free.

For the last ten years men in great numbers have been requesting appointment to cargos of their choice. By 1961, the practice of
requesting cargos had become so popular that the moletik held
waiting lists as long as 20 years for some positions; that is, some
men had requested specific cargos for the year 1981. This expansion of requests for cargos is discussed in detail in Chapter 15.

Because of this relatively new pattern, the moletik have been re-
lieved of some of the burden of seeking out candidates whom they
could appoint. Some cargos, however, are not very popular and
are seldom requested. Mayor is never requested, apparently because it does nothing to enhance the prestige of the incumbent in
the community; in fact, many individuals are appointed to it as
a punishment for poor behavior. The moletik share the responsibility for the appointment of the eight Mayores with the civil officials. In theory, four Mayores are the messengers of the civil officials and four serve the moletik. In practice, they are used interchangeably.

Careers in Public Life

The reputation a man makes in the three sectors of public life in
Zinacantan is the face he presents to the community. Only a handful of adult Zinacantecos go through their adult years without participating in at least one of the three.

The curers receive the most distinctive type of respect for their
participation in public life. Their reputations are usually greatest
in the hamlets where they live, but the most important curers are
known throughout the township. Their all-important resource—the
power to communicate with the native deities and cure sickness—
provides them with their renown. Only a small percentage of Zinacanteco adults are curers.

The civil officials, with the exception of the Presidente, do not
necessarily continue to receive respect after they have served their
terms of office. However, most of them are men who can continue
to command respect for the same qualities that originally caused
them to be selected for public office. Only a small percentage of
Zinacanteco adult males hold civil office, and those who do not

know Spanish are usually excluded completely from such service.

The cargo system is the only sector of public life in which almost all Zinacanteco males participate in some degree.[9] The cargo-holder, as I have pointed out elsewhere (Cancian 1964), receives a very special kind of prestige and respect, which is principally dependent on the amount of money he spends in the service of his cargo or cargos.

The public service of the curer is usually known to a limited number of people, and service as a civil official is limited to a small proportion of the population. The cargo system, on the other hand, provides a single standard by which all adult males may be compared on their participation in public life. For this reason (and others to be discussed later) the cargo system is the key to the community-wide social structure of Zinacantan. Cargo service is the most important single determinant of a man's position in the community.

The few individuals who do not take any roles in public life are usually at the bottom of the social scale in Zinacantan. In some cases, men who participate as civil officials or curers find themselves excluded from the cargo system because their other roles preclude the accumulation of money necessary to pass a cargo—but this is rare. A few men who for some reason never accumulate the funds for a cargo consistent with their self-image find alternative paths to prestige in curing and civil offices. Some gain prestige through informal political activity. In most cases, however, men who are successful curers and civil officials also participate in the cargo system. A man's reputation in the community is a composite of that made in the performance of various roles. The outstanding men are characterized by important participation in two or three sectors of public life.

[9] The precise degree of participation is discussed at length in Chapter 11.

Four

The Cargos

The expressed purpose of the religious hierarchy is to guarantee performance of rituals for the saints in the local Catholic churches. Tradition dictates that these rituals be performed, and it is believed that harm will come to the community if they are not performed. When a man takes a cargo for a year he is responsible for part of the ritual, and is thus doing a service for the community. Most Zinacantecos believe that the saints will favor him if he performs his duties well, and punish him if he does not.

Every year 55 Zinacantecos serve cargos in the religious hierarchy. The rights and duties of each cargo are set by tradition and do not vary with the incumbent from year to year. However, the rights and duties vary greatly between cargos. Each cargo has a distinct sphere of responsibility and a distinct name. This chapter describes the organization of the hierarchy and the general activities and responsibilities of the cargoholders. It is divided into five sections. The first describes the levels of service in the hierarchy; the second discusses the principles by which the various cargos are ranked within the levels and their subdivisions. The last three sections are devoted to the specific cargos on the first level, the second level, and the third and fourth levels. The cargos, and the auxiliary personnel described in Chapter 5, are represented in Figure 1. Table 2 offers a summary of the organizational features described in the five sections of this chapter.

Levels of Service

The levels indicate an order of service. After serving a first-level cargo, a man may pass a second-level cargo, then a third-level

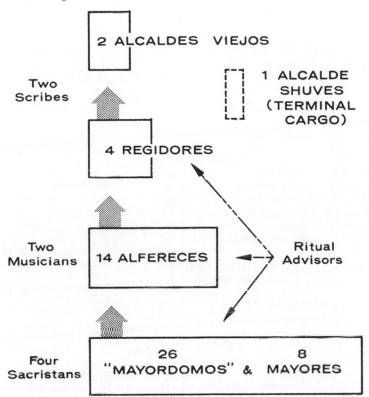

Figure 1. The religious hierarchy in Zinacantan. Shown are 55 cargos on four levels, and four types of Auxiliary Personnel.

cargo, and then a cargo on the fourth and final level. This order of progression is very rigidly set in Zinacantan. There are 34 cargos on the first level, 14 on the second level, 4 on the third level, and 3 on the fourth level. A complete career of four cargos might be, for example, Mayordomo Santo Domingo, Alferez Natividad, First Regidor, and Senior Alcalde Viejo. Because there are fewer positions available at the higher levels, the "incomplete" career is of course the rule.

There are four apparent exceptions to this description of the levels and the order of progression. The first three are not seen as exceptions by Zinacantecos, and are merely artifacts of my effort to make a simple initial statement.

TABLE 2

The Four Levels of Cargos

Code Numbers	Spanish Names[a]	Code Numbers	Spanish Names
FIRST LEVEL[b]		**SECOND LEVEL**	
Mayordomos		*Junior Alféreces[c]*	
A8S–A8J	San Sebastián	B11	San Sebastián
A9S–A9J	San Antonio	B10	Santa Rosa
A2S–A2J	la Virgen del Rosario	B9	San Jacinto
A6S–A6J	Santa Cruz	B12	San Pedro Mártir
A5S–A5J	Santo Domingo	B3	San Antonio
A3S–A3J	Sacramento	B7	la Virgen de Soledad
Mayordomos Reyes and Mesoneros		B1	San Lorenzo
A7S–A7J	Mesonero	*Senior Alféreces*	
A1S–A1J	Mayordomo Rey	B8	San Sebastián
Cargos of Salinas		B6	la Virgen de Natividad
MRSa1	Mayordomo de la	B5	la Virgen del Rosario
	Virgen del Rosario	B4	San José
	(1)	B2	la Santísima Trinidad
MYSa1	Mayor de Salinas (1)	ADC	la Divina Cruz
Cargos of Navenchauc		ASD	Santo Domingo
	Mayordomo de la		
	Virgen de Guadalupe	**THIRD LEVEL**	
Cargos of Apas		*Regidores*	
	Mesonero (1)	C4	Regidor Cuarto
	Mayordomo Rey (1)	C3	Regidor Tercero
Cargos of the Easter Season		C2	Regidor Segundo
A4S–A4J	Pasionero	C1	Regidor Primero
Cargos of the Fiesta of San Lorenzo		**FOURTH LEVEL**	
A10S–A10J	Capitán	*Alcaldes Viejos*	
Mayores		D2	Alcalde Viejo Segundo
A11	Mayor (eight ranked	D1	Alcalde Viejo Primero
	positions)	*The Terminal Cargo*	
			Alcalde Juez (Shuves)[d]

NOTE: In the text that follows I begin to refer to each cargo mentioned by the code numbers listed in this table. I would like to use the names of the cargos throughout, but have found that readers, even those who have done research in Zinacantan, often have trouble remembering which cargo is which. The code numbers convey essential information concisely. The first letter indicates the level of service (from A for the first level to D for the fourth level). The next number represents position on the prestige ranking that is developed in Chapter 8 (from 1 for the highest prestige, downward). The final S or J found after some references to first-level cargos indicates whether the cargo is senior or junior. Thus, A1 denotes the pair of Mayordomos Reyes, and A1S denotes the Senior Mayordomo Rey. Nine of the 55 cargos have no code numbers; these are the six first-level cargos that are served outside the ceremonial center, the Alferez Santo Domingo, the Alferez Divina Cruz, and the Alcalde Shuves. Letter abbreviations useful for reporting data in the appendixes have been assigned to the cargos served in Salinas, and to Alferez Santo Domingo and Alferez Divina Cruz. Shortened forms of some of the first- and

(1) The Alferez Divina Cruz is one of the Alferez group and may be served as a second cargo. Usually, however, it is served by a man who has already passed two cargos. It is, then, either a second- or a third-level position. In recent years, apparently because of conditions of supply and demand, it has been exclusively a third-level cargo.

(2) The Alferez Santo Domingo may be served as a second, third, or fourth cargo. In recent years it has seldom been served as a second-level position. Note in Table 2 that the Alferez Santo Domingo and the Alferez Divina Cruz are the ranking Alfereces.

(3) The Alcalde Shuves is always a terminal cargo. That is, a man who passes it is considered to have completed his service and is not eligible for further cargos. It is a minor post and carries little prestige. The typical incumbent is a very old man who passed a minor first-level cargo in his youth and then avoided service in the hierarchy; too old and too poor to consider normal progression through the system, he is given this cargo and allowed, in effect, to slip away from the course of the normal cargo career. An incumbent who was typical in spirit but atypical in previous history served the cargo in 1962: he had served three cargos previously, but had the unique record of having been removed from two of these because of his habitual drunkenness and misbehavior. He apparently requested Alcalde Shuves in an effort to make amends. Having passed it, he died.

(4) The only true exception in the system is often made with respect to the junior of the two fourth-level Alcaldes Viejos. This position is sometimes served by a man who has passed only two cargos previously. It is my idea that most men who have had the

---

second-level cargo names will be used in the text; e.g., Senior Mayordomo de la Virgen del Rosario (A2S) will appear as Senior Mayordomo Rosario (A2S).

a Tzotzil names for the cargos are given in the Glossary.

b Unless otherwise specified parenthetically, each name here denotes two positions, a senior and a junior.

c The senior-junior order of the Alfereces is that indicated above. San Sebastian Junior is the most junior and Santo Domingo the most senior. They are paired as are the Mayordomos, e.g., Santa Rosa is the junior of Natividad and Santisima Trinidad is the junior of San Antonio. There is, however, one exception in the walking order. It is exactly like the senior-junior order indicated above, except that the San Antonio walks behind the Virgen de Soledad.

d The name Alcalde Juez is known to very few Zinacantecos, and is almost never used. In order to avoid confusion with the Alcalde Juez of the civil government, I use the mixed term Alcalde Shuves in the text.

resources and endurance to pass three cargos will not settle for the junior post on the fourth level. Thus the cargo has few takers. In 1962 the cargo was filled by a man who was appointed after two previous cargos. He was an old resident of the ceremonial center; and because of his ability to speak and write Spanish, had served on many committees and as Scribe (see Chapter 5) during his lifetime. Informants recognized the exception made in appointing him, but rationalized it by saying that because of his service in many capacities, he deserved to complete his cargos in an honorable fashion. This type of reasoning would not give sufficient excuse for making an exception in the case of the Senior Alcalde Viejo.

In summary then, the levels of progress are rigidly set. However, because of the particular characteristics of the Alferez Santo Domingo and the Alferez Divina Cruz positions, it is more accurate to say that there are 12 cargos on the second level, five or six on the third level, and two or three on the fourth level. Alcalde Shuves is really served without regard to level.

Senior and Junior

Who is senior[a] and who is junior[a] is almost always a question of great importance in Zinacantan, whatever the situation. When drinking formally, the older person is served first and is bowed to as he toasts the younger.[1] He extends his hand touching the younger's forehead, and thus indicates that the latter may raise his head. When the younger person is served, he bows to the older as he speaks the words of toast. If two persons meet on a path, the

---

[1] Unless otherwise specified, "a drink" or "drink" refers to aguardiente, the distilled sugarcane liquor that is most commonly drunk by Zinacantecos. It is usually served in a one-ounce shot glass and drunk immediately so that the glass may be returned to the server, who then passes on to the next person. In the form purchased from Ladino distributors and illegally from Chamulas, it is about 40 proof. For distribution at rituals one or more parts of water are usually added. Nevertheless, in many rituals a participant is offered eight to ten shot glasses of drink within half an hour. All cargoholders and all prudent observers carry an empty bottle and a small funnel when attending such a ritual. Except on very special occasions and when drinking informally with friends, it is perfectly proper to accept the drink and pour it into the bottle for later consumption. The important thing is to accept the gift and properly toast one's fellow drinkers. Drunkenness is frequent and usually tolerated, but it is never admired or considered something to boast about.

younger stops to let the older pass, and if they are walking together, the older walks ahead.[2]

In the hierarchy the ranking according to the senior-junior distinction applies to the cargos—and apparently to the saints they represent—not to the relative ages of the men who occupy the cargo roles. Two types of senior-junior differentiations are made. First, on each of the first two levels of progress the cargos are divided into senior-junior pairs (see Table 2). Thus there is a Senior Mayordomo San Antonio and a Junior Mayordomo San Antonio. Among the Alfereces, the Alferez San Lorenzo is the junior partner of the Alferez Santo Domingo. Among the Mayordomos these senior-junior pairs do ritual together, and on both levels the pairs enter and leave office together. In all there are six junior and six senior Mayordomos, and seven junior and seven senior Alfereces.

The second employment of the senior-junior distinction involves the groups of six and seven cargos mentioned immediately above. The cargos within each group are ranked from most senior to least senior—from one to six for each group of Mayordomos and from one to seven for each group of Alfereces. Thus, among the senior Mayordomos (see Table 2), it is possible to say that the Senior Mayordomo Sacramento is more senior than the Senior Mayordomo Santo Domingo. This second principle of ranking is most clearly evident in seating and walking orders. In contrast with everyday practice, the senior walks *last* in a procession of cargo-holders. In a procession of Mayordomos, the Junior Mayordomo San Sebastian walks first. The sixth man behind him is the Junior

---

[2] Men of approximately the same age simply shake hands when drinking, and do not stop for each other when meeting on the path. The age limits are not fixed absolutely and depend on the persons and the situation. A difference of three or four years is usually recognized, and finer distinctions are made on more formal occasions.

Women are generally treated as junior. That is, they always stop on the path for any man, and they walk behind all men. Women are served their drink only after all the men have been served, except that a very old woman may be served before an unmarried man. In bowing behavior, however, the principle of age holds without regard to sex, except that men and women do not shake hands.

The bound morphemes *bankil* ("senior") and *iȼ'in* ("junior"), which are used in describing cargos, also appear in kin terms: *hbankil* means "my older brother" and *kiȼ'in* "my younger brother."

Mayordomo Sacramento. Then come the musicians, who walk between the junior and the senior groups. Following them is the Senior Mayordomo San Sebastian, the most junior of the seniors; and last in the procession comes the Senior Mayordomo Sacramento, the most senior of the seniors.

As will be noted later, especially in Chapter 8, this ranking is important to the reputation that a given cargo has in the community. It is also important in interaction among cargoholders, since the senior always has authority over the junior.

The role and not the man is usually most important in ritual. For example, in speaking with each other on ceremonial occasions, the cargoholders use the name of the cargo, not the name of the person. Thus the Mayordomo San Sebastian will toast the Mayordomo Rosario: "I drink, Rosario," and will be answered "Drink, San Sebastian."[3] This pattern is so strong that cargoholders who serve together often do not know each other's full names. The custom of addressing by role name rather than by personal name also extends to the interaction between the cargoholders and the various kinds of auxiliary personnel (musicians and helpers) described in the next chapter.

First-Level Cargos

The burden of performing day-to-day ritual falls on the cargoholders of the first level (A). The Alfereces (B) appear at only the most important fiestas, and the principal duties of the Regidores (C) and the Alcaldes Viejos (D) are more administrative in nature, though they too have many ritual obligations. The cargoholders of the first level change the flowers and light the candles in the six churches and chapels in Zinacantan. They sweep the floors and tend to the garments of the saints. Like the cargoholders of the upper levels, they have elaborate ceremonial meals, and at the more important fiestas they have complex ritual obligations, but the duties that distinguish them from the other cargoholders are those they perform from day to day. The 34 cargos of the first level are discussed according to their natural subdivisions—those

[3] In determining who will bow to whom, however, age overrides cargo rank.

dictated by the saints and the buildings that they serve. They are divided into eight groups (see Table 2).

(1) *The Mayordomos.* The twelve Mayordomos care for the two churches in the ceremonial center and the saints in them. The principal church is that of San Lorenzo, the patron saint of Zinacantan. In their regular duties there, the Mayordomos are aided by the Sacristans and the Church Committee (see Chapter 5), who tend to such matters as opening and closing the building and ringing the bells. The Mayordomos of San Sebastian (A8) are themselves responsible for opening and closing the second church, that of San Sebastian. The Mayordomos work together in major duties such as changing the flowers inside the churches and at their doorways and changing the layer of pine needles that is spread over the floors. At the time of the flower change—which takes place every two to three weeks, depending on the fiesta schedule—they first do the church of San Lorenzo and then pass on later in the same day to the church of San Sebastian.

The Senior Mayordomo Sacramento (A3S) is the "boss" of the group of twelve men as they undertake these tasks.[4] Most of the individual tasks, such as changing flowers at the altar of a particular saint, are assigned by custom to a particular Mayordomo, and the Senior Sacramento (A3S) has only the responsibility of seeing that they are carried out. If some special task must be done, he has the authority to decide who will do it. In general the cargo of Senior Sacramento (A3S) is occupied by a man who has the ability to supervise, or at least fancies himself to have it.

In the ordinary interplay of events, the Junior Mayordomo Sacramento (A3J) also has a modicum of authority over the other junior Mayordomos. However, if the Senior Mayordomo Sacramento (A3S) is absent or too drunk to supervise properly, the authority passes on to the Senior Mayordomo Santo Domingo (A5S). Though perhaps in theory the authority would pass from the Senior Santo Domingo (A5S) to the Senior Santa Cruz (A6S) if the need arose, informants refuse to consider this a possibility.

[4] The Mayordomos of Sacramento are associated with San Lorenzo, the patron saint of Zinacantan.

Beyond this, only the Junior Mayordomo San Sebastian (A8J) is further distinguished from the rest of the group. As the most junior of the junior Mayordomos, he is required to pour the drinks on certain ritual occasions.

At each fiesta there is a pair of Mayordomos (senior and junior) who have more responsibilities than the others. As sponsors[a] of the fiesta they must provide more than a proportionate share of sky-rockets, candles, and other articles necessary for the celebration. Some Mayordomos are sponsors of more and bigger fiestas than others. This type of division of labor among the Mayordomos is recorded in Appendix D, where the ritual calendar is given.

(2) *The Mayordomos Reyes and Mesoneros.* The Mayordomos Reyes (A1) and the Mesoneros (A7) are responsible for the chapel that is located in one corner of the walled churchyard of San Lorenzo. The chapel houses a single image—that of the Señor de Esquipulas. Their normal duties involve ritual observances each Sunday (as described in Chapter 6) and general care of the chapel during the week. The Senior Mayordomo Rey and the Senior Mesonero serve for a month and then are replaced by their respective juniors for a month, alternating through the year. The Mesonero is responsible for seeing that the chapel is swept each day, and both he and the Mayordomo Rey contribute candles to be lighted for the saint. They are both officially in service throughout the week, but if either one has a special obligation or other business he may ask the other to do the duty of both for a day or two. In questions of authority the Mayordomo Rey is very much in command. All four of these cargos are served for the calendar year and have additional ritual responsibility during the fiesta of San Sebastian in the January following their service.

(3) *The Cargos of Salinas.* The Mayordomo de la Virgen del Rosario is responsible for the care of the single image of the Virgen del Rosario in the small church in Salinas. The Mayor de Salinas has obligations to the chapel of Esquipulas in Zinacantan and the salt well in Salinas, more than to the church there.[5]

---

[5] There is a small salt well in Salinas, the water of which is boiled down to make salt. The quantities produced are too small for commercial exploitation,

(4) *The Cargos of Navenchauc.* In the hamlet of Navenchauc there is a small church that houses the image of the Virgen de Guadalupe. A pair of Mayordomos take care of this church. The church, the image, and the cargos are of comparatively recent origin. The cargos were established about 1954.

(5) *The Cargos of Apas.* The chapel in the hamlet of Apas is even more recent than that in Navenchauc. It was built in 1962, and the cargos were to be officially served for first time in the calendar year 1963. Since the chapel is for the Señor de Esquipulas, the cargos are called Mayordomo Rey and Mesonero. Because the hamlet is small, its leaders decided[6] it could provide only one of each cargo.

(6) *The Cargos of the Easter Season.* The Pasioneros (A4) are cargos of the Easter Season.[7] The incumbents enter at Carnaval and end their obligations with the end of the observances after Easter. Their saint is Santo Entierro. Their responsibilities are distinct from those of other first-level cargoholders and do not include the care of churches.

(7) *The Cargos of the Fiesta of San Lorenzo.* The Capitanes (A10) serve only during the fiesta of San Lorenzo—four days. The

---

but the Mayor is responsible for extracting a small amount of salt and taking it to the chapel of Esquipulas in Hteklum every two weeks. It is divided among the Mayordomos Reyes, the Mesoneros, and the officials of the civil government. I assume that this custom is a vestige of a tribute paid by Salinas to Zinacantan. Before the present form of civil government was established in 1899, the Mayor may have had civil authority in Salinas. Some informants indicated that the Mayordomo Rey and the Mesonero may have had civil authority before this change; and the Mesonero still carries a small nightstick similar to that used by the eight Mayores or policemen. Both Mayordomos Reyes are still ceremonially given civil authority when they travel to Salinas for the fiesta of the Virgen del Rosario in October.

Salt is a very important trade item in highland Chiapas, and the Zinacantecos are by tradition the salt merchants of the area. For connections between trade and the black Christ, or Señor de Esquipulas, see Borhegyi (1954).

Zinacantecos have a myth that relates the story of how San Lorenzo sent people and the Virgen del Rosario to Salinas to take care of the salt well.

[6] See note 3, Chapter 14.

[7] Here and in later chapters I use "Easter Season" to refer to the period that includes what is normally called "Lent" and the "Easter Season." That is, "Easter Season," as I use it, refers to the period beginning with Carnaval and ending with the celebration of the Sagrado Corazon de Jesus (see Appendix D).

cargo is a minor one, both in expense and in the prestige that accrues to the person who passes it. It seems to exist mostly as an embellishment on the ritual for the fiesta of the patron saint.

(8) *The Mayores.* The eight Mayores (A11) are as much a part of
the civil government as of the religious hierarchy. The post counts
toward progress in the hierarchy and is thus included here as a
cargo. The Mayores are responsible for sweeping the town hall
and for doing errands for both the civil officials and the moletik
(C and D). They also act as policemen. The cargo requires almost
no expenditures, and service in it may hurt rather than enhance a
man's position. After their year of service, the Mayores have special
roles in the fiesta of San Sebastian in January.

In summary, there are three distinct types of cargos on the first
level. The first type is responsible for the everyday ritual. It includes the Mayordomos, the Mayordomos Reyes and the Mesoneros in the ceremonial center, and the six cargos that are served
in outlying hamlets. The Pasioneros and the Capitanes, whose
terms are less than a year, and who have ritual duties not associated with continuing care of a particular church or chapel and
the saints in it, are a second type. The eight Mayores are a quite
distinct third type.

Second-Level Cargos, the Alfereces

The Alfereces have no responsibility for care of the saints or buildings comparable to that of the first-level cargoholders. Besides
their appearances in the Easter Season, when they participate in
processions, they come to Hteklum for only seven major fiestas a
year, and at each one of these a pair of them is changed for new
incumbents. Thus the Alfereces are what might be called a major
embellishment at major celebrations. They dance in front of the
churches, they participate in processions, and they invite the whole
community to a party (see Chapter 6) when they enter their
cargos. A major part of their efforts is devoted to meals to which
they invite one another, and to ceremonial visits to one another's
houses.

When pressed for comparison of the duties of the Alfereces and the Mayordomos, informants are generally at a loss. "Who knows why there are Alfereces?" one of them said. "They just get together and dance in each other's houses. The Alfereces just get together to make fiesta; they don't have to watch over anything. It was always this way—the Alfereces never had anything different—for it is this way and you can't change it."

These comments are supported by observation. The Alfereces are not workhorses of the hierarchy, as are the first-level cargoholders, nor are they responsible administrators like the moletik (C and D).

Though most of their activities are done as a group with all members participating equally, there are some special duties. The Alferez Santo Domingo and the Alferez Divina Cruz provide more than a proportionate share of the hospitality given on the ceremonial rounds, and the Alfereces San Lorenzo (B1), Trinidad (B2), and San Antonio (B3) have greater burdens than the others because the fiestas for which they are responsible are bigger than most.

During the year the image of Santo Domingo in the church of San Lorenzo is taken on visits to major fiestas in other communities. On two of these trips Alfereces, as well as the normal group of Mayordomos, accompany the saint. On the trip to San Lucas, in the hot country below Zinacantan, two pairs of Alfereces go. They are the Alferez Natividad (B6) and the Alferez Santa Rosa (B10), and the Alferez Rosario (B5) and the Alferez San Jacinto (B9). At a certain point on the trail to San Lucas they hold a swearing-in⁶ ceremony among themselves and "convert" the former pair temporarily into Regidores—so that Zinacantan is symbolically represented by a pair of Alfereces and a pair of Regidores. This trip is made for the fiesta of October 18 in San Lucas. Similarly, for the fiesta of August 15 in Ixtapa, from whence comes the salt supply for the region, the Alferez Santo Domingo and the Alferez San Lorenzo (B1) go as Regidores, and the Alferez Trinidad (B2) and the Alferez San Antonio (B3) go as Alfereces.

These last two pairs also have special roles at the fiesta of San Sebastian in the January after they have finished their cargos.

Third- and Fourth-Level Cargos, the Moletik

The group of cargoholders known as the moletik includes the four Regidores of the third level (C) and the two Alcaldes Viejos of the fourth level (D). Even though they are spread over two levels of progress in the hierarchy, many of their duties are performed by the group as a whole. These duties may be divided into administrative and ritual parts.

As administrators of the cargo system they are responsible for appointing cargoholders, or sending out notices of impending obligations to those who have volunteered and know that their names are on the lists for certain cargos. In the last decade the waiting lists have grown to such an extent that the moletik's task of finding incumbents has been considerably reduced, but recruitment of incumbents is still a problem for some of the lesser cargos. Then, too, they are responsible for problems that have not been reduced significantly by the increasing number of volunteers. If a man who has already been named to a cargo finds himself inadequately prepared at the last minute before entering, they must help him to make his arrangements. As a last resort they may have to donate firewood or make a temporary loan so that he will be able to carry out his duties properly. If a man dies during his cargo they must find a replacement or make special arrangements for the performance of the ritual until the new term begins. In these things they work together.

In theory they serve for alternating two-week terms. The Senior Alcalde Viejo (D1), the First Regidor (C1), and the Second Regidor (C2), together with the Senior Scribe (see Chapter 5), alternate with the other three moletik and the Junior Scribe. In fact, the Senior Alcalde Viejo (D1) must be available continuously to handle problems, and many of the other officials participate during their off-terms if they have nothing else to do. The Senior Alcalde Viejo (D1) and the First Regidor (C1) hold the positions of authority, and thus their presence is essential more often than that of the others.

The Senior Alcalde Viejo (D1) has in his house an altar where a sacred picture of San Sebastian is kept in a chest. Every 14 days the flowers decorating the altar are changed, and all the moletik (C and D) participate. Each in turn provides the flowers for this ceremony. The Alcaldes Viejos (D) provide the candles lighted at the altar, with the Senior (D1) providing the larger share of them.

The group also performs together in functions that may be seen as combining administration and ritual. At the change of Mayordomos they go to the house of the incumbent and observe the counting of the "rosary" of coins and ribbons, certifying that it has all the money it did when the cargoholder received it the year before. For the change of Alfereces they perform the swearing-in (see Chapter 5).

The Regidores (C) and the Scribes go out to the hamlets and make collections for payment of the Masses said at fiestas. In most cases the Regidores also take on a disproportionate share of the searching and visiting necessary to find an incumbent for a cargo that is not filled by a volunteer. Until 1962, of course, the Regidores also had to serve as civil Regidores when the need arose (see Chapter 3).

As the chief official in the hierarchy, the Senior Alcalde Viejo (D1) has an additional important obligation. The three annual public ceremonies performed by the curers for all of Zinacantan begin with a meeting at his house—and he must formally receive this group.[8]

All the moletik (C and D) have special roles in the fiesta of San Sebastian after their year of service.

The Terminal Cargo, Alcalde Shuves

Finally there is Alcalde Shuves, the terminal cargo that is served without regard to level. The Alcalde Shuves is principally active during Carnaval. He accompanies the Pasioneros (A4) on their rounds and gives a sweet gruel[6] made of corn and brown sugar (see Chapter 6) to all who come to his house at a specified time.

---

[8] His lightest duty is perhaps the custody of the official Zinacantan branding iron. Zinacantecos who want to brand horses with it usually present him with a small bottle of drink when requesting its loan.

Five

Auxiliary Personnel

The cargoholders do not perform their duties unaided. In fact, their advisors, musicians, and other helpers always outnumber them at least two to one. These people, to whom I have given the general name "auxiliary personnel," can be divided roughly into two classes: (1) those who contribute special skills and knowledge, and (2) those who, in an almost perfectly literal sense, lend a hand. The former group includes the Sacristans,ᵃ the Musicians of the Alfereces,ᵃ the Scribes,ᵃ the Ritual Advisors,ᵃ the Women's Advisors,ᵃ and the Special Musicians.ᵃ The second class includes the ordinary musicians and helpers, some of whom have special roles. In this chapter a listing and description of each type of auxiliary personnel is followed by a discussion of recruitment for these roles and rewards given persons who serve in them.[1]

Ritual Advisors

The Ritual Advisor is a master of ceremonies for the cargoholder. He knows what, when, and how tasks must be done, and tells the cargoholder or his helpers to do them. He knows what things are needed and tells the others to get them. And he makes appropriate speeches to other cargoholders and Ritual Advisors when his cargoholder is working with them.

A man who passed Capitan (A10), the four-day cargo served during the fiesta of San Lorenzo, described his relation to his Ritual Advisor in this way: "For days before the fiesta the Ritual Advisor

---

[1] A complete list of the auxiliary personnel of the Senior Mayordomo Rey for 1960 is found in Appendix C.

told me what to do. I did not really know what was going on, but the fiesta was very gay. I had to drink a lot and dance a lot, and that's all I remember. I did just what I was told. The Ritual Advisor would say, 'Take a bottle and go and visit so-and-so. Now do this. Now take a bottle and do this.' I hardly knew what happened during the fiesta."

This is a case of extreme submission to the Ritual Advisor, for the Capitan cargo is a uniquely short one and the cargoholder had little chance to gain experience. Most cargoholders are accompanied by a Ritual Advisor only at the important points in their year-long cargo. The Mayordomo, for instance, is accompanied by his Ritual Advisor for a few days on each of the following occasions: when he enters his cargo; when he holds the special celebration of the sacred chest on the altar in his house; when he is sponsor of an important fiesta; when the group of Mayordomos participates in an annual fiesta known as the "killing of the saints"; and when he leaves office. An Alferez has a Ritual Advisor on only three occasions during his year of service: when he enters, when it is his turn to invite all the Alfereces (B) for a meal, and when he leaves office. The Regidores (C) have Ritual Advisors only when they enter office, and the Alcaldes Viejos (D) do not have them at all.

The responsibilities of the Ritual Advisor when the cargoholder is entering and leaving office include going to the sacred mountains to pray to the gods that the cargo will be served well, and to ask pardon for inadequacies in the performance. Similarly, the Ritual Advisor speaks to the other cargoholders when the man he is representing leaves office. He asks pardon and expresses the hope that they are satisfied with the manner in which his charge has carried out his duties. The importance of the Ritual Advisor as a speechmaker and representative is reflected in the alternative Tzotzil name for the role: *htak'avel,* "he who answers."

All Ritual Advisors must have passed at least two cargos; there is no other formal requirement for the position. A Ritual Advisor need not have passed the cargo for which he is advising. If he does not know exactly what is required, it is his responsibility to learn it before the cargo begins. Thus, Ritual Advisors are usually recruited by the cargoholders at least six months in advance. A cargoholder who finds himself temporarily without a Ritual Advisor may ask one of the moletik (C and D) to help him.

Mariano, an informant who has served as a Ritual Advisor, says that one does not learn much about being a Ritual Advisor while serving as a Mayordomo (A). One begins to learn while watching what is done during one's Alferez (B) cargo. And one really learns well as a Regidor (C), for then one goes to pick up all the Alfereces (B) in their houses at the time of swearing-in (see Chapter 6). The important thing to learn, according to Mariano, is the talking. This is what really counts and what really has to be done correctly.

Sacristans

There are four Sacristans for the church of San Lorenzo in Zinacantan. One part of their job is the same as that of any sacristan in a Catholic church. They open and close the building, ring the bells, and tend to certain of the ritual objects. In these duties each one serves every fourth week in regular alternation.[2] More frequently and more importantly they are involved in the ritual of the Mayordomos. They know special prayers that must be said on certain occasions—for example, when the Mayordomos count rosaries, bring them to the church, and place them around the necks of the saints. In times past, it is said, the Sacristans knew much more than they do now. Then they even chanted at the Masses.[3]

The Sacristans serve a number of years in their posts, and all can read some Spanish. Their long experience makes them important

[2] In addition to the Sacristans there is a church committee, which was established at the request of the priest a number of years ago. This committee is more directly under the priest's control when he visits Zinacantan than are the Sacristans, who have traditional attachment to the Mayordomos. It seems to be discharging some of the duties performed by the Sacristans in the past, but I have no clear data on what it does. Its current head, an important man in Zinacantan, seems to define the range of its activities.

[3] It is said that the Sacristans who had such skills served until the late 1930's. The last group of such men were full adults at the time and were drunk too often for the taste of the priest who visited Zinacantan. He asked that they be dismissed and younger men appointed. Since then Sacristans have been much younger and have generally served shorter terms. Usually they leave the post before or soon after they are married.

advisors to the Mayordomos when the Ritual Advisors are not present. Because they are able to read the church calendar, which is printed in Spanish, they are also responsible for telling the Mayordomos the dates on which they must perform rituals.

Musicians of the Alfereces

The Musicians of the Alfereces are much more than simple musicians. Because they serve year after year with the changing groups of Alfereces (B), they have greater experience than any of the cargoholders and are given great respect and authority as advisors.

There are two Musicians, whose duties occupy them for roughly 35 days each year. At present, the first, the violinist, has served for more than thirty years. The second, the guitarist, was appointed fairly recently after a previous guitarist was unable to do the job properly. Unlike the musicians of the other cargoholders, who serve for just a year (or even less when the duties cause great inconveniences for them), the Musicians of the Alfereces go through a swearing-in ceremony, and are expected to serve for life. While the violinist gives every indication of being able to do so, two or three guitarists in the last decade have proved unable to perform properly through the extremely long ritual rounds.

Scribes

The two Scribes are attached to the six moletik (C and D). They are chosen for their ability to read and write Spanish. Their duties include keeping a list of all adult males who must pay fiesta taxes, writing out notifications of appointment to cargos, and keeping the lists of people who are waiting for cargos.[4]

The Scribes are appointed for terms of one year that coincide with those of the moletik. They are often appointed for a second consecutive term, and many of them serve as many as three times in the course of a lifetime. Like all the other auxiliary personnel

---

[4] Among their other responsibilities is the keeping of land records for those Zinacantecos who request their services. From all indications this service is seldom requested, for most of the land records are kept by the Secretario Municipal. Their function as keepers of land records was probably more important in the years before the turn of the century, for then the moletik had some civil duties also.

in this first of the two classes, they are not mere underlings of the cargoholders they serve. Their judgment is respected: witness the fashion in which the Scribes discuss whether to jail the Senior Alcalde Viejo (D1) for his poor performance of ritual (Chapter 6).

Women's Advisors

The Women's Advisor, the old woman who directs the cooking in the kitchen of the cargoholder and serves special foods on certain ritual occasions, might be identified as the ritual advisor of the women. She is responsible for knowing the requirements in food and serving for various fiestas. Certain women are known to be especially capable of directing the women's work for specific cargos.

Special Musicians

These Special Musicians are comparable to the Musicians of the Alfereces in many ways. There are two of them, a violinist and a guitarist, and their appointments are theoretically permanent.[5] They serve different cargoholders at three different fiestas. At the fiesta of San Sebastian they play for the "jaguars"[a] (the former Alferez Trinidad [B2] and his junior, the former Alferez San Antonio [B3]). During the Easter Season they serve with the Pasioneros (A4), and during the Christmas Season they serve with the Mayordomos of Rosario (A2), who are sponsors of the fiesta.

Musicians and Helpers

In addition to the very specialized auxiliary personnel discussed above, each cargoholder has a number of other helpers, who are usually recruited by the cargoholder himself or by a senior-junior pair of cargoholders. Lacking the authority or special knowledge of the various types of auxiliary personnel already mentioned, they are normally the underlings of the cargoholders. Since they need fewer skills, they are more readily replaceable than the very specialized people, and their commitments to serving are not as binding.

The most skilled of this class of helpers are the Musicians.[a] The

[5] However, they are not sworn in like the Musicians of the Alfereces.

moletik (C and D) and all the first level (A) cargo-pairs (senior-junior) who serve on a year-long basis have three musicians—a violinist, a harpist, and a guitarist. They are present for flower changes and other rituals in the homes of the cargoholders, and for almost all the rituals performed in and around the church. For many occasions the moletik (C and D) also need a flutist and two drummers. The Alfereces (B) need a flutist and drummers only when entering and leaving their cargos, and it is generally arranged so that the old incumbents[a] recruit them and they serve both the old and new incumbents.[a]

Special Helpers[a] serve the moletik (C and D), the Mayordomos Reyes (A1), and the Mesoneros (A7).[6] Like the General Helpers[a] mentioned below, the Special Helper runs errands, serves food, and pours drinks. He is distinguished from the others by the fact that he makes a stronger commitment to aid a cargoholder who will require more frequent services. In addition, if he cannot serve for a particular occasion, he is responsible for finding his own replacement. The cargoholder is responsible for going to the town hall and informing the civil officials that two persons are his Special Helpers. He requests that their service be recognized, and that they be exempted from other community service during the year. No other helpers, not even the Musicians, are entitled to this exemption.

Among the General Helpers there are special roles, but people may be used in them interchangeably. Thus among the General Helpers there is a drink pourer who goes from person to person serving drinks. Among the General Helpers' wives who help in the kitchen, one woman is responsible for pouring the drink from the large container in which it is stored to the bottles carried about by the drink-pourer.

Another helper role, that of Cannoneer,[a] falls into the General Helper class and is usually served by the same person all year. The Cannoneer fires a miniature cannon during rituals. Powder is packed into the bore with a stick, and a little is fed into a fuse hole. Then the fuse is lighted, usually with a cigarette, and the cannon is

[6] One informant claimed that the Mayordomos also have Special Helpers, but I am inclined to believe the informant who said they did not, for he is a former Mayordomo.

held at arm's length until it goes off. The explosion is deafening
even at 15 or 20 feet, and the job of Cannoneer requires some skill,
a good deal of courage, and strong eardrums. The explosions are
often used as signals between groups of cargoholders who are
starting off on coordinated ritual rounds from different points.
People who live in the ceremonial center are often able to tell what
point a ritual has reached simply by listening for the sequence of
cannon shots.

Recruitment and Rewards of the Auxiliary Personnel

Making any substantial request or asking any substantial favor in
Zinacantan involves presenting a bottle of drink to the person so-
licited. Requesting that a person help with a cargo is no exception
to this rule. For very special roles, such as that of Ritual Advisor,
a few pieces of sweet bread are also included with the gift. Acceptance of the gifts signals acceptance of the request, and the bargain
is usually sealed with at least some of the drink that has been given.

The Scribes are recruited by the moletik (C and D) well before
they are to enter service, and with the understanding that the
Senior Scribe is found first and has the right to choose the person
he would like as Junior Scribe. The Sacristans also name the replacement when one of their number leaves his post, but the drink
used in requesting the services of the new Sacristan is provided by
the Mayordomos. The Alfereces recruit their Musicians, and the
Special Musicians are recruited by the cargoholders they serve.
All other helpers and the regular Musicians are likewise recruited
by the cargoholders they serve.

Kinship is important in the recruitment of auxiliary personnel,
except in the cases of the specialized personnel who serve a group
of cargoholders rather than a single individual. This seems to be
true for two reasons: (1) Kinsmen are more easily approachable
by the cargoholder, more easily obligated to him, and more likely
to enter into a reciprocal agreement in which they will receive
similar aid when passing a cargo. That is, they are in many ways
more closely bound to the cargoholder. (2) The behavior and
capacities of individual kinsmen are likely to be better known to
the cargoholder, and they are more likely to have already worked

together. The probability of disruptive conflict within the group of helpers is thus reduced considerably, for the interpersonal relations and the lines of authority have already been tested.[7]

When a man has few kinsmen he can depend on, he retreats to the second line of defense, his ritual kinsmen,[6] and recruits many of his helpers from among them.[8]

Service as helpers of a cargoholder also has rewards for the kinsmen. Though they have to work very hard for parts of the period during which they are helping the cargoholder in the ceremonial center, there is ample time for them to wander about enjoying the fiesta and the preparations for it. The women obviously see the meals and ceremonial activity as a party. Some talk with keen anticipation about the great amount of drink that will be poured and served, and the fantastic number of tortillas that will be eaten. The fiesta at which kinsmen come together to aid one of their number is often an occasion for the strengthening of family ties.

Most of the auxiliary personnel, kin or not, seem to agree to serve because they want to participate in the entertaining activities of the fiesta. Serving a cargoholder enables them to be close to the center of things and furnishes them with a free supply of drink and food—not a small consideration for many men. Furthermore, the specialized personnel get varying amounts of recognition and prestige.

All auxiliary personnel receive maintenance while serving at a fiesta. That is, the helpers and their families, who accompany them, eat and sleep at the house of the cargoholder. Among the specialized personnel, the Scribes are treated with special consideration. They are invited to meals at the houses of the moletik (C and D) when they could just as easily go home to eat, and it is the responsibility of the moletik to provide better-than-average meals on these occasions. The Sacristans, the Musicians of the Alfereces, and the Special Musicians receive great amounts of food and gifts. The

---

[7] Chapter 9 includes further discussion of the advantages of having kinsmen as helpers.

[8] The Alferez whose entrance to his cargo is discussed in Chapter 6 is an example of a man who had virtually all kinsmen for helpers. The list presented in Appendix C illustrates the use of ritual kinsmen to a much greater degree.

Sacristans get huge bags of fruit at certain fiestas, and substantial amounts of drink, which they may take home and sell if they wish. The Musicians of the Alfereces and the Special Musicians receive so much food and drink that they usually have helpers to carry it away for them. Beyond this, they are paid in money for their services, receiving amounts comparable to half a day's pay for a laborer for each of their days of playing.[9]

Added to the cargoholders, the auxiliary personnel greatly increase the number of people participating directly in the ritual activities at any given fiesta. For large fiestas, such as those of San Sebastian and San Lorenzo, the combined number is 300 or more. Though the number of cargoholders who bear the burden of expense is limited, a great number of Zinacantecos—perhaps 600 a year—contribute time and energy to the staging of fiestas.

[9] In another place (Cancian 1964) I have discussed the rewards and social position of the specialized auxiliary personnel in greater detail.

Six

Ritual

Ritual is the principal product of the hierarchy, and the performance of ritual is the principal duty of the cargoholder. Alone, the cargoholder offers a candle and prays before the altar in his house. Together with dozens of other cargoholders, he does his part in the massive fiestas for San Sebastian in January and for San Lorenzo in August. For these two great fiestas thousands of Zinacantecos come to Hteklum to see the processions and many other attractions. Indians and Ladinos from other communities come to sell food and household wares in the marketplace. Horse traders appear for the most important days. A band is hired. A priest comes to say Mass. Drink, beer, soda pop, and food are sold in more than 20 temporary stalls in the marketplace. A merry-go-round stands out in the middle of it all. Ritual kinsmen meet and drink together. Disputes are settled at the town hall. New clothes, representing weeks and months of weaving and plaiting, are displayed. Young men dressed in their finest lean against the church wall in small groups and eye the girls who scurry back and forth between family groups. Fighting drunks are hauled away to be judged by civil officials who may not be very sober themselves. The Alfereces sponsor horse races, and there are fireworks displays paid for by voluntary donations.

Virtually all the cargoholders are active in some ritual during the two largest fiestas. There are a few formal meetings between the groups of cargoholders (Mayordomos and Alfereces, for example) that normally operate independently during the rest of the year, but for the most part they are engaged in the same patterns that they follow all year. It is the simultaneous presence of all cargo-holders, the few special events, and the crowd that make these fiestas extraordinary. The totality of ritual activities at one of these fiestas is too complex to describe in the space available here.[1] Appendix D is a calendar of all the important rituals in the annual round. In this chapter I will describe two basic ritual patterns in some detail. Each pattern may occur either virtually alone, in a small fiesta, or amid the complex of activities found at the two fiestas mentioned above.

The first is performed in a 24-hour period each weekend by the Mayordomo Rey (A1) and the Mesonero (A7). It is a tiny cele-bration held for the Señor de Esquipulas, an image in the small chapel near the church of San Lorenzo. Not many people gather for such a celebration, although a few hangers-on, mostly little boys, often come in the morning hours. The average Zinacanteco is at home in his hamlet, or traveling to San Cristobal to buy and sell, or off in hot country working his fields—secure in the knowl-edge that the appropriate ritual is being performed by the incum-bent cargoholders. The twelve Mayordomos of the main church may be attending to the saints if their schedule calls for it, or they may be changing flowers on the altars in their houses. If they have no commitments in the ceremonial center for a day or two, some may have left a kinsman to light candles for the small image or sacred chest in their houses in Hteklum and rushed off to their homes in the hamlets to bring back food or seek out someone who will lend them enough money to buy the meat, candles, and drink needed for the next fiesta.

Account of the Regular Weekend Ritual of the Mayordomo
Rey (A1) and the Mesonero (A7) Given by Antonio,
the Senior Mayordomo Rey for 1960

Late Saturday afternoon the assistants arrive at the house of the Mayordomo Rey. The Musicians appear alone to play on instru-ments supplied by the Mayordomo Rey—violin, harp, and guitar.

[1] John Early, S.J., has done an intensive study of ritual associated with the religious hierarchy (1965).

The two Special Helpers come with their wives and children. The Women's Advisor comes to direct the work of the women. (Antonio's sister, and his little daughter who lives with her, also come to help with the women's work.) They all eat a simple meal of beans and tortillas and go to sleep.

Before dawn they are awake. The Musicians tune their instruments while the women begin to make tortillas and the helpers set up the table and spread the tablecloth. The Mayordomo Rey goes from person to person formally requesting that they do him the favor of carrying out their part of the duties. A helper follows him and gives each one the first drink of the day.

Soon the Mesonero arrives with his two Special Helpers (one of whom happens to be his son). He presents a bottle of drink to the Mayordomo Rey and states that he has come to help prepare the rosary of the saint. The Mayordomo Rey places the bottle at the head of the table (east end) and adds one of his own.

Then they put on their formal dress and begin to prepare the rosary. (The rosary is made up of coins and ribbons and is kept in a cloth bag in the saint's chest. The chest rests under an arch of flowers on an altar in the corner of the room.) The Mayordomo Rey opens the chest and takes out the bag. The straw mat is taken from the altar and spread on the floor. When the rosary has been placed on the mat the helper of the Mayordomo Rey gives each person a drink. He is followed by a helper of the Mesonero.

Next they count the rosary. The Mayordomo Rey counts each coin, and the Mesonero moves a kernel of corn from one pile to another for each peso counted by the Mayordomo Rey. (The corn is received with the rosary when the cargoholders take office. If the cargoholder is fortunate, his count will come out higher than that of the previous cargoholder. No one knows what makes the count change. For the rosary of the Mayordomo Rey and the Mesonero the count is usually 328. Their saint has a larger rosary than any other saint.) After the rosary is counted it is put back in the bag, and a round of drink is poured. The bag is returned to the chest, and another round of drink is poured.

With this round of drink the Mayordomo Rey asks the Mesonero, the Musicians, and the helpers to sit down to a meal with him. After the meal there is another round of drink, with which they are asked to accompany him to the chapel in the center of Hteklum. The rosary is again taken from the chest and they go to the chapel, the Mayordomo Rey carrying the rosary in the front of his robe like a woman with an apronful of apples. A round of drink marks the arrival at the chapel, and then the rosary is taken from the bag and placed around the neck of the saint. Then follows another round of drink.

By this time it is 6 or 7 A.M. The Musicians play and the Mayordomo Rey and the Mesonero dance in the chapel. The dancing involves three rounds of drink—at the beginning, middle, and end of the dance. Each round is signaled by a special song. About 10 A.M. they go outside the chapel and eat a meal, usually of pork and tortillas.

Meanwhile the moletik (C and D) and the Scribes have been sitting at the table inside the chapel for most of the morning, talking over cargo matters and waiting for anyone who might arrive to ask for a cargo or discuss problems relating to his cargo. They are included in all the rounds of drink, but they do not eat with the Mayordomo Rey and his party.

If there is time after the meal they may dance a bit more inside the chapel, less formally and without drinking. At 1 P.M., or a little before, there is a round of drink. The Mayordomo Rey takes the rosary off the saint and returns it to the bag. (Someone must always watch to be sure that the rosary is taken off by 1 P.M., for if it is not, the Mayordomo Rey and his party will be strongly reprimanded by the moletik. If the Mayordomo Rey is too drunk to remove it, the Mesonero may do it for him. Antonio is proud of the fact that he was never too drunk to do his duty.)

A round of drink marks the departure from the chapel, and another marks the arrival at the Mayordomo Rey's house. The return of the rosary to the chest is followed by a round of drink and a meal of meat, bread, and sweet gruel. The helper pours a final drink, and the Mayordomo Rey thanks all the participants for their help and asks them to return the next weekend. By 5 or 6 P.M. they have all left for their homes.

The First Days of a New Alferez

The second ritual pattern to be described in this chapter is the change of Altereces that takes place at the fiesta for the Virgen del Rosario in October. Almost identical ceremonies take place on six other occasions during the year when the other pairs of Alfereces are changed, and very similar procedures are followed at the end of the year when all the officials who served during the calendar year are changed.

What follows is divided into four parts. Part (1) is based on observations made between 2:30 P.M. and the middle of the evening when the Alferez's party arrived at the chapel of the Señor de Esquipulas, where the swearing-in ceremony is performed. Part (2) is an adaptation of Domingo's description of the essential features of the swearing-in ceremony. Part (3) describes what I observed at this ceremony, and part (4) describes the giving of sweet gruel to the public the following day.

(1) *An Alferez Prepares for Swearing In.* I arrived at the Vaskis house a few blocks above the church at about 2:30 P.M. Shun Vaskis was to be the Ritual Advisor for his son-in-law, Maltil, who was to enter as Alferez Rosario. Besides Shun and Maltil, 21 others were present when I arrived:

Petul Vaskis, Shun's son, a
   helper
Lol Vaskis, Shun's son-in-law, a
   helper and Cannoneer
Manvel Ko?, Shun's son-in-law,
   a helper
Marian, a Hteklum man, a
   helper
Two boys about 15, probably
   Maltil's sons, helpers
Two boys about 10, probably
   Lol's sons, helpers
Pil, Shun's wife

Maruch, Maltil's wife
Shunka, Manvel's wife
A very old woman, the
   Women's Advisor
Tinik, Petul's oldest daughter
Two adult women, apparently
   relatives of Maltil
A girl about 12, probably Lol's
   daughter
A girl about 10, probably Lol's
   daughter
A girl about 3
Three babies

When I arrived Shun was resting inside and Maltil was resting outside. They both had been very drunk the day before and were tired.

The other men were outside getting haircuts from Marian. The women were busy cooking, but they were not yet hurried. Pil and Tinik, who live in the same house, were on one side of the fire, the others on the opposite side.

I talked with the men for about half an hour, arranged to come back at night for the swearing-in ceremony, drank a sample of sweet gruel, and left.

When I returned about 6 P.M., Maltil was standing on a straw mat in the middle of the room. Petul was dressing him in the elaborate costume of a new incumbent. Shun was observing from a nearby chair and giving advice. When they were finished one of the ten-year-olds poured a round of drink.

After the dressing we all sat talking for a time and then ate. I ate in a group with Lol, Petul, Manvel, and one of the ten-year-olds. Maltil sat alone and did not eat. Shun ate alone facing the fire. The fifteen-year-olds ate a little later. Marian arrived from an errand and ate last of all. The food was beans and tortillas.

About 7:30 the men started to go to sleep. The women were still eating. The entire household was spread out on straw mats by the time Manvel and I stopped talking and lay down at 8. About 8:20 there was a stir of activity when Maltil had to attend to personal needs and asked for help in undoing his complicated costume.

At 8:30 I got up and sat with Maltil, smoking. Fifteen minutes later Petul, who had been resting outside, rushed in to say that the Regidores were coming. All got up quickly. Within minutes only a few yawns and a few strands of hair that women had not finished arranging betrayed the fact that the group had just awakened. The Regidores arrived with their flutist and drummers in the lead and a little group of boys carrying pails (for sweet gruel received but not drunk) trailing behind. The official party—the Regidores, the flutist, and the drummers—stopped in front of the cross in the patio to pray briefly. Then the Regidores went on to the door of the house to greet the Ritual Advisor (Shun) and the new incumbent (Maltil), whom they were to accompany to the swearing-in ceremony. Shun and Maltil stood in the doorway, facing out. Shun, who stood to Maltil's left, received each Regidor first; then the Regidor passed on to Maltil. Both men exchanged "prayer-greetings" with each

Regidor.[2] After the prayer-greeting the Regidor passed on to the helper who stood ready to pour him a drink. After another short prayer-greeting they all entered the house and sat on the benches prepared for them, with Shun sitting on a chair facing the line of them. There they received a drink, then sweet gruel, and then a cigarette. While the drink and sweet gruel were given to helpers and hangers-on in the yard, the group inside made small talk; then the entire group except Shun left for the chapel, stopping briefly to pray at the patio cross before leaving the yard.

We entered the churchyard at 9:25 and the Regidores called a halt to pass a bottle and cigarettes. After a few minutes of joking, we proceeded to the chapel. The Regidores delivered Maltil to the door and left to get the other new incumbent, the Alferez San Jacinto (B9), while the officials inside swore in Maltil. Maltil's Cannoneer set off a great blast outside the chapel and continued to fire at regular intervals all through the ceremony.

(2) *The Swearing-in Ceremony: Domingo's Account.* The new incumbent enters the chapel, goes to the far end of the table, and stands facing the altar (Figure 2). The wooden staffs carried by the officials as symbols of office are on the table, with their heads pointing toward him. The Senior Alcalde Viejo stands, faces the new incumbent, and they begin a prayer-greeting—which the Senior Alcalde Viejo leads.[3] When finished the Senior Alcalde Viejo sits down, and the Junior Alcalde Viejo immediately stands and repeats the same procedure. Then it is done by the First Regidor, and so forth, crisscrossing down the table to the Fourth Judge.

When these prayer-greetings are finished the new incumbent kneels, touching his bowed head to the table, and prays. The Senior

---

[2] I will use the term "prayer-greeting" to refer to a whole class of formalized conversations between persons in ritual contexts. Both speak at the same time, with a prayer-like intonation. The speeches are almost always interval-markers in a ritual, and are most often greetings at the beginning and end of important segments. The wording of the speeches is not absolutely set, but the general content seems to be fairly generally known, though younger people and women often mumble their way through them. The person in the senior role (usually the older person) sets the pace, and the junior person responds, usually following a few words behind.

[3] A text of the prayer-greeting between the Senior Alcalde Viejo who is about to leave office and the entering Senior Alcalde Viejo is found in Appendix E.

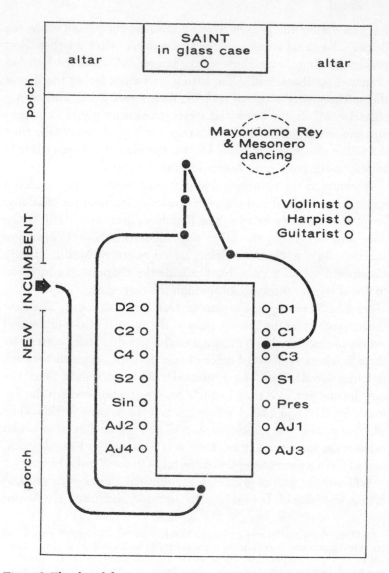

Figure 2. The chapel during a swearing-in ceremony. Starting at the top of the table, the following pairs face each other: Alcaldes Viejos 1 and 2; Regidores 1 and 2; Regidores 3 and 4; Senior and Junior Scribes; Presidente and Sindico; Alcaldes Jueces 1 and 2; Alcaldes Jueces 3 and 4. The six circles in the new incumbent's path indicate his place at various points in the ceremony.

Alcalde Viejo leaves his seat and comes to the new incumbent's side. He blesses the new incumbent and then turns to the altar to pray.

Then the new incumbent goes to the altar to pray and to light a large candle, kneeling and crossing himself three times as he approaches the altar. When his prayer is done he turns his back to the altar and faces the table. There is another, shorter, exchange of prayer-greetings with all the officials. With this the swearing-in is complete, and the wrapping of the new incumbent's headcloth is changed to that of a cargoholder in office.

His helpers bring forth a bottle of drink, a gourd of coffee, and a piece of bread, and he presents these to the Senior Alcalde Viejo. Then he repeats the process for the junior side of the table, giving the same to the Junior Alcalde Viejo. The drink is poured by a helper, the coffee is passed from hand to hand, and the bread is broken and distributed by the Mesonero. After everyone at the table has been served, the Mayordomo Rey, the Musicians, the helpers, and the spectators each get a bit of drink, coffee, and bread.

Meanwhile, the new incumbent goes to sit between the First Regidor and the Third Regidor, and the group is ready for the next swearing-in. The second new incumbent sits between the Second Regidor and the Fourth Regidor when his swearing-in is complete. After the ceremony is over, each new incumbent is invited to a special meal of chicken in the house of the man he has replaced.

(3) *Swearing-in Ceremony, October 6, 1961.* Maltil, the new Alferez Rosario, entered and went to the foot of the table. Seated on the senior side of the table were the Senior Alcalde Viejo, the Senior Scribe, and the Presidente; on the junior side were the Junior Alcalde Viejo, the Junior Scribe, and a Judge. The Regidores had gone off to get the other new incumbent, and the other civil officials were said to be tracking down a man accused of murder.

The Senior Alcalde Viejo was very drunk and made it through the prayer-greetings and the blessing only with the aid of his fellows at the table. Staggering, he made commands that lagged behind the responses of the new incumbent, who was sober and primed for the performance. By 10:30 the swearing-in was finished, and the group sat talking as they waited for the arrival of the new Alferez San Jacinto. After several exchanges of drinks I found myself sitting at the end of the senior side of the table at the Presidente's side.

The Regidores and the new incumbent arrived, and he went to the foot of the table while the Regidores took their seats. The new Alferez San Jacinto was even more sober and ready than the new Alferez Rosario had been, but all the officials at the table were in various states of drunkenness. The Alferez Rosario, the Judge, all the Regidores, and the Senior Scribe were able to operate without any difficulty. The Junior Alcalde Viejo was a bit drunker than this group. The Junior Scribe was a good bit drunker still, and the Senior Alcalde Viejo and the Presidente were present in body only.

The ceremony started and the Senior Alcalde Viejo managed his first prayer-greeting. He finally was told to sit down. The Scribes were talking with each other across the table, saying, "Why go on with this farce?" They all got through the first prayer-greeting. Then the Senior Alcalde Viejo was too drunk to go to the foot of the table for the next part of the ceremony, the blessing. Finally his fellows helped him to get there, but he could not do the blessing properly. As he bungled along, the others, especially the Scribes, tried to persuade the Junior Alcalde Viejo to come down and take over. He refused, saying that the Senior Alcalde Viejo was doing well enough. They gave up on the Junior Alcalde Viejo and persuaded the First Regidor to take over. He handled the blessing and the prayer efficiently—and the Senior Alcalde Viejo was pushed back to his seat. That done, the new incumbent went to the altar.

The Junior Scribe leaned across the table to tell me that the Senior Alcalde Viejo would be sent to jail for his inability to carry out his duties, but the Senior Scribe insisted that he should be pardoned and taken home to rest.

The new incumbent turned to face a very unholy group for the second exchange of prayer-greetings. All managed to get through it except the Presidente, who had fallen asleep on my shoulder and could not be awakened.

When the Alferez San Jacinto was finally seated and passing out cigarettes, Shun Tsu stormed in. He had been Senior Alcalde

Viejo in 1957 and, in addition to being the Ritual Advisor of the new Alferez San Jacinto, was a very powerful political leader in Zinacantan. He gave the Senior Alcalde Viejo a thorough dressing-down but did not suggest jailing him. Finally, just before the group staggered to the altar for the final prayers before leaving, the Senior Alcalde Viejo was taken home by two young men.

It should be added that the behavior of the Senior Alcalde Viejo at this ceremony was extraordinary. As far as I could tell, it came just short of causing a serious scandal. The Senior Alcalde Viejo, who was a very respected man and had made a reputation for not drinking excessively during his previous three cargos, had been going on binges for a number of weeks. This pattern is not uncommon as a cargoholder reaches the end of his year of service. However, shortly after this incident, the Senior Alcalde Viejo resolved to drink nothing stronger than beer. He held to his resolve through the remaining rituals of the ceremonial year; when I saw him last, eight months after his cargo was over, he was still holding to it.[4]

(4) *Giving Sweet Gruel.* Sweet gruel is a drink made of finely ground corn, water, and brown sugar. The day after the ceremony in the chapel the new Alferez gives a large cupful to fellow cargo-holders who pay a formal visit to his house, and to any other person who wishes to partake of the special treat. Below is my description of the giving of sweet gruel at Maltil's house on October 7, 1961.

We arrived to find the yard full of people. The moletik and the Alfereces were arranged on junior and senior benches facing each other in front of the house. Shun and Shun Tsu, the Ritual Advisors of the new Alfereces, sat in chairs facing the ends of the benches. They talked with the Alcaldes Viejos, who sat on the first seats on their respective sides. We were invited into the house, where the women were busily filling gourds with sweet gruel. They immediately put my wife to work.

The Ritual Advisor for each side gave a blessing, and the sweet gruel for the seated cargoholders was brought out by the male

---

[4] The Senior Alcalde Viejo was Lucas, the rich farmer discussed in Chapter 7. When his son-in-law became a Mayordomo Rey (A1) in 1964, Lucas served as Ritual Advisor. He began drinking again, and died shortly after a week-long binge in early 1964. Some Zinacantecos attributed his death to witchcraft thrown by a man who was jealous of Lucas's power in his home hamlet.

helpers. The cargoholders drank what they were offered, or poured it off into buckets carried by the little boys who follow them around on such occasions, and returned the gourds. While the seated party talked, the helpers served the Mayordomos, who were standing to the side in an informal group. Then they all left, the seated group stopping to pray briefly at the patio cross on the way out, and the Mayordomos wandering off. Helpers rushed forward to take the benches to the house of the Alferez San Jacinto for a similar offering of sweet gruel.

Long after the officials left, the helpers were serving sweet gruel to people who waited outside. Young women were served last, it seemed. Six men were involved in passing out sweet gruel. Two ran from the house to the groups of people, carrying a full gourd in each hand. Two others alternated between this task and carrying empty gourds back to the house; and the last two stood at the edge of the crowds, passing the gourds from the carriers to the receivers, and seeing that each person received a gourdful and that all gourds were collected and returned as efficiently as possible. Most of the gourds were fairly full when received by the visitors. Toward the end a few people got short rations—and some of the sweet gruel from the bottom of the pot was lumpy. In all, at least 200 people received about a half-liter of sweet gruel each—so about 100 liters, or more than 25 gallons, were given to the visitors.

The mood and behavior of the principal figure changed over the two days described above. Before the swearing-in Maltil was quiet, tense, and very submissive to those who were dressing him. The whole household was on edge. Seeing him before the ceremony, I wondered how such an apparently weak-willed man could have achieved the economic success necessary to become Alferez Rosario. At the chapel both he and the other new incumbent performed their roles in the ritual with a rigid intensity indicating a fear that they would be unable to handle the very jumbled situation. It was not until I saw Maltil the next afternoon at the giving of the sweet gruel that I realized how much he and his household had been in the grip of stage fright the night before. At the giving of the sweet gruel he was totally in command of the situation and of himself, and showed the force of personality his position implied.

Seven

The Zinacanteco Corn Farmer

Sponsoring a ritual is very expensive for the cargoholder. Chapter 8 gives details on his expenses, and the present chapter gives background helpful in understanding these details.

Corn (maize) farming is the principal occupation of Zinacantecos. Below I begin with the facts about corn farming that are common to all Zinacantecos.[1] Since I want to show the possibilities for acquiring differing amounts of wealth, the later sections of the chapter concentrate on three representative corn farmers: one unsuccessful, one moderately successful, and one wealthy.

General Background

Zinacantan is in the highlands of Chiapas, a cold-country zone where yields from corn farming are consistently too low to make serious commercial exploitation possible. However, the township borders on the lowlands of the Grijalva River valley; and this access to productive land in a hot-country zone is an important factor in making Zinacantecos the principal corn farmers among the highland Indian groups that frequently use San Cristobal as a market center. Since the walk to hot country from almost all points in Zinacantan requires the better part of a day, Zinacantecos go there for periods ranging from a few days to several weeks to work their fields.[2]

[1] This statement holds for the ethnographic present, 1962, and for a number of years before it. The years since have seen a number of important changes in corn farming and marketing, and more change seems imminent. The trends are described in Cancian (1965).
[2] Stauder (1961) gives an excellent description of these trips, the preparations for them, the groupings of people involved, and the work in hot country.

Zinacantecos have access to three kinds of land. The first is that in cold country. Almost without exception, each family owns small cornfields around its house. This land is seldom enough to take care of more than a very small proportion of the family's yearly needs. Most men work it in spare moments. A few Zinacantecos have extensive lands in cold country, but I know only one instance in which these provide the principal support of a family.

Some 850 Zinacanteco families have plots of land in the Ejido. The Ejido is land distributed to farmers under the Mexican government's land-reform program.[3] Much of the Ejido land is located in the temperate-country[6] zone between Zinacantan and hot country. In almost all cases the fertility and productivity of this land are marginal from the point of view of commercial exploitation. Though the intent of the land-reform program was to give each individual enough land to make him economically self-sufficient, this ideal has not been achieved in Zinacantan. Ejido plots provide full support for very few families.

The relatively productive hot-country land supports almost all the commercial production of corn by Zinacantecos and a good proportion of production for household consumption. Zinacantecos are not property-holders in hot country. They rent from Ladino landowners whose holdings have survived the land reform program. Though limited in size by Mexican law, most of these holdings are large enough to accommodate several Zinacantecos, who may rent land together. For the most part, these lands are in the Grijalva River valley between Totolapa and Chiapa de Corzo. Some Zinacantecos travel to still more productive lands near Venustiano Carranza, but the greater distance tends to make farming these lands uneconomical, especially for the small operator.

All farming is done by the milpa system of shifting cultivation. Trees and underbrush are cut from a piece of reforested land and burned, after which the corn is planted with a digging stick. The land is usually farmed during the year it is cleared and for three or four following years. When land is farmed for more than that period

---

[3] Edel (1962) presents a detailed study of the Ejido program in Zinacantan, emphasizing its history.

without being allowed to reforest, yield falls off, and lower-than-standard rents are often arranged with the owners.

Almost all Ejido land and private property in Zinacantan has been cut and burned. From the point of view of fertility it usually lies fallow much less than the optimal proportion of the time. Land that has lain fallow long enough to grow sizable trees is known as rozadura, in reference to the process of cutting and burning it. Land that has been very recently used is called rastrojo, in reference to the cornstalks left from the previous harvest.

Land is measured by two systems. Zinacantecos seldom use the Mexican system of reference by area, in which the hectare (100 by 100 meters) is the unit. Because much of the land is so hilly and stony that parts of it cannot profitably be planted, amounts of land are gauged by volume of seed planted. In Mexico as a whole, corn is more and more coming to be measured by weight rather than by volume, but in Chiapas the following volume measurements are still most commonly used:[4]

> Caldera = one metric liter
> Cuarto = five calderas (five liters)
> Almud = three cuartos (15 liters)
> Fanega = 12 almudes (180 liters)

Land is generally measured by the almud of seed put into it, and rent is calculated on this basis. A hectare of land will generally take about an almud of seed if a normal proportion is lost to stony spots and hilliness. If the land is good, a hectare is usually planted with four cuartos of seed, i.e., 1.33 almudes.

Rent is almost universally paid in kind at the rate of two fanegas of corn for each almud of seed planted. On certain types of government land it is possible to rent by the hectare at only 25 per cent of

---

[4] These are the units used by Zinacantecos and many others in the area. Ladinos more often use two other related units: the litro, which is four cuartos (20 liters); and the fanega-litro, which is 12 litros (240 liters). When the two types of fanegas are discussed together, the one listed in the text is called fanega-chica to distinguish it from the fanega-litro. When Zinacantecos say "fanega" they mean fanega-chica.

One American bushel is equal to approximately 35 liters of volume. Thus a fanega (chica) is approximately 5.14 bushels.

the above rate, but this land is accessible to very few Zinacantecos. There is also some privately owned land that produces low yields and is available at low rents.

Yield varies tremendously, depending on the quality of the land and the vicissitudes of climate. Yields as low as three fanegas per almud planted occur in very bad years and on very poor land. In these cases landowners are usually forced to adjust the rents. An average yield in hot country is eight fanegas. A good one, which is usually expected in the first year of planting rozadura, is 12 fanegas. Fifteen fanegas is an excellent yield, and 20 fanegas a yield that very few Zinacantecos have in a lifetime of work.

Some Zinacantecos sell corn to each other for home use, but most of the corn they grow for profit is sold in the San Cristobal market to Ladinos and to Indians from other townships. Some is also sold in Chiapa de Corzo.

When a Zinacanteco has harvested his crop he has three outlets for his surplus. He may sell to a middleman; he may sell to the government; or he may keep the corn and sell it himself in small quantities during the year. Many Ladinos who have trucks to transport corn or places to store it buy crops at harvest time on speculation. The price they offer is generally too low to be attractive unless the farmer is in great need of cash or has special problems that make transporting the corn to his own home for storage too expensive. A small group of Zinacanteco middlemen has appeared recently. However, unlike the Ladino middlemen, they usually buy corn in small quantities and make an immediate profit through resale in the San Cristobal market.

An independent agency of the national government has in the last few years established a system of corn warehouses in Chiapas. This agency will buy corn at a standard price throughout the year, but the paper work, quality control, and other complications of dealing with the agency have made it unattractive to most Zinacantecos, especially the large majority who do not speak Spanish.[5]

---

[5] Young (1962) has made a study of the government corn-buying system and gives details on the factors that make it an unattractive outlet for Zinacanteco producers.

Most Zinacantecos take the third alternative. They transport the corn to their houses in the highlands and store it until they are ready to sell. The price of corn in San Cristobal market varies from 1.80 pesos per cuarto at harvest time to an extreme high of 4 pesos in August, before the harvests are in.[6] The strategy of the average Zinacanteco is to hold his corn as long as he is able to live without selling, and to sell at the highest possible price. Those who succeed in holding significant amounts until August watch the market very carefully for the peak of prices. When he is ready to sell at the San Cristobal market, a Zinacanteco takes the corn there, pays a small fee for a place to sit with his bag of corn, and sells in small quantities, usually one cuarto, to individual buyers.

The amount of corn consumed in the home varies greatly, depending on the size and appetite of the family. The poverty of some families keeps their consumption down, but the Zinacanteco who lacks tortillas with any regularity is a very poor one indeed, and a very exceptional one. Many Zinacantecos "invest" their corn in raising a small number of chickens or pigs, the former primarily for home consumption and the latter primarily for sale. This investment is not normally considered part of home consumption. An average nuclear family will use between three and five fanegas of corn for tortillas in a year.

The Agricultural Cycle

The agricultural cycle begins in January or February, when the winter rains have stopped. If a man is going to work land that has been lying fallow for many years, he must cut the undergrowth and trees. This is done in January or February. If the land has been used the year before, he has simply to gather up the stalks left at the last harvest. This is usually done in April. In either case he burns the debris at the peak of the dry season in April.

In late May, when the summer rains are just beginning, he seeds. About a week later, if all goes well with the rains, he reseeds some

[6] The price of corn is about 2 pesos for the first half of the year. It usually rises to 2.50 in the early part of the summer, and often to 3.50 through most of August. In exceptional years it reaches 4 pesos in August and early September.

few places that have not taken well. Usually this is a minor job, but
in 1962, for instance, lack of rain threatened a disaster and some
Zinacantecos were still considering a third seeding in early August.

June and July usually see the corn growing rapidly and an
equally rapid growth of weeds. Two weedings are done, one beginning just before the middle of June and the other beginning about
the middle of July. During the first year on a newly cleared field
only one weeding is necessary. After the weedings the fields need
little attention until October. However, where the land will support them, many Zinacantecos plant beans among the rows of corn
in early September. In October the corn is "doubled"; that is, the
stalk is broken so that the food supply of the ear from the stalk is
cut off and the ear dries. The ear is left pointing downward so that
it has natural protection from rains, which might otherwise rot
the grain.

The harvest may take place in December or January. The corn
is husked in the process of gathering, so that only the ear is brought
to the central location. There the grains are taken off the cobs by
beating with a pole. For this process the ears are placed in a net
bag or on a cowhide sieve supported by a platform.

The grain is then bagged and prepared for the trip home. Until
recently all Zinacantecos transported their corn with horses or
mules. However, the improvement of roads in Chiapas has made
trucking more important every year, and it may soon be the chief
means of moving corn.

Table 3 lists the approximate amount of work necessary for each
of the steps in the agricultural cycle reviewed above.

The basic work that must be done on any milpa amounts to 30
man-days per almud seeded plus 1.5 man-days for every fanega
harvested. These figures should be considered "high minimums."
That is, very few people can work so as to reduce them substantially. Very good land, which is hard to find, may reduce them
somewhat. On the other hand, inefficient operations can make the
time required considerably longer than Table 3 indicates. It should
be noted that the figures do not include travel time between Zinacantan and hot country. This can be important, especially for the

TABLE 3
Labor Costs in Corn Farming

From preparing land to doubling (man-days per almud seeded)		Second weeding (if not new land)	8
Cutting and gathering . . 10–14		Doubling	2
or		Approximate Total[a] . . .	30
Gathering stalks and burning	3	*Harvest* (man-days per fanega harvested)	
Seeding	3	Gathering	1
Reseeding	1	Taking grain off cobs . . .	0.5
First weeding	12	Total	1.5

[a] Calculating either new land with no second weeding or old land with no cutting and burning.

man who is working very little land and has to spend two days traveling (round trip) in order to work just a few days in hot country.

At weeding time in June and July, the work load is so great that a man can keep up with it himself only if he has less than two almudes seeded. Unless he has a very large family, any Zinacanteco who is growing corn commercially hires workers at this time. Many of the workers are Zinacantecos who have not planted much corn, but the greater proportion seem to be men from the neighboring township of Chamula. Since the Chamulas are land-poor and have even less convenient access to the hot-country land than do the Zinacantecos, many of them seek day work all through the year. Workers are also hired at other points in the agricultural cycle, but they are most crucial at weeding time, when the corn is still small and can be ruined if not weeded immediately.

Workers are not paid for traveling time, but are fed during the days of traveling. The cost of feeding a worker for a day is approximately 1 peso (8 cents U.S.), and he is paid 5 pesos. Thus a man-day in hot country is worth about 6 pesos. The 30 days of work put in on an almud of milpa before harvest are thus worth 180 pesos, and the work of harvesting costs 9 pesos per fanega. An almud of seed that produced an average yield of eight fanegas would cost 252 pesos in labor on the field itself.

In my calculations on the economics of corn farming I have used a standard price of 2.50 per cuarto for the sale of corn. Obviously some people make more and some make less. The selection of 2.50 as an average is supported by the fact that hired hands are commonly paid in cash at 5 pesos a day or in kind at two cuartos a day.

Transportation, equipment, and many other lesser expenses add to the cost of the corn produced by Zinacantecos. These factors, more than the actual cost of labor, determine the profit a farmer can make, and they vary from person to person more than does the labor cost. They are among the crucial factors distinguishing the three cases examined below.

Three Zinacanteco Corn Farmers

The salable surplus and profit from a year of corn farming varies tremendously among farmers. The following discussion of three cases is meant to show the possibilities for differentiation in wealth and to suggest the factors that produce success or failure in commercial corn farming. Besides these cases, general statements of informants, observation, and a number of other cases recorded in less detail support my conclusions.

(1) Domingo does not like to work the milpa. During the year in which the data on his corn farming was gathered he worked half-time as an informant for the Harvard Project, principally as my informant. Because he received an income of about 2,000 pesos from this work, he was able to live quite well despite the commercial failure of his farming. The practices that caused his farming to be an economic failure are extreme instances of those that undermine the efforts of other poor Zinacanteco farmers. Domingo is 24 years old and lives in a small house very near his father's. He moved there only recently, having lived with his mother for almost all the time since his parents separated shortly after his birth. His father had no children by his second wife, and Domingo has no siblings. Domingo married a girl from a nearby hamlet and they have a baby son.

The people of Hteklum, where Domingo lives, have a reputation for being poor corn farmers. They sometimes claim that the relative gaiety of life in the ceremonial center makes the isolation, dirt, and heat of hot country more disagreeable for them than for the people who live in the outlying hamlets.

(2) Juan is a full-time corn farmer. That is, he spends 200 to 250 days a year attending to his milpas and selling corn. He is about 38 years old and lives in Paste, near hot country, with his wife and three small children. Juan's house is very near those of his father and three brothers. He is past Presidente of the township and a powerful political leader. Because of his political responsibilities, Juan looked into the research that anthropologists were doing in Zinacantan, and ended by working as an informant from time to time. He earns about 200 pesos a year from this work. The sale of drink, soft drinks, and cigarettes, a supply of which he sometimes keeps in his house, also yields a few pesos a year.

(3) Lucas lives in Apas. A very successful full-time corn farmer, he passed Senior Alcalde Viejo in 1961. He is 55 years old and the father of 11 living children—seven sons and four daughters. Most of his children are already married, but two sons and two daughters remain single and live with him and his wife. Only the milpas he farms in hot country are included in the calculations made below. However, he also farms a considerable amount of land that he owns in Apas. This land probably gives him an additional profit of 500 to 1,000 pesos a year. Like Juan, he sometimes maintains a small store in his house.

Table 4 gives a summary of the financial aspects of a corn-farming year for Domingo, Juan, and Lucas. For Domingo I have very accurate records of expenses, based on a notebook he kept, on my almost daily conversations with him, and on my visits to his fields in hot country. The figures for Juan are based on his reports of the previous year's work. For Lucas I have only estimates. His estimates, however, are very good, if consistency with statements of other informants can be taken as an indication of accuracy. My own observations also indicate that his estimates are correct. The discussion that follows refers to, interprets, and supplements Table 4.

Although Domingo seeded 25 per cent less than Juan, he harvested more, principally because he did all of his work on land in hot country, and most of it on rozadura. Juan planted at three

TABLE 4
Farming Accounts of Three Zinacantecos

CORN

Production, Expenses, and Profit[a]	Domingo	Juan	Lucas[b]
Seeded	9	12	30
Harvested	900	828	2,880
Paid in rent	148	72	180
Corn taken home	752	756	2,700
Net production[c]	743	744	2,670
Idealized cost of workers	($765.00)	($927.00)	($2,520.00)
Actual cost of workers	937.05	845.00	2,520.00
Gifts for workers	123.45	50.00[b]	100.00
Voluntary gifts	36.00	—[d]	–
Transportation	427.65	–	600.00
Tax	20.00	–	–
Subtotal	1,544.15	895.00	3,220.00
Contingencies (5%)[e]	77.20	44.75	161.00
GRAND TOTAL EXPENSES	1,621.35	939.75	3,381.00
Value of Net Product	1,857.50	1,860.00	6,675.00
Profit	236.15	920.25	3,294.00
Unit Cost	2.18	1.26	1.27
Unit Profit	.32	1.24	1.23

BEANS

Production, Expenses, and Profit[a]	Domingo	Juan	Lucas[b]
Seeded		10	24
Harvested		118	288
Paid in rent		–	–
Beans taken home		118	288
Net production[c]		108	264
Idealized cost of workers		($198.60)	($480.00)
Actual cost of workers		–	480.00
Gifts for workers		–	20.00
Transportation		–	64.00
Total		–	564.00
Contingencies		–	–
GRAND TOTAL EXPENSES		–	564.00
Value of Net Product		540.00	1,320.00
Profit		540.00	760.00
Unit Cost		–	2.14
Unit Profit		5.00	2.86
TOTAL PROFIT, CORN AND BEANS	$236.15	$1,460.25	$4,054.00[f]

NOTE: All idealized calculations and all calculations of value of products are made on the basis of figures given in the text.

a Figures for the first five items in each left-hand column are given in cuartos (five liters of volume). The remainder are given in pesos (8¢ U.S.).

b Estimated figures. All figures for Lucas are my estimates except for the amounts seeded and the rent paid, which he reported to me.

c Amount of corn produced in excess of the amount invested in rent and seed.

d Dashes in any column indicate that the farmer had no expenses for the item in question.

e The 5% listed for contingencies is meant to cover such things as replacement of equipment and ceremonies performed in the fields to ensure good harvests. Actually, Domingo spent more than this because he had to invest in much new equipment. The others no doubt spent less. This 5% probably does not cover all the expense of replacing horses and mules when they die. The animals are usually purchased after an especially good harvest with the "surplus" profit. The year presented here (1961) was not an exceptionally good one for any of the three farmers.

f Lucas's total profit, taking into account the fact that he probably does his own labor on beans, is 564 pesos higher, or 4,618.00 pesos.

locations. He seeded one almud on Ejido land in cold country and got a return of only three fanegas. Two almudes planted on Ejido land in temperate country yielded 12 fanegas, and one almud planted on rented land in hot country yielded eight fanegas. Lucas's yield is calculated as eight fanegas per almud planted, which, as can be seen in the cases of Domingo and Juan, is a fair average for hot country.

Although Domingo paid more rent than either Juan or Lucas, he paid a little less than the normal two fanegas per almud seeded, for two reasons: (1) The rastrojo he planted had been used for many years and the owner accepted less than full rent. (2) He managed to convince the owner of the rozadura that he had seeded less than he actually had. Juan paid full rent for the land in hot country on which he planted one almud, but the remaining three almudes of his seeding was done on Ejido land, for which there is no rent. Lucas, in a manner that is not entirely clear to me, managed to obtain rights to plant areas of government-held land for which the very low rent of six almudes per almud planted is charged.

In sum, Lucas had advantages in both quality of land (yield) and amount of rent paid, while Domingo had no such advantage on rent, and Juan seeded land of poor quality.

Labor costs in the production of a crop are an important part of the investment the farmer makes each year. The idealized cost of workers shown in Table 4 is calculated from the figures presented earlier in this chapter (180 pesos per almud seeded, plus nine pesos per fanega harvested). The important fact, of course, is the actual cost of workers. The actual cost should be below the idealized cost because the farmer's own work is not included in the figure for actual cost. Despite this fact, Domingo's cost for workers was higher than the idealized cost calculated for him. Part of this disparity is explained by the fact that a good share of his effort was devoted to clearing rozadura, an expense that would not be repeated in full in future years. However, much more of the disparity is explained by the inefficient manner in which Domingo organized his work. Often he had to give workers full pay for short days and travel time. Juan paid workers 82 pesos less than the idealized cost.

The approximately 14 days of his work that this amount would cover is certainly much less than he actually devoted to his fields. His labor costs were raised by the fact that the stony, poor land of the Ejido plots is hard to weed.[7] Because I have no actual figures, Lucas is charged the full idealized cost. In fact, because he and his sons did the work, his actual labor cost was probably much lower than the one listed.

Because he has few relatives and little experience in corn farming, Domingo had higher costs for recruiting workers than did Juan and Lucas. Normally an employer has to give a bottle of drink when asking a man to work for him, and a good meal when the worker returns from hot country. Domingo made more trips to hot country and stayed there for shorter periods, and thus spent a proportionately greater amount on meals. Moreover, he did not have a long-term arrangement with workers as did Juan and Lucas. Recruiting workers each trip cost him time and money for drink.

Only Domingo gave "voluntary gifts" to workers while they were traveling to and from hot country. These gifts were usually given because Domingo had to ask workers to carry heavy loads over long distances. Juan and Lucas have horses to carry food and tools to hot country, and do not have to ask such favors.

Transportation costs contributed most to Domingo's failure. Part of his high expenditure for transportation is attributable to bad management, another part to his lack of horses, and a third to the fact that he lives further from hot country than the other two and must pay higher rates to have his corn brought home. Bad management is reflected in the extra trips he made to hot country and the extra bus fares he paid on those trips. The same lack of horses that made it necessary to give "voluntary" gifts to workers also made it necessary to pay bus fare part of the way to hot country. A worker can be expected to walk all the way if horses carry the food and equipment, but not if he has to carry a load.

[7] For the weeding of one of the Ejido plots Juan reported a number of days so high that I suspect an error in my notes. Adjustment of this figure to the average required for this type of work reduces Juan's labor cost so that the difference between the ideal and the actual costs covers much of his work. This adjustment is not made in Table 4.

Because of the greater distance, transportation of corn from hot country to IIteklum costs 25 to 50 per cent more than transportation to Apas or Paste.

Juan had no cost for transportation because he and his brothers pool their horses and help each other bring up the harvests. Juan pays for this advantage to some extent, for he must take a turn caring for the horses at their pasture, which is some distance from the family home. Since the Ejido land, where he did most of his farming, is closer to his house than is hot country, Juan has an added advantage.

Lucas has enough horses to carry food and tools to hot country, but it would be impractical to maintain the large number required to transport his great harvests, so he pays others to bring his corn home. The 600 pesos listed for transportation went entirely for the transport of 2,700 cuartos (75 fanegas) at 8 pesos per fanega from his fields to his home. Similar service to Hteklum usually costs 12 pesos per fanega.

The government tax on the transport of corn out of a producing region was paid only by Domingo, for he was the only one of the three to employ a truck to carry his harvest home. Farmers using horses can avoid the tax stations along the road.

The profit realized from the year's labor indicates most clearly the varying success of the three efforts that have been reviewed. Domingo's profit, which represents 65 working days and 32 traveling days of his time, is a very low 236.15 pesos. His unit cost is 2.18 pesos per cuarto of net production. This cost is so high that he would have been able to buy the corn more cheaply had he had cash on hand at harvest time. A good part of Domingo's harvest went into home consumption and feeding chickens and a pig, but he did manage to sell some of his surplus in August of 1962. He received a little more than 3 pesos per cuarto—thus his actual profit was a bit higher than calculated in Table 4.

Juan and Lucas had much lower unit costs than did Domingo. Lucas's saving on rent was a major factor in lowering his costs, and Juan's savings on both rent and transportation helped lower his expenditures. Though Juan saved money on transportation, the particular arrangements he makes with his brothers in order to do so limit the total amount he can transport (and produce). Thus Lucas's system yields a higher total profit.

Both Juan and Lucas made additional profits from beans. Domingo did not think his land suitable for a bean crop and decided it would be a poor investment.[8] Juan planted beans at each of the three locations at which he farmed. Lucas planted beans only on part of the corn land he seeded in hot country. The eight almudes of beans that he seeded were put into land that had already taken about four almudes of corn. Although I have calculated his profits from beans as if the work had been done by workers, it was probably done by Lucas and his sons. Their work probably added at least 1,000 pesos to his profits, bringing them to over 5,000 pesos.

At least half of Juan's "profit" is needed for the day-to-day expenses of his family. He would be lucky to have 700 pesos to spend on "luxuries," emergencies (such as sickness), long-term investments (such as a new house), and service in the cargo system. Even with his larger family, the comparable figure for Lucas is probably closer to 3,000 pesos.

Summary

The factors that distinguish the three men discussed above are crucial to the success or failure of any corn farmer in Zinacantan.

Besides poor management, which is reflected in Domingo's general approach to corn farming, the reasons for his failure are principally the following: (1) lack of special arrangement for renting land; (2) lack of investment in horses and corn;[9] and (3) distance of his home from hot country.

---

[8] Many Zinacantecos hesitate to plant more beans than they need for home consumption. It is universally recognized that really huge profits can be made from beans, but that there is a great risk in planting beans. While it takes a very bad year to make the corn crop a total loss, the bean crop is ruined completely much more often. On the other hand, in a lucky year beans will produce two fanegas for every almud planted, yielding an enormous profit. Since the average "good" return on beans is only 12 to 1 on seed (as opposed to about 100 to 1 for corn), one is risking food as well as work when planting beans.

[9] For instance, Domingo had to make a special trip to hot country to harvest enough corn so that his wife could prepare food for the workers going to harvest the rest of his crop. Had he kept reserves of corn, this expensive trip would have been avoided.

Excluding the large number of men who have Ejido land, the proportion of Zinacantecos who have the connections and ability necessary to make special arrangements for land is very small. Many are successful corn farmers without such special arrangements—even though they must pay normal rents. Thus, although Domingo is at a disadvantage here in comparison with Juan and Lucas, on the whole his costs in rent represent what is normal for Zinacantecos.

Because he was starting out anew and because he is not really interested in corn farming, Domingo did not have the equipment and the horse he would have needed to run an efficient operation. The lack of these raised his expenses considerably, for he had to pay bus fare for workers and give them gifts for carrying their own food. Domingo's reason for not having made these investments is special, but the lack of these investments is typical of the poor and unsuccessful farmer in Zinacantan. Initial poverty, inefficient management of money, and poor luck all contribute to keeping some Zinacantecos from ever making these investments. Young men often break this cycle of poverty through inheritance or through long periods of wage work and careful management of money. However, a few periods of family sickness or a few bad crops can nullify any efforts to acquire the necessary capital.

The fact that Domingo lives in Hteklum and has to travel farther to hot country is of considerable importance, I think. Most Zinacantecos, while recognizing the fact that the people of Hteklum are the poorest corn farmers, do not fully recognize the advantage in travel time and transportation of the product held by the people of the hamlets closer to hot country.

Neither Juan nor Lucas is burdened with the disadvantages that plague Domingo. Although they are both successful, there is a great difference between them. Juan runs what may be characterized as a conservative operation—an effort to hold his ground securely. The minimizing of risk and expenses is the key to his success. He produces corn at a very low unit cost, but the special arrangements necessary to achieve this low unit cost make it impossible for him to expand his operation. Juan is typical of a class of farmers who run "holding" operations, depending on low costs and the value of their own work for much of their success. Domingo's father and his stepmother's brother Mariano are also of this type. They plant in several locations in hot country and cold country so that the necessary weeding can be done on different dates. Thus they can do much of their own work, while a man who does all his planting in hot country must hire workers to get the weeding done at the optimal time. They own horses and make extra efforts to recruit laborers whom they can pay ten per cent less than the usual rate. They plant Ejido land or land that is rented at a very low rate, thus cutting the risk if the crop is bad, but limiting profit because the average yield is lower. The more successful of these conservative operators have enough profits to participate in the cargo system, but they are usually limited to the less expensive cargos.

Lucas is rich. He runs a large and efficient operation. The value of his own work is not crucial to his success, though he increases his profits by working himself and having his sons work for him. A very bad crop would hurt him because he invests a great amount each year. However, he keeps a substantial reserve, so that even the worst crop would not ruin him. For instance, in 1962, when many Zinacantecos had given up after both the seeding and the reseeding had dried up, Lucas was making plans to seed a third time—especially because the failure of the crops of others would raise the price of corn and increase his own profits if he could harvest anything approaching a decent crop. He represents the rich, the people who depend on size of operation for profit. Many inherit such an operation, but the organizational ability that is required to maintain it is beyond the capacities of some.

Lucas's large family was no doubt a great asset to him. However, the style of operation is not limited to those who have this advantage. One young man who is establishing himself on a large scale has hired a Chamula at 7 pesos a day to oversee other Chamula workers. Though this arrangement reduces his margin of profit, he is apparently making a success of it.

In sum, substantial profits can be made by commercial corn farming in Zinacantan, though the risk is high. Hard work and efficient management are rewarded by economic success—if one has some luck besides. Despite the apparent openness of the system, few actually are able to become rich without at least some of the advantages the rich already have. It is possible, through conservative farming practices, to minimize risk, but these practices also limit profit.

In the following chapters the three types that have been reviewed here will appear again and again, participating in the cargo system in a manner determined by their wealth.

Eight

Cost, Authority, and Prestige

The costs of the various cargos differ widely. The approximately 50 pesos spent by the Mayor (A11) can be managed by any Zinacanteco. However, the more than 14,000 pesos that are spent by the Mayordomo Rey (A1) in a year of service would be a very great burden even for Lucas. Neither Domingo nor Juan could ever afford to serve as Mayordomo Rey.

The cost of each cargo is fairly public knowledge, and the relative cost of the various cargos is even more widely known. Since the expenses of the various cargos are substantially different, the observer, native or anthropologist, has public evidence upon which to assess an individual. From the point of view of the participant, the cargo system can be a clear way to communicate his abilities and his self-image to his fellows. The cost of a cargo and some other factors, including its traditional rank or authority, determine the prestige that accrues to the person who serves it. In this chapter I am primarily concerned with documenting the absolute and the relative cost of the various cargos, and with constructing scales that rank the cargos of each level according to cost and prestige.

The Cost of Cargos

While the total expenses of the cargos vary, the items for which outlays are made are similar for all cargoholders. Food and drink—or, perhaps more correctly, drink and food—for fellow cargoholders and for auxiliary personnel account for most of the cargoholder's budget. Meat (including chicken and pork as well as beef), corn, beans, bread, brown sugar, and candles fill out the list of major items. Vegetables, eggs, spices, cigarettes, and matches normally account for a few pesos at any ritual event. Permanent items like pots, lanterns, and musical instruments may be either borrowed or purchased, depending on the financial condition of the cargoholder and his plans for future use of the items in other cargos. Table 5 lists the expenses for five cargos.

TABLE 5

Expenses for Five Cargos

Cargo	Drink	Other Purchases	Home Goods Consumed[a]	Total Expenses
A1S 1960	5,880.00	6,125.30	2,289.60	14,294.90
A8S 1952	1,400.00	1,030.50	910.50	3,341.00
A7S 1961	875.00	1,360.00	120.00	2,335.00
B7 1952	410.00	164.00	255.40	829.40[b]
C1 1957	560.00	103.00	493.00	1,156.00[b]

NOTE: All figures are based on reports of goods purchased and consumed. They are in pesos, calculated at 1960–61 standard prices

[a] Market value of goods produced in the home and consumed in observance of cargo ritual.

[b] These figures are from the same informant, Mariano, who passed both these cargos. Both are certainly too low, but by what percentage it is hard to estimate. As for the other figures, the one for A1S 1960 is very accurate; and those for A8S 1952 and A7S 1961 are probably accurate within 10% to 15%.

The Senior Mayordomo Rey (A1S) for 1960, by fortunate coincidence, was bilingual and probably the most Ladinoized Zinacanteco participating in the cargo system. A very intelligent and thoroughly self-conscious man, Antonio made an excellent informant on many aspects of the cargo system. Especially for calculations of the expenses of cargos, his virtually unique ability to write and keep accounts was valuable. His cargo is the most expensive in the entire Zinacantan cargo system. A cargo for the rich, it entails expenses that total more than ten times the annual income of a relatively prosperous Zinacanteco like Juan. A moderately expensive first-level cargo is that of Mayordomo San Sebastian (A8), which was passed by Manuel in 1952. Table 6 compares the expenses for Senior Mayordomo Rey and Senior Mayordomo San Sebastian.

I have two kinds of information about the expenses of cargos:

TABLE 6

More Detailed Expenses for Two Cargos

Type of Expenditure	A1S 1960	A8S 1952
Drink	5,880.00	1,400.00
Meat	3,984.00	497.00
Bread	529.60	140.00
Sugar	532.00	142.50
Candles	250.00[a]	116.00
Miscellaneous	296.70	—
Permanent items	533.00	—
Subtotal	6,125.30	895.50[b]
Corn	1,740.00	367.50
Beans	220.00	135.00
Chickens and eggs . . .	129.60	408.00
Coffee	200.00	135.00[a]
Subtotal	2,289.60	1,045.50
GRAND TOTAL	14,294.90	3,341.00

NOTE: All figures are in pesos and are calculated at 1960–61 standard prices.
  [a] Estimated figure.
  [b] A8S reported spending nothing on permanent items and only a negligible amount in the miscellaneous category.

(1) statements of informants and friends about their own cargos, and (2) statements of cargoholders reported by reliable informants. Information gathered in either of these ways is often hard to evaluate systematically, for the statements refer to different aspects of the economics of a cargo. Some reported the debts they had at the end of the year of service. Others reported the cash they spent, but did not consider corn and other household items as expenses. Only one informant, a man widely recognized as a rich and enterprising type, ever gave a money figure that included the calculation of corn and other household items consumed as well as cash spent. Some of the less systematic statements are presented in Table 7. The figures are listed as received from informants. No adjustments are made for the general inflation over the years.

The Cost Scale

The ideal way to establish the absolute and the relative cost of cargos would be to have every cargoholder in the hierarchy during

TABLE 7
Expenses and Debts of Cargoholders

Cargo	Information
A1J 1961	7,000 debt
A1S 1962	6,000 debt
A2S 1958	5,500 debt in cash, plus corn
A8J 1959–60	3,000 debt plus 952.50 in corn and beans
A8S 1960–61	4,000 spent in all, 3,000 debt
A10S 1952 (ca.)	Less than 1,000 spent in all
ASD 1962–63	9,000 plus corn (anticipated)
ASD 1960–61	9,000 spent in all
B1 1956	6,000 spent including corn
B1 1952 (ca.)	3,400 spent in all
B2 1955–56	4,800 spent in all
B12 1958 (ca.)	1,500–2,000 plus 900 in corn
All C and D (except D1) . . .	2,000 to 4,000 (many estimates)
D1	3,000 to 5,000 (many estimates)

NOTE: Information listed, in pesos, as received (not adjusted for 1960–61 standard prices).

a given year give a detailed list of his expenses. Most of the cargo-holders would not know their expenses in such detail, however. And, since most of them would consider such a question from an anthropologist an intrusion, attempting such a procedure would have diminished rapport. The absolute costs of some cargos were determined as described above. The most obvious and practical alternative for systematically determining the relative expenses of cargos was to have a number of informants rank the cargos of each level by expenses. This was done, and the results are presented in Table 8.[1]

These data were gathered from the various informants at different times during the field stay. Some were gathered as general ethnographic information before I conceived of the purpose to

[1] Note that six first-level cargos and two Alfereces are not included in the Cost or Prestige Scales that follow. For the first level, the six positions served in outlying hamlets are excluded for two reasons: (1) except for the two in Salinas, they are very recent, and informants (and the average Zinacanteco) have very little information about them; (2) only people from the hamlet itself normally see the incumbent serving his cargo. Alferez Santo Domingo and Alferez Divina Cruz are left out because they are not normally served as second cargos.

TABLE 8

Informants' Estimates of Relative Expenses of Cargos, First and Second Levels

FIRST LEVEL

Informant	A2	A6	A5	A8	A3	A9	A1	A4	A7	A10
A 1		2.5	4	5.5	2.5	5.5	1	1.75[a]	5.5	7
B 1		2	3	4	5.5	5.5	1	2	5.5	7
B 1		2	3	4	5.5	5.5	0[b]	3.5	2.5	7
C 1		2.5	5	2.5	5	5	1	1	7	8
D 1		2	3	5	5	5	1.5	1.5	5	5
E 1		2.5	2.5	5	5	5	[c]			
F 1		2.5	2.5	6	4	5				
Mean A–D . 1		2.2	3.6	4.2	4.7	5.3	.9	1.95	5.1	6.8
Mean A–F . 1		2.29	3.29	4.57	4.64	5.22	[c]			

SECOND LEVEL[d]

Informant	B1	B2 B3	B6 B10	B5 B9	B4 B12	B7	B8 B11
A 1		2	5	5	5	5	5
B 1.5		1.5	5	5	5	5	5
B 1		2	3.5	3.5	6	6	6
C 1		2	4	6.5	4	4	6.5
C 1		2	4	4	6.5	6.5	4
F 1		3	6/7	4/7	2/?	5	7
Mean[e] 1.08		2.08	4.58	4.67	4.75	5.25	5.59

NOTE: The cargos from Salinas, Navenchauc, and Apas are not included because not all informants have knowledge about them.

[a] The informant was unclear whether it should be rated with the "1" group or with the "2.5" group.

[b] The rankings for A1, A4, A7, and A10 were always taken after those for the Mayordomos (A2, A6, A5, A8, A3, A9), and informants compared these cargos to the Mayordomos. The "0" ranking for A1 results from the informant's placing it clearly above A2.

[c] Informants E and F did not give rankings for cargos A1, A4, A7, and A10.

[d] Since Alferez Santo Domingo and Alferez Divina Cruz are not usually served as second-level cargos, they are not included here.

Since senior and junior cargoholders generally work together they are listed as pairs. The senior usually spends a bit more, but only informant F (Antonio) considered this a factor in making his ratings. Informant F's different ratings for senior and junior are listed thus: s/j.

[e] Taking informant F's rating for the senior.

which they were to be put. Note that two of the rankings for both first- and second-level cargos are by informant B (Domingo), and two of the rankings for second-level cargos are by informant C (Manuel). Though these informants are not always perfectly consistent with themselves, they are by far the most reliable informants, and their opinions deserve to be given double weight.

In estimating the cost of first-level cargos (Table 8), informant agreement is high. The three cases of serious disagreement can be explained: (1) Informant A's rating of Mayordomo Sacramento (A3) as equal to Mayordomo Santa Cruz (A6) probably results from the high prestige (see below) of Mayordomo Sacramento. He was not a sophisticated informant, and perhaps did not fully understand the effort to rank on simple cost. (2) Informant B's rating of Mesonero (A7) as more expensive than Mayordomo Santo Domingo (A5), a very high rating, is perhaps accounted for by the fact that his father was about to enter as Mesonero. Much of their conversation must have been devoted to the problems of financing the cargo. (3) Informant C's ranking of Mayordomo San Sebastian (A8) as equal to Mayordomo Santa Cruz (A6) is probably best explained by the fact that he served as Mayordomo San Sebastian and felt the expenses he had undergone more intensely than the expenses of other cargos, which were simply reported to him in conversation with friends.

The clearest pattern in the rankings of second-level cargos (Table 8) is that the first three are universally considered more expensive and that the last nine are essentially lumped together as equal. This pattern fits all information available about absolute cost. While there are certainly differences in cost among the lower nine, all indications are that they are so small they would not substantially affect anyone's choice of a cargo. Wealth seems to enter into the service of these lower nine cargos in a different way. Alferez San Jose (B4), Alferez Rosario (B5), and Alferez Natividad (B6) are the most senior, and are most desired for that reason. They tend to be served by richer persons, who ask for them in advance. The lower six, which are more often filled by appointment, tend to go to poorer persons, who do not have enough confidence in their economic resources to ask for a cargo years ahead of the time of service.

The ranking of cargos by cost is presented in simplified form in Table 9. This Cost Scale will be important in testing some of the hypotheses about the cargo system to be presented in Chapters 9 and 10.

Authority, Prestige, and the Prestige Scale

Factors other than cost are important in determining the respect and deference given a cargoholder for his service. This is clear from the way Zinacantecos talk about cargos and act toward cargo-holders. For example, Domingo, when talking about which cargo he would like to serve, dismissed Mayordomo San Sebastian (A8), Mayordomo San Antonio (A9), and Mesonero (A7) as undesirable in comparison with Mayordomo Sacramento (A3); but with respect to cost they are essentially equal. Zinacantecos are much more impressed by someone who has passed Alferez Natividad (B6) than by someone who has passed Alferez Santa Rosa (B10), but the difference in cost is minimal. The best label for this other

TABLE 9

The Cost Scale

First Level[a]			Second Level		
high	A1	Mayordomo Rey	high	B1	San Lorenzo
	A2	Virgen del Rosario		⌈B2[c]	Santisima Trinidad
	A4	Pasionero		⌊B3	San Antonio
	A6	Santa Cruz		⌈B6	Natividad
	A5	Santo Domingo		⌊B10	Santa Rosa
	A8	San Sebastian		⌈B5	Virgen del Rosario
	A3	Sacramento		⌊B9	San Jacinto
	A7	Mesonero		⌈B4	San Jose
	A9	San Antonio		⌊B12	San Pedro Martir
	A10	Capitan		B7	Virgen de Soledad
low	A11[b]	Mayor		⌈B8	San Sebastian (Senior)
			low	⌊B11	San Sebastian (Junior)

[a] Senior and junior are not distinguished for the first-level cargos.
[b] A11 requires insignificant expenditures.
[c] Bracket indicates that the two cargos occupy the same rank on the Cost Scale.

quality of cargos is "prestige." Prestige is the total value of the performance as seen by Zinacantecos. It is the deference and respect a man will receive because of his cargo service, the variable on which he can compare himself with others who have also passed cargos.

Prestige is an elusive quality, difficult to measure in any systematic way. A younger man of high prestige seems to hesitate slightly before bowing to an older man of low prestige. A man of high prestige seems to be bolder than usual when talking to or about a man of low prestige. However, I found no way comparable to the informant ratings on cost to rate cargos on prestige. After talking with dozens of Zinacantecos about cargos, and observing dozens of interactions between persons who had passed different cargos, I simply found myself thinking in terms of a hierarchy of cargos based on prestige.

For the most part, the prestige ranking I thought appropriate can be seen as a combination of the cost and the authority of the cargos. Authority is indicated by the traditional ranking within each level and by the senior-junior relationships in the pairs of cargos. The authority dependent on this traditional ranking has two aspects. The first is the actual authority in giving orders that is

TABLE 10

The Prestige Scale

First Level			Second Level		
high	A1	Mayordomo Rey[a]	high	B1	San Lorenzo
	A2	Virgen del Rosario		B2	Santisima Trinidad
	A3	Sacramento		B3	San Antonio
	A4	Pasionero		B4	San Jose
	A5	Santo Domingo		B5	Virgen del Rosario
	A6	Santa Cruz		B6	Natividad
	A7	Mesonero		B7	Virgen de Soledad
	A8	San Sebastian		B8	San Sebastian (Senior)
	A9	San Antonio		B9	San Jacinto
	A10	Capitan		B10	Santa Rosa
low	A11	Mayor		B11	San Sebastian (Junior)
			low	B12	San Pedro Martir

[a] Senior and junior are not distinguished for the first-level cargos.

exercised by certain roles over others, e.g., the Senior Mayordomo
Sacramento (A3) over the other Mayordomos. The second is the
rank revealed by the walking order, e.g., the Alferez Rosario (B5)
over the Alferez Natividad (B6). The second type is potential authority and is in fact never exercised.

Even though both aspects of authority are relatively easily observed, the construction of a prestige scale is not without problems;
e.g., how is the prestige value of cost to be integrated with the
prestige value of authority? Moreover, in a few cases, idiosyncratic
features of particular cargos seemed to override the ranking that
could be made on the basis of cost and authority. These problems
cannot be solved in any perfectly systematic fashion with the data
I have available. Given this situation, I will describe the construction of the Prestige Scale, giving reasons as I make each step.
Though this procedure is lengthy, it has the advantage of revealing
the points at which the ranking depends most on essentially sub-
jective judgment. In the section following this, I will present systematic evidence that validates the rankings I make immediately
below.

Since cost is the most important factor in determining the prestige of most cargos, the Prestige Scale (Table 10) is based primarily on the Cost Scale (Table 9).

In the Prestige Scale of first-level cargos no distinction is made
between the members of senior-junior pairs. The distinction does
have some importance. For instance, the senior usually spends a bit
more than the junior. And, in conversations with me, persons who
had passed a senior cargo would usually state the fact of its senior-
ity in mentioning the cargo they passed, while persons who had
passed a junior cargo were much more likely to mention the name
of the cargo only, avoiding the senior-junior distinction. However,
informants describing the cargo careers of other people were often
unable to remember whether a senior or a junior position had been
passed. This fact makes lumping the senior and junior members of
pairs together desirable for two reasons. First, the forgetting by informants suggests that the distinction is not crucial. Second, the
forgetting by informants means that I could not gather data that

would make such a distinction useful even if I did build it into the scale. When I refer to a cargo in the scale for the first level, I mean the senior-junior pair—two actual positions in the hierarchy.

In the Prestige Scale for first-level cargos, only three cargos were deliberately changed from the position they held on the Cost Scale—Mayordomo Sacramento (A3), Mayordomo Santo Domingo (A5), and Mesonero (A7)—but of course the relative and absolute positions of many other cargos are affected by these changes.

The cargo of Mayordomo Sacramento (A3) has been moved from seventh position to third. Third position for Mayordomo Sacramento is surely appropriate. It is the only cargo among the Mayordomos that always exercises authority over the others. It is also the highest in the traditional ranking and is associated with San Lorenzo, the patron saint of Zinacantan. In conversation, informants who are too poor for Mayordomo Rey (A1) and Mayordomo Rosario (A2) show a great preference for this cargo.

The moving of Mayordomo Santo Domingo (A5) from below Mayordomo Santa Cruz (A6) in the Cost Scale to above it in the Prestige Scale is the second change. This is justified by the fact that Mayordomo Santo Domingo is second in traditional ranking, and occasionally exercises authority comparable to Mayordomo Sacramento's over the other Mayordomos. The data gathered in casual conversations also support this change, especially because of the ambivalent attitude toward Mayordomo Santa Cruz (see below).

Mesonero (A7) was moved above Mayordomo San Sebastian (A8) on intuition. In general, I judged, people talked about Mesonero as if it were more prestigious than Mayordomo San Sebastian. One of the reasons for this may be the fact that the Mesonero is associated with the highly prestigious Mayordomo Rey (A1). However, if Mesonero is really more prestigious than Mayordomo San Sebastian, the difference is slight and thus the shift in ranking not very important.

As a whole, the Prestige Scale for the first-level cargos may be viewed as constructed in uneven steps—though the data on the size of these steps are too uncertain to be used in the statistical treatment in later chapters. Mayordomo Rey (A1) and Mayordomo

Rosario (A2) are so immensely expensive and prestigious that people who look up at them from below do not quibble about the difference. The prestige of Mayordomo Sacramento (A3) is also very great, but it is dampened a bit by the unimpressive expenditures the cargo involves. Pasionero (A4) and Mayordomo Santo Domingo (A5), though a distinct step below the upper three, command exceptional amounts of prestige. They are perhaps the Buicks of the cargo world. Mayordomo Santa Cruz (A6) has something of the status of a Cadillac in a community of academics—admittedly expensive, but somehow out of place. The fiestas the cargo is responsible for are very often out of the standard pattern (see Appendix D). Its expenses do not buy it the prestige one might expect; people are ambivalent about it. This ambivalence, which I could never come to understand with any confidence, is one of the most important reasons for moving it down the Prestige Scale beneath the secure position of Mayordomo Santo Domingo (A5).

Mesonero (A7), Mayordomo San Sebastian (A8), and Mayordomo San Antonio (A9) are all very respectable cargos. Service in them is a substantial effort that is recognized by the community. Their considerably lower expenses do not go unnoticed, however. If a rich man tried to pass them off as his contribution to cargo service, he would lose more than he would gain in the eyes of the community, but a moderately wealthy person receives respect for serving them. One rich man who began his career as Mayordomo San Sebastian (A8) was the subject of disparaging comments in Zinacantan. He continued his cargo career by serving the relatively inexpensive Senior Alferez San Sebastian (B8); but shortly after that cargo he was pressed into service as Alferez Divina Cruz by the moletik.

Capitan (A10) is a very long step below the three cargos mentioned above. A very poor man can show his good will and indulge his desire to participate in fiestas by serving it, but he is unlikely to pass on to higher cargos. Mayor (A11) is never requested, nor is it ever accepted with any feeling of pride. Many are appointed Mayor to force them to make a decision about the cargo system. Faced with the prospect of serving this lowest of all cargos, they commit themselves to another cargo in order to avoid the shame.

Other kinds of delinquency are also grounds for appointing a person Mayor. Since the delinquency that brings on the appointment is sometimes just a youthful folly, a few men who begin as Mayor go on to relatively distinguished cargo careers. However, most of those who pass Mayor never attempt another cargo.

The construction of the Prestige Scale for the second level (Table 10) involves more complications, since the Cost Scale does not make the distinctions as sharply as it does for the first-level cargos. In general I relied more heavily on the authority principle (senior-junior) in ranking the second-level cargos.

Alferez San Lorenzo (B1) is clearly the most prestigious of the twelve Alfereces on the second level. Alferez Trinidad (B2) and Alferez San Antonio (B3) are less prestigious, but much higher than the remainder of the list, especially because of their higher cost. Alferez Trinidad (B2) is placed above Alferez San Antonio (B3) simply because it is the senior of the pair.

The next three ranks are filled by Alferez San Jose (B4), Alferez Rosario (B5), and Alferez Natividad (B6). They are placed here because as senior Alfereces they have more authority and spend a bit more money than their respective junior partners. Their order goes from most senior to least senior in the traditional ranking.

Alferez Soledad (B7) is moved above the Senior Alferez San Sebastian (B8) because of clues gathered in conversations, but I am not certain of this ranking. The remainder of the Prestige Scale is arranged according to the traditional ranking, except for Alferez San Pedro Martir (B12), which is lowered to the last position. This too was done on the basis of conversational clues. In addition, Alferez San Pedro Martir (B12) seems to be the Alferez most often forgotten when informants are asked to list the Alfereces. Many informants could recall the names of all the Alferez positions except this one.

The spaces between the steps of the Prestige Scale for second-level cargos are more uneven than those for first-level cargos. Alferez San Lorenzo (B1) is highest. Alferez Trinidad (B2) and Alferez San Antonio (B3) are lower, but enormously more prestigious than the remainder of the list. Alferez San Jose (B4), Alferez Rosario (B5), and Alferez Natividad (B6) command a prestige perhaps equivalent to Pasionero (A4) and Mayordomo Santo Domingo (A5) on the first level. That is, they are solid but not stunning. The remainder of the list is not easily distinguishable, but I have the distinct impression that Alferez Soledad (B7), Senior Alferez San Sebastian (B8), and Alferez San Jacinto (B9) are considered less minor than the truly minor Alfereces: Santa Rosa (B10), Junior San Sebastian (B11), and San Pedro Martir (B12).

Differences in prestige on the third level are less important for the purposes of this study. The six cargos may be described as falling into three classes. Alferez Santo Domingo and First Regidor (C1) are very prestigious. Alferez Divina Cruz and Second Regidor (C2) are quite prestigious, and Third Regidor (C3) and Fourth Regidor (C4) are prestigious. On the fourth level, Alferez Santo Domingo (sometimes served as a fourth cargo) and the Senior Alcalde Viejo (D1) may be described as very prestigious, while Junior Alcalde Viejo (D2) is simply prestigious. The terminal cargo, Alcalde Shuves, is of a completely different and lower order of prestige than any of the other third- or fourth-level cargos.

Validation of the Prestige Scale

Many attempts were made to have Zinacanteco informants "construct" a prestige scale for me, as they had constructed a cost scale. Though Zinacantecos constantly behave in ways that indicate that they defer to and respect their fellows according to the criteria described above, no informant was able to conceptualize the notion of prestige consistently enough to produce a prestige scale. Any direct attempt to ask about the relative prestige of cargos drew either a statement about the relative cost (which is public knowledge) or a retreat to the cultural ideal that all cargos are in service of the saints, and all service of the saints is equally virtuous. This ideal blocked every attempt to get direct estimates of relative prestige of cargos from informants. Thus there was no direct way to get evidence that the prestige-ranking of cargos I had intuitively made coincided with the ranking made by Zinacantecos.

In this situation, errors made by informants in describing the cargo careers of other Zinacantecos became important. With other purposes in mind (see later chapters) I had collected statements from more than one informant (or more than one statement from a single informant at different times) about the cargos passed by many men in Zinacantan. In some cases informants disagreed. In all but a very few of these cases of disagreement, it was possible to make systematic decisions about which statement to accept as correct and which to label erroneous. This was done on the basis of a predetermined order of preference of informants—Manuel, for example, was considered more accurate than Antonio. In a few cases kinship or proximity of residence overrode the general ranking of informants in deciding which report to label as erroneous. That is, even an unreliable informant was considered more apt to know the cargos of his immediate family. Thus I have a number of cases about which I can say, "Individual number 1 in fact passed cargo Y, but the informant says that he passed cargo Z."

When arranged on the Prestige Scale these errors tend to be very close to the actual cargo held by the person about whom the questions were asked. That is, the informant who did not have correct information did not make a random guess. He apparently guessed in terms of some general impression of the cargoholder's prestige in the community.

The 38 erroneous statements about first-level cargos and the 73 erroneous statements about second-level cargos are presented in Tables 11 and 12, respectively. The distribution of cases is shown in Table 13. For the first level 31.6 per cent of the cases are in the 18.2 per cent of the cells closest to the diagonal and 52.6 per cent of the cases are in the 34.6 per cent of the cells closest to the diagonal. Application of a binomial test to these data shows that the distribution would have happened less than one time in 20 if all the informants had been guessing randomly.[2] The correspond-

---

[2] In calculating the probability that the distribution occurred by chance, the *number* of cases falling in cells adjacent to the diagonal (or within two) is compared with the *number* falling further from the diagonal. Under the null hypothesis the distribution is random; i.e., the cases adjacent to the diagonal (or within two) are not a significantly greater proportion of the total number of cases than are the cells adjacent to the diagonal (or within two) of the total number of cells. For the test (actual figures from Table 13, First Level, adjacent to the diagonal) p equals proportion of the total cells (.182); r equals number of cases falling in these cells (12); and n equals total number of cases (38). The cumulative probability for this distribution and all more extreme ones was read from tables (Aiken *et al.* 1955).

ing probability for the second-level cargos is much more satisfactory—less than one time in 100,000.

While both of the Prestige Scales I have constructed yield statistically significant distributions of errors, there is a possibility that some other ranking might be more appropriate. In the case of the data for the first level there are obvious changes that would

TABLE 11

Informants' Errors: First Level

(N = 38)

CORRECT POSITION / ERRONEOUS STATEMENT	A1	A2	A3	A4	A5	A6	A7	A8	A9	A10	A11
A1		–	1	–	–	–	–	–	–	–	–
A2	3		2	–	–	–	–	–	–	–	–
A3	–	1		–	4	1	–	–	–	–	–
A4	–	2	–		(2)	–	–	1	–	–	–
A5	–	–	–	–		1	–	–	1	–	–
A6	–	–	1	1	(2)		1	–	–	–	–
A7	–	–	–	–	–	–		–	–	–	–
A8	–	–	1	–	1	–	–		–	–	–
A9	–	–	(1)	–	6	–	–	–		–	–
A10	–	–	–	–	–	–	–	–	–		–
A11	–	–	–	–	1	–	4	–	–	–	

NOTE: Entries in parentheses are less than expected for those cells.

TABLE 12

Informants' Errors: Second Level

(N = 73)

CORRECT POSITION / ERRONEOUS STATEMENT	B1	B2	B3	B4	B5	B6	B7	B8	B9	B10	B11	B12
B1		3	1	–	–	–	–	–	–	–	–	–
B2	–		–	–	2	2	–	–	–	–	–	1
B3	–	1		–	–	–	–	–	–	–	–	–
B4	1	4	2		8	7	(1)	–	(1)	–	3	–
B5	–	–	–	1		2	–	–	–	–	–	–
B6	–	(2)	–	2	5		1	–	4	1	–	–
B7	–	–	–	–	–	2		–	–	–	–	–
B8	–	–	–	–	–	–	–		–	–	–	1
B9	–	–	–	–	–	–	–	1		–	–	–
B10	–	–	–	–	2	(1)	–	2	1		1	–
B11	–	–	–	–	–	–	–	–	–	2		–
B12	–	–	–	–	(1)	(1)	1	–	1	1	–	

NOTE: Entries in parentheses are less than expected for those cells.

TABLE 13

Analysis of Informant Errors, First and Second Levels

Proximity to Diagonal	Number of Cases	Percentage of Total Cases	Percentage of Total Cells	P less than
First Level ($N = 38$)				
adjacent	12	31.6	18.2	.05
within 2[a]	20	52.6	34.6	.02
Second Level ($N = 73$)				
adjacent	30	41.2	16.7	.00001
within 2[a]	47	64.5	31.9	.00001

[a] Includes all cells adjacent to the diagonal and all cells adjacent to them; e.g., for row 5 "within two of the diagonal" includes the cells in columns 3, 4, 6, and 7.

yield a distribution closer to the diagonal—i.e., if A9 were placed in position six and A6, A7, and A8 dropped to positions seven, eight, and nine. In the case of the data for the second level these alternative arrangements are less obvious. In both cases, however, there is no major change that can be justified in terms of the other information available about the cargo system. I attribute the "imperfections" in the distributions to the fact that the sample is small, and I do not feel that the Prestige Scale should be modified.[3]

A more serious possible objection to the conclusions I am about to draw may be stated in the following form: the ordering may be correct, but my reasons for making it may be incorrect. That is, the manner in which I combined cost, authority, and a few idiosyncratic features may be said to yield an appropriate ordering by chance. For instance, on the second level, B5 and B6 are adjacent in the ritual walking order as well as in my Prestige Scale. It is possible that the informant confused them, not on the prestige dimension that I postulate, but simply by their position in the line as he remembers it. While some of the errors may be explained by such

[3] The most glaring imperfection in the data for the first level is the six cases in the cell at row nine, column five. Five of these actually involve only two individuals and repetitions of erroneous statements about them by the same informant (Manuel) at different times. How the informant got his mistaken idea I do not know, but I felt that each repetition had to be counted as an independent case since the errors were made at intervals so great (one or two months) that it is unlikely that he was merely covering for his previous mistake.

alternative principles, there is no one such principle or combination of principles that I can think of that orders all the errors as well as the prestige dimension.

Since the Prestige Scale was constructed prior to and without regard to this analysis of errors, I feel relatively safe in drawing the following conclusions from the data:

First, I conclude that Zinacantecos, though they will not openly discuss it, actually do perceive cargos in terms of relative prestige, and are apt to remember the approximate prestige of an individual even when they have forgotten the particular cargo he passed in the process of achieving it.

Second, I conclude that the Prestige Scale as presented in Table 10 is a fairly accurate ranking of the cargos in terms of the prestige they bring to the person who passes them.[4]

---

[4] This discussion of the validation of the Prestige Scale appeared as part of an article in the *American Anthropologist* (Cancian 1963), and is used here in revised form with the permission of the editor.

Nine

Financing Cargo Service

No Zinacanteco is able to pay the expenses of a cargo out of cash on hand. He is expected to be in debt when he finishes his cargo. A man's skill in handling his debts is one of the keys to his success in the cargo system. When a man overextends himself he is unable to recover fast enough to take another cargo in his lifetime. On the other hand, if he puts too little of his wealth and talents into his cargo, he is subject to criticism from the community. This chapter is devoted to three aspects of the problems of financing and managing a cargo: (1) the beliefs about gods, money, and cargos; (2) the system of loaning money to cargoholders; and (3) the role of kinsmen, especially brothers and sons, in facilitating the performance of the duties of a cargoholder.

Gods, Money, and Cargos

The cargo must be a financial burden to the cargoholder, and he must accept this burden in good spirits, happy that he is sacrificing for the gods and the saints. When he is short of money his fellows must help him by giving him loans. These norms are expressed time and again by Zinacantecos in statements of ideals and in interpretation of events involving cargoholders.

God sees your heart, says Domingo. If you spend for your cargo with a happy heart, God will help you and you will spend less in the end. If you are unhappy about the burden of your expenses, your punishment will be misfortunes that make you spend more.

Martin says not to worry about the expenses of your cargo—if you enter happy for the opportunity to serve, the money will come from somewhere.

Manuel recounts that when he was about to finish serving as Mayordomo San Sebastian, he saw his replacement arrive with eight jars full of money. It was as much as Manuel had spent on the entire cargo. The man said he would pass the cargo without debt; he would not have to struggle. Before long his punishment came. His wife did not help him well: she did not always light the candles for his saint when he went away. The man began to drink and spent more and more on drinking. His wife spent money, who knows for what, for they had exactly the same expenses for the cargo as any other incumbent. In the end he was as much in debt as Manuel had been when he left the cargo—some 1,500 pesos.

Manuel says: "If one is very rich and doesn't spend money for cargos, and refuses to lend money to cargoholders, lying and saying that one has nothing, then one will end the year in debt anyway, for that will be God's punishment for not respecting Him to the best of one's ability, and for not helping others who want to respect Him, and for lying to them. The punishment may be sickness, or any number of misfortunes, but in the end the money will go, for it cannot be kept from God. For example, a man from the hamlet of Nachig lost his money when he lied to a cargoholder in this way."

People will just talk if you have money and don't take a cargo, says Manuel. That's all they will do—but they might talk a lot. Antonio, who passed Mayordomo Rey, says, "For instance, if I had twelve mules and didn't want to pass Mayordomo Rey, then the people would say that God would punish me later with sickness or loss of the riches that I have."

Antonio is a Ladinoized man who is proud of being more sophisticated than other Zinacantecos. He says that some people believe that a man will be punished by the saints with sickness or poverty if he doesn't pass his cargo well. They think God will help a man with his crops if he passes in good spirits.[1] "I think that good crops are the result of hard work, no matter what the saints do,"

[1] Domingo's father had an exceptionally good harvest the year he passed his cargo, despite the fact that his cargo duties prevented him from giving a normal amount of attention to his fields. Domingo sees this as a favor from the saints.

says Antonio. "I took my cargo so that I would not lose face in public."

Antonio expresses the norms about cargo service in relation to the approval or disapproval of other Zinacantecos, while Manuel and Domingo and most other Zinacantecos relate these norms to a complex system of beliefs about the gods, wealth, good fortune, and punishment. However stated, the norms of Zinacantan society dictate participation in the cargo system for all who have the means to participate.

Given this norm, it is important to ask, I think, whether it is met in practice—whether all wealthy Zinacantecos do in fact participate to a high degree in the cargo system. To answer this question purely on the basis of interviews about a limited number of cases would be difficult; for if the belief system and the reaction to non-participation is as I have described it, then the cases most prominent in the minds of informants will be those of persons who have broken the norms. For the first of many times in this chapter and those that follow, I will turn to an extensive sample of individual cases in an attempt to avoid this kind of distortion. These samples were gathered with more or less attention to avoiding bias. The Paste Economic Sample, which is used to answer the present question, is one in which it was impossible to insure randomness of cases, but it still provides, I think, more information than would a handful of cases intensively analyzed. The gathering of the data is described in detail in Appendix A.

If the norm is the practice, then all wealthy people should take many cargos. To test this hypothesis, two variables from the Paste Economic Sample are compared: amount of corn seeded in hot country in the year the sample was taken as a rough measure of wealth and compared with participation in the cargo system.[2]

The results of the comparison, which are presented in Table 14, confirm the hypothesis that the norm is the practice in Zinacantan. Of the 37 men included in the Sample, eight have three or more

[2] This participation is rated high or low by the system described in footnote 4, p. 104–5.

TABLE 14

Wealth and Participation

(N = 37)

Degree of Participation	Wealth: Almudes of Corn Seeded in Hot Country			
	1	2	3	4
High	8	8	6	2
Low	7	6	–	–

almudes of corn seeded in hot country, and all eight of them are among those who participated in the cargo system to a high degree. On the other hand, the 29 men with two almudes or less seeded in hot country are distributed fairly evenly among the high and low participators. Two almudes is the most an average farmer can seed in hot country if he cannot plan to hire workers for the weeding (see Chapter 7).

The crudeness of the data used here to measure wealth prohibits any complex conclusions, and certainly some exceptions would appear if more detailed information were available. But it is clear that in general Zinacantecos with exceptionally high economic resources participate in the cargo system to a high degree.

Borrowing Money for Cargo Service

Ideally, a man who enters a cargo has already accumulated half the cash necessary for his year's expenditures. If he has much more than half it may mean that he is not making an effort that is in keeping with his wealth. If he has less than half it may mean that he is overextending himself and will have a difficult time repaying his debts. There are, of course, exceptions to this standard. A man on the waiting list for a particular cargo might wait some years, and save more than needed; or he might find the cargo open immediately because of the default of another, and accept it before he is fully prepared. In general, however, it is considered normal and proper to borrow about half the money needed for a cargo. These loans are made at the moment the money is needed, and so it is expected that a man will reach the middle of his term before seeking loans. If he seeks loans soon after entering his cargo, those he approaches for money will know that he was grossly under-prepared.

Loans to cargoholders are always given without interest, and on a fairly long-term basis.[3] Money is usually borrowed from kinsmen and friends, but there is another important factor that determines whether a man is likely to loan money to help another with a cargo. This is the lender's status with respect to his cargo career. If he is expecting to take his first cargo in a few years, or has long since passed a first cargo and is likely to take a second one, he is a good prospect for the cargoholder who is seeking a loan. Prospective cargoholders do not hoard the money they expect to use for their cargos but rather lend it out to other cargoholders in anticipation of repayment at the time they will need it for their own cargos. Thus, the prospective cargoholder will loan amounts of money ranging from 50 to 500 pesos to various individuals during the years before his cargo—all with the specific understanding that he will be paid back when he needs the money for his own cargo ex-penses. On the other hand, the cargoholder who is borrowing money will seek to borrow from several persons who will expect to be repaid at various times in the future (i.e., when their cargos come up), thus securing for himself the advantage of gradual re-payment.

There is another very important principle governing the seeking and giving of loans. As far as I can tell, no cargoholder is expected to dip deeply into his capital reserves before asking for loans. Many Zinacanteco farmers, especially those who run the larger opera-tions, set aside a certain amount of corn with which to pay workers during the next agricultural cycle. If they were expected to reduce these reserves before asking for loans, they would find themselves

---

[3] Most other loans in Zinacantan are given on a relatively short-term basis. Many are given to be paid when the harvest is in. Normally, interest is not charged among friends and relatives if the loan is needed to meet a family emergency. If interest is charged it can be as high as 20 per cent per month. As far as I know, Zinacantecos do not borrow from each other for investment in corn farming. Government agencies do offer loans to farmers at moderate rates of interest, but the procedures for securing such loans are too complex for most Zinacantecos.

in a very difficult position later, for they would not have the capital needed to produce the crops that would pay their cargo debts. However, lenders do not require that the cargoholder be destitute before asking for a loan. Rich or poor, a man is not required to alter his economic style of life when he passes a cargo. It is his profits, not his capital, that he pours into cargo service. On the other hand, of course, the profits dispersed in cargo service cannot be used to expand his capital reserves.

It is also expected that a man will liquidate all his debts from previous cargos before passing another one, and that he will have half the expenses of his next cargo ready before he enters it. In 1962 a man well known in the community acted against this expectation. He had many debts, but people did not press him, apparently because he was thought to be a powerful curer and witch. Having passed Alferez Trinidad (B2) in 1957, he immediately placed himself on the waiting lists for Alferez Santo Domingo in 1962. Many people knew that he was not free of debt, and he told me in January 1962 that he did not know where the money for his next cargo would come from. In the spring of 1962 the man who was to enter Alferez San Lorenzo (B1)—the junior partner of Alferez Santo Domingo—threatened that he would not enter if the curer were to be the Alferez Santo Domingo, for the curer still owed him 200 pesos from 1957. In the end they entered together. I do not know how the conflict was resolved, but I am certain that a man who was less valued as a curer, and less feared for his powers of witchcraft, could not have flouted custom with such impunity.

Antonio, the Mayordomo Rey (A1) for 1960, had something approaching an ideal pattern of borrowing. He received 12 loans from fellow Zinacantecos. Three were from a friend and two ritual kinsmen who were aiding him in anticipation of, or in return for, aid he would give or had given them during their cargos; four were from kinsmen; and the remaining five were from ritual kinsmen. He had a large debt with the Ladino woman who sells drink in the ceremonial center, and a smaller debt with a rancher who sold him a steer on credit. Two features of his borrowing are very close to the ideals described above: (1) he borrowed for the first time on June

20, just a few days short of the middle of his term; (2) all the Zinacantecos he borrowed from were either his relatives or his ritual
kinsmen, except for one, a friend who made him the loan on a
reciprocal basis.

Antonio's pattern of borrowing also has some unusual features.
First, his total debt, 4,010 pesos, is relatively small considering the
cargo passed. This is explained by the fact that he was very well
paid as a schoolteacher for years before his cargo, and made additional profits in agriculture during the same period. He is very rich.
Second, he took no loans from siblings. Antonio has only one
brother, a poor man with whom he does not get on very well.
However, because of his wealth, his political power in days past,
and his ability to deal with the Ladino world, Antonio has more
than 100 ritual kinsmen, who make up in part for his lack of siblings. An examination of the auxiliary personnel recruited by Antonio for his cargo (Appendix C) will also reveal the manner in
which ritual kin have replaced siblings for some other support
needed by the cargoholder.

Brothers, Sons, and Cargos

The aid given by brothers and sons is important in handling the
economic and organizational problems involved in cargo service.
As shown by Antonio's case, it is not impossible to complete a cargo
without the aid of close kinsmen; but although ritual kinsmen and
friends can give most of the aid that close kinsmen can, having
brothers and grown sons is an advantage. Below I will try to demonstrate this fact in two ways: first, by reviewing informants' statements about the manner in which kinsmen can help, and second,
by analyzing census data from three hamlets.

When asked to enumerate the ways in which brothers could help
a cargoholder, Juan responded with the following list: (1) They
can serve as helpers at fiestas. (2) They can go to buy things in
San Cristobal. (3) They can bring things to you from home in the
hamlets. (4) They can be sent to hot country to buy meat. (5)
They can help work your land in hot country, either by themselves
or simply by directing your workers.

When challenged with the idea that nonkinsmen could also take care of all these tasks, he noted that brothers would more readily do them and that brothers would do a number of things that other people would not. Brothers will loan you corn and money when you need them, he said, and not press for their return. If you don't have brothers to borrow from, says Juan, you have to work furiously in the few years after a cargo to pay off your debts. Brothers will wait until they have a cargo themselves or until you are easily able to pay the debt.

Brothers may even give you days of work in hot country to help farm your corn. They will want the work returned only when they pass their own cargos. Furthermore, they certainly will watch over your fields when you cannot go to hot country. Others cannot be trusted to do this as well.

Domingo, who has no brothers, emphasized the fact that friends can do almost everything that brothers can, but he readily admitted that it is not easy to find friends to do such tasks and make such sacrifices. Antonio, who does not get along with his brother, also emphasized the fact that friends and ritual kinsmen can help, but he noted that even ritual kinsmen cannot be expected to loan money for an unspecified period.

If brothers really do give a man an advantage in handling the financial and organizational problems of passing a cargo, then those who have many brothers should participate in the cargo system to a greater degree than those who have few brothers. This hypothesis is tested in Test 1, Table 15. The 136 cases include all patrilocal males over 45 years of age in the hamlets of Paste, Apas, and Hteklum.[4]

---

[4] The compilation of the distributions on which Table 14 and the three Tests in Table 15 are based presented a particularly difficult problem because the participation of an older man is not directly comparable with the participation of a younger man, the older man having had more time in which to serve cargos.

For the Tests, the following procedure was adopted to compensate for the differences in opportunity. The sample ($n = 136$) was divided into three age groups: 45–54, 55–64, and 65 and older. Each of these groups was divided into high and low halves on cargo performance and on number of relatives, yielding three sub-samples, each distributed in a 2 x 2 table. These tables were superimposed, yielding a single table on which the test was performed. For

TABLE 15

Kinship and Participation in the Cargo System: Tests
(N = 136)

Number of Indicated Kin	Participation		Results
TEST 1. BROTHERS	High	Low	
Two or more	36	24	$\chi^2 = 2.55$, P < .10
One or none	34	42	57% for
TEST 2. SONS			
Two or more	36	21	$\chi^2 = 4.59$, P < .025
One or less	34	45	60% for
TEST 3. BROTHERS AND SONS			
Three or more	44	28	$\chi^2 = 4.90$, P < .025
Less than three	26	38	60% for

The data presented in Test 1, Table 15, is distributed as hypothesized, but the confirmation of the hypothesis is weak at best, for such a distribution would occur slightly less than one time in ten even if the hypothesized relationship did not exist.

It should be emphasized that the finding implies that an advantage is gained by *all* members of a large male-sibling group, not simply the more obvious truth that a man has an advantage if all his brothers devote all their efforts to helping him. That is, the summary statement of the result of Test 1, Table 15, is not: A group of brothers can aid one of their number to participate more in the cargo system than any man who is alone. Rather, the statement is: All brothers in a group of brothers will tend to outperform any individual who has fewer brothers. The importance of being able to efficiently organize the work involved in cargo service is emphasized by these data. All members of a male-sibling group can help

---

the cargos the dividing points between high and low were: ages 45–54, A9–A10; ages 55–64, B3–B4; age 65 and older, C4–B1. For relatives, the dividing points were the same for all age groups—brothers: two or more, one or none; sons: more than one, one or less; brothers and sons: three or more, less than three. Appendix B, Note 1, reviews the statistical procedures followed in these tests. For Table 14, where the sample is smaller, the dividing points for cargos set with the larger sample described above were adopted.

all other members, while a man who is alone must take the trouble to seek aid from people who are not so closely bound to him.[5]

Sons should give a man many of the same advantages that brothers do, some to a greater and some to a lesser degree. Sons, especially those who are young and still economically dependent on their fathers, cannot be expected to make loans. On the other hand, as helpers and substitutes in hot country, they can give aid that does not need to be reciprocated in the direct manner necessary with brothers. While the expenses of their courtship and marriage can be a great burden for a family, in the end they are probably an economic advantage because of the labor they contribute without pay.

In Test 2, Table 15, the same sample of 136 individuals is used to test the hypothesis that a man having many sons will participate in the cargo system to a greater degree than a man having few sons. In order to reduce the distorting effect of sons who are not old enough to be of significant help to a cargoholder, I have weighted married sons one and unmarried sons one-half. The advantage of having a number of sons is clearly confirmed by these data.

Combining the close kinsmen that an individual has (brothers and married sons weighted equally at one and unmarried sons weighted one-half) gives a slightly stronger confirmation of the hypothesis, as shown in Test 3, Table 15.

When the data are examined more carefully it becomes apparent that the support for the hypotheses confirmed above comes mostly from the cases of men between 45 and 54, while the advantage for older cargoholders is less. Apparently these younger cargoholders depend more on their kinsmen for a good start in the cargo system, while other factors are more important in determining how far a man will go in his later years.

[5] Vogt (1964) has pointed out that the kinship and residence group beyond the nuclear family (of procreation or of orientation) has important corporate functions in Zinacantan. With the data from the Paste Census it was possible to test for a relation between the size of the larger kinship or residence group and the degree of participation in the cargo system. No significant relationship was found.

Ten

Economic and Social Stratification in Zinacantan

Zinacantan society is stratified along social and economic lines. Participation in the cargo system reflects an individual's economic rank and determines, in large measure, his social rank. Since I have chosen to give the label "stratification" to the phenomenon I am describing, I will define that term more precisely before reviewing the evidence for the existence of the patterns it denotes.

Definition of Stratification

"Stratification" as I use it denotes the patterns of social and economic ranking in which individuals and families maintain their position over time. It should be emphasized that this definition has two components: (1) the existence of significant differences, and (2) the persistence in the same relative rank by individuals and families over significant periods of time. This general definition should be clear enough, except for the terms "significant differences" and "significant periods of time." That is, how much stratification really deserves to be called stratification? This question is difficult to answer both because any answer would have to be couched in comparative terms and because ideological as well as scientific considerations will influence the response of most readers to any answer. Since my purpose is to describe the situation in Zinacantan as accurately as possible, and thus to make this case available to those who will interpret it in a larger context, I will not attempt to answer the question in absolute terms. I have chosen to call Zinacantan society stratified because the differences that are described below are very significant to Zinacantecos.

The data presented in this chapter are meant to show that the differences persist over significant periods of time; i.e., that individuals and families tend to hold their rank. Before proceeding to the analysis, however, the differences themselves must be defined more carefully. For a variety of reasons, economic ranking must be distinguished from social ranking: (1) economic ranking as I use it is a much simpler concept than social ranking, and evidence for or against its existence is easier to interpret; (2) there are questions about the consequences of the cargo system in Zinacantan and in other Middle American Indian communities (see Cancian n.d.) that will receive clearer answers if the distinction is made; (3) economic ranking is merely reflected by patterns of participation in the cargo system, while social ranking is in large measure determined by this participation; (4) social ranking, as I will try to show, is more important to Zinacantecos than economic ranking.

Economic ranking is defined by the Cost Scale of cargos described in Chapter 8. Chapters 7 and 8 together show that the differences in cost among cargos represent very significant differences for Zinacantecos. Only a few can afford the most expensive cargos. For instance, Juan, who might have 700 pesos surplus income a year from corn farming, could not hope to shoulder the 14,000-peso burden involved in serving Mayordomo Rey (A1). Nor is he so poor that he would have to accept appointment to the Mayor (A11) position, which can be served with trivial expenditures. As Chapters 7 and 8 show, not every interval between ranks in the Cost Scale can be taken as significant; but the Cost Scale as a whole represents a significant range.

It should be emphasized that service in the cargo system does not itself determine a man's economic rank. It merely reflects his economic capacity. He must accumulate his wealth elsewhere. In fact, in demonstrating by cargo service that he is wealthy, the individual actually disperses his wealth. This feature of the system will receive more detailed attention later.

Social ranking is defined by the Prestige Scale of cargos described in Chapter 8. The subtleties and difficulties involved in accepting this ranking as a measure of social position are discussed at length there, and the validity of the ranking made in the Prestige Scale is demonstrated principally through the analysis of informant errors. The consistency with which the Prestige Scale orders data throughout the remaining chapters is further evidence of its soundness.

Rank on the Prestige Scale is less than a complete measure of an individual's community-wide social standing. In Chapter 3, I argued that, from the point of view of the entire community, performance in the cargo system is by far the most important determinant of social standing. Of course, what an individual does in other sectors of public life may add to or subtract from his social standing based on cargo performance. But the number of men who receive respect and deference for their performance as public officials (or "politicians") or as curers is limited when compared with the number that participate in the cargo system.

With this background on the first component of the definition of stratification (the existence of significant differences), it is possible to state two hypotheses about the second component (persistence over time), which may be tested with the data to be presented below. I go directly to the statement of the alternative hypotheses.

Hypothesis of economic stratification: Individuals and families will maintain consistent rank on the Cost Scale over time.

Hypothesis of social stratification: Individuals and families will maintain consistent rank on the Prestige Scale over time.

The Individual and His Cargo Career

Most Zinacantecos serve only one cargo during their lifetimes. That cargo is one of the 34 first-level positions. A good number go on to take one of the 12 second-level cargos; and a few of these go on to third- and finally fourth-level cargos. Only one man each year emerges as Senior Alcalde Viejo. Under this system individuals may be distinguished from each other in two ways: they may be ranked according to their performance on their first cargos; and they may be ranked according to the number of cargos they take.

If the cargo system had no importance in Zinacantan society one might expect to find no relation between the rank of first cargo and the rank of second cargo, if a second cargo were served at all. Alternatively, in a hypothetical equalitarian society that happened to have cargos of differing ranks, one would expect to find an inverse relation between first and second cargo; for the man who happened to serve a low-ranking first cargo would take a high-ranking second one, showing the equality between him and the man who served his high- and low-ranking cargos in reverse order. However, in a stratified society one would expect that a man who began in a high-ranking cargo would continue in similar cargos; and this is what has been hypothesized for Zinacantan.

Furthermore, since each level of the hierarchy has fewer cargos than the level below it, the difference between individuals should be made even clearer. Those who begin in high-ranking cargos should continue in the hierarchy, while those who begin in low-ranking cargos should be less apt to take second, third, and fourth cargos. Several tests of the hypotheses of stratification are presented below, with a minimum of discussion.

Table 16 shows data on the first two cargos of all men aged 55 and older in the hamlets of Hteklum and Apas. Censuses show 32 men aged 55 and older in the two hamlets. Two of them have

TABLE 16

Cargo Careers of Men Aged 55 and Over

$(r = .62)$

		A1	A2	A3	A4	A5	A6	A7	A8	A9	A10	A11
						FIRST CARGO						
	B1	–	2	–	–	–	–	–	–	–	–	–
	B2	–	–	1	–	1	–	–	–	–	–	–
	B3	–	1	–	–	–	–	–	–	–	–	–
	B4	1	–	–	–	2	–	1	–	–	–	–
SECOND CARGO	B5	1	1	1	1	–	–	–	–	–	–	–
	B6	–	1	–	–	–	–	–	–	–	–	–
	B7	–	–	–	1	–	–	–	–	–	–	–
	B8	–	–	–	–	–	–	–	–	–	–	–
	B9	–	–	–	–	–	–	–	–	–	–	–
	B10	1	–	–	–	–	–	2	–	–	–	–
	B11	–	–	–	–	–	–	–	–	–	–	1
	B12	1	–	–	–	–	–	–	–	2	–	–
	None	–	–	–	1	1	–	2	1	–	1	2

Lucas at the fiesta of San Sebastian, after passing Senior Alcalde Viejo.

Domingo's wife and son. Domingo's father's house is in the background.

The women of Manuel's family.

A curing ceremony at an altar overlooking Hteklum.

A newly appointed mayor at the fiesta of San Sebastian.

The scribes check the waiting lists.

A young man at the town hall.

de año de 1971

Manuel Vasquez Shuljol mayordomo Rey 1ª P. Parte.
Antonio Hernandez Min Mayordomoffe ± P. Sequentic.
Mariano Martinez Hernandez Mayordomo Sacramento 1º
P. Bochojbo.
Sebastian Lopez alferez San Lorenzo Navenchauc +
jose Juan Perez acienda Mayordomo virgen de Rosario 1ª
P. jobchenom
Andres Perez Hernandez alferez San ticima Trinida
P. Patocil.
Pedro Perez bts. alferez san antonio Buavenchauc.

Part of a page from the waiting lists kept by the scribes in 1961.

Shun Vaskis

Mariano

Domingo

Antonio

Manuel

The Valley of Hteklum from the air.

passed no cargos. Among the thirty that have passed at least one cargo there is a clear tendency for those who have passed high-ranking first cargos to take high-ranking second cargos, and for those who have taken low-ranking first cargos to take no second cargo, or at most a low-ranking one.

These data, arranged according to the Prestige Scale as they are in Table 16, were analyzed statistically. Test 1, Table 17, shows the two-by-two table that results when the distribution is divided in half on each variable.[1] As shown by the chi-square presented with the table, the distribution is different from chance at the .01 level of significance. The hypothesis of social stratification is strongly confirmed by these data. When the data are rearranged according to the Cost Scale and a similar statistic calculated, the hypothesis of economic stratification is also clearly confirmed (Test 2, Table 17). However, the confirmation is not as strong as that for the data arranged by the Prestige Scale.

Because of field conditions it was impossible to gather more censuses of the type analyzed immediately above.[2] However, it was possible to gather much more information on men who had passed two, three, or four cargos. (See Appendix B, pp. 205–10.) This information does not show as clearly as that given above that men who begin in low-ranking cargos tend to drop out of the cargo system without further service. It is possible to see, however, that there is a very rigid type of progression from level to level in the cargo system.

In Test 3, Table 17, it is clearly shown that men who take two cargos tend to take a second cargo that is as prestigious as their first. Here only a very simple two-by-two table is presented so that the line of argument will not be lost in a mire of complex matrices and statistics. As can be seen from a glance at the complete distribution (Appendix B, p. 209), more complex analysis of the data would yield even stronger confirmations of the hypothesis of social stratification. For example, an analysis that uses more ethnographic information about the significant gaps in prestige between cargos

[1] The procedures followed in the statistical analysis are described in Appendix B, Note 1.
[2] Problems in gathering the data are discussed in Appendix A.

TABLE 17

Cargo Careers: Tests

Rank of Second Cargo	Rank of First Cargo		Results
TEST 1. PRESTIGE (N = 30)	High	Low	
High	11	4	$\chi^2 = 6.56$, P < .01
Low	3	12	77% for
TEST 2. COST (N = 26)[a]			
High	9	4	$\chi^2 = 2.46$, P < .10
Low	4	9	69% for
TEST 3. PRESTIGE (N = 145)			
High	48	26	$\chi^2 = 15.1$, P < .0005
Low	22	49	67% for
TEST 4. COST (N = 145)			
High	48	26	$\chi^2 = 9.29$, P < .005
Low	27	44	63% for

[a] Division of the sample in half on performance on the second cargo yielded an ambiguous result because there were an equal number of cases on each side of the middle cargo and four cases of that middle cargo. In the table presented above these four cases are dropped to give an unambiguous test. The two tests on the original sample yield chi-squares of 1.34 and 3.23, significant at less than .15 and .05 respectively.

yields a chi-square of 44.92 (df = 1) and a contingency coefficient of .50.

Test 4, Table 17, presents the analysis of the same data rearranged according to the Cost Scale. Again the hypothesis that the individual will maintain a consistent rank throughout his career is strongly confirmed. And again, as in Tests 1 and 2, Table 17, the confirmation provided by the data arranged by the Cost Scale is not as strong as that provided by the data arranged by the Prestige Scale.

Although almost all Zinacantecos take a first cargo, and many reach the second level of service, no more than six reach the third level of service each year. It is possible to show that those who reach the higher-ranking third-level cargos have more prestigious and expensive previous careers than those who reach the lower-ranking third-level cargos, but reaching any third-level cargo is a very great distinction in Zinacantan. Thus, the data presented in Table 18 are arranged to show that men who reach third-level cargos of any kind tend to be those who have had high-ranking previous careers.

The percentages shown in the Prestige Scale column of Table 18 are calculated in the following way. The most prestigious "paths" to a third cargo are those that involve very high-ranking first and second cargos. The upper five per cent may be visualized as the extreme upper left corner of Table 16. The next lower 15 per cent in prestige (cumulatively 20 per cent) are the paths a little further away from the upper left corner of the table.[3]

TABLE 18

Paths to Third-Level Cargos

(N = 82)

Paths, Ranked by Prestige Scale	Cargoholders Using These Paths	Paths, Ranked by Cost Scale	Cargoholders Using These Paths
Top 5%	30%	Top 5%	32%
Top 20%	74%	Top 20%	59%
Top 50%	89%	Top 50%	90%

If access to a third cargo were random, it would be expected that the upper five per cent of the paths (calculated by prestige or cost) would yield only five per cent of the actual incumbents of third cargos. As is shown in Table 18, this is decidedly not the case. Men who serve third cargos have very distinguished previous careers. The hypothesis of social stratification is so clearly and strongly confirmed that no statistic is shown. Note that the Cost Scale column of Table 18 strongly confirms the hypothesis of economic stratification. Again, the confirmation by the Cost Scale is not quite as strong as the confirmation by the Prestige Scale.

The ultimate achievement in an individual's career in the cargo system is the attainment of the position of Senior Alcalde Viejo. Thirty-four men take a first cargo each year, but only one of them is likely to reach Senior Alcalde Viejo eventually. The results pre-

[3] The calculation for Tables 18 and 19 is fully explained in Note 2 of Appendix B, and the data are found on pp. 208–10 of Appendix B.

TABLE 19

Paths to Senior Alcalde Viejo (D1)

(N = 22)

Paths, Ranked by Prestige Scale	D1's Using These Paths
Top 5%	41%
Top 20%	73%
Top 50%	95%

sented in Table 19 show that the previous careers of the men who reach this top position involve only the more prestigious cargos. The patterning, as would be expected, is even more rigid than that for careers which lead to third cargos.[4] The analysis of previous careers of Senior Alcaldes Viejos by the Cost Scale also yields a very significant patterning of data. Again, this patterning is not as rigid as that produced through analysis by the Prestige Scale.

In sum, the social and economic stratification in Zinacantan is clearly reflected in men's careers in the cargo system. The data on individual careers unmistakably show that men who distinguish themselves socially and economically in early cargo service go on to maintain their position and to increase the distance between themselves and their fellows.

Stratification Over Generations

Testing for the maintenance of social and economic rank by families over generations is more complex than the testing done above on individual cargo careers. The examination of limited data yields patterns that can be interpreted in a number of ways. There are family dynasties, and families that have been poor as long as anyone can remember; there are men who have established themselves in the last generation, and men who seem to be falling far below the positions of their fathers. A handful of carefully selected cases does not lead to a clear and inevitable interpretation, as it did in

[4] For the first two cargos, the careers of men who eventually reach First Regidor (C1) are essentially the same as those who eventually reach Senior Alcalde Viejo (D1).

the analysis of individual careers. Only a statistical test on a rather large sample can yield a satisfactory answer to the question of stratification over generations.

The majority of men in Zinacantan today take their first cargo after age 45, so by the time a man's own cargo career takes shape, his father may well be dead and forgotten by most informants. Despite this difficulty, it was possible to get information on the fathers of 103 men who have passed at least one cargo. This is recorded on p. 210 of Appendix B. The hypothesis that a son will maintain the rank held by his father is tested with these data. The hypothesis of social stratification is clearly confirmed (Test 1, Table 20).

Test 2, Table 20, shows the data arranged by the Cost Scale. The test yields a chi-square of 2.65, significant at the .10 level—at best a weak confirmation of the hypothesis of economic stratification. It would indicate that it is not easy for a father to pass on economic advantages to his sons; and this interpretation fits those made by anthropologists studying other communities in Middle America (see Cancian n.d.). They have said that landholdings and other economic advantages are so fragmented by the inheritance system, which gives an equal share to each child, that economic advantage is difficult to maintain over generations. This is a possible interpretation, and it has some validity for Zinacantan.

Despite these results of the simple analysis of data, closer analysis of the original data reveals considerable economic stratification

TABLE 20

Fathers' and Sons' First Cargos: Tests
(N = 103)

Rank of Father's First Cargo	Rank of Son's First Cargo		Results
	High	Low	
TEST 1. PRESTIGE			
High	32	18	$\chi^2 = 7.07, P < .005$
Low	19	34	64% for
TEST 2. COST			
High	26	19	$\chi^2 = 2.65, P < .10$
Low	23	35	59% for

in Zinacantan over generations. Many of the cases that do not support the hypothesis of economic stratification involve Mayordomo Sacramento (A3) and Mayordomo Santa Cruz (A6). As was pointed out in Chapter 8, the relationship between the expenses and the prestige of these cargos is rather anomalous. Mayordomo Sacramento is very prestigious despite its low cost. Neither the moletik, in appointing a man to this cargo, nor the man who seeks to serve it are primarily concerned with economic resources. Mayordomo Santa Cruz, on the other hand, is very expensive, but the prestige accruing to those who pass it is very low considering its expenses. This may indicate that the person who passes it is deficient in some way, though relatively rich. In sum, there is reason to think that neither of these cargos reflects the economic capacities of its incumbents very accurately. The clear-cut pattern of economic stratification is best seen without them. Removing either one of them from the total sample is enough to yield a distribution with a chi-square significant at better than the .05 level. Removing them both lowers the probability to less than .01, and clearly confirms the hypothesis of economic stratification.

In sum, data arranged by the Prestige and the Cost Scales confirm the hypotheses of stratification over generations. Families tend to maintain their social and economic position over time.

Social Stratification and the Selection of Spouses

The existence of social stratification in the public life involved with the cargo system has been clearly demonstrated above. I have argued, essentially on the basis of the evidence used in constructing the Prestige Scale, that this stratification is "significant" to Zinacantecos: important to the men and their families in everyday interaction in all aspects of Zinacantan life. If this stratification is as important as I have claimed, it should be reflected in the choice of partners for the most intimate and prolonged of social contacts, marriage. It is thus hypothesized that spouses will come from families of similar social standing. The hypothesis is tested with data from a census of the hamlet of Apas (Appendix B, p. 210, and Note 3). In this test social standing is measured by performance in the cargo system (Prestige Scale), with two cargos being considered more prestigious than one of any kind. Results of the analysis, presented in Table 21, confirm the hypothesis: spouses do tend to come from families of similar social standing. There are thus two conclusions to be drawn from this test: (1) there is social stratification in Zinacantan outside the realm of the cargo system; and (2) cargo performance, as it is rated by the Prestige Scale, is an important determinant of position in this stratification.

Some Case Materials

The extensive samples analyzed above support generalizations about Zinacantan society as a whole, but in making such analyses one tends to lose sight of the individual Zinacantecos whose cargo careers either support or go against the generalizations. With the case materials presented below I hope to give the reader a fuller understanding of the meaning of the generalizations for the individual Zinacanteco, and to show something of the range of actual cases that are subsumed by the generalizations. In addition, I hope that this relatively intensive case material will demonstrate the complexity of the situation in Zinacantan, and thus make it clear that reliable generalizations about Zinacantan society can be drawn only from extensive samples like those used earlier in this chapter.

It might be well to begin with some cases that represent notable exceptions to the patterns of stratification. The First Regidor in 1961, for instance, had previously served as Mayor and Alferez Natividad (A11-B6-C1). I do not know the details of his case, but I suspect that he was appointed to Mayor because of some offense

TABLE 21

Stratification and the Selections of Spouses: Test
(N = 57)

Prestige Rank of Wife's Father	Prestige Rank of Husband's Father		Results
	High	Low	
High	19	11	$\chi^2 = 2.95$, P $< .05$
Low	10	17	63% for

committed as a young man—something that he overcame dramatically in later years. He appears to be capable of reaching Senior Alcalde Viejo. If he manages it he will be a very notable exception, for in my records of 22 careers leading to Senior Alcalde Viejo, Mayordomo San Antonio (A9) is the lowest starting point.

This most inauspicious beginning was made by Lorenzo Perez, perhaps the most important leader of Zinacantan a generation ago. After passing Mayordomo San Antonio, a cargo that normally means the end of a career (or at best a career ended after service in a low-ranking Alferez position) Lorenzo Perez went on to Alferez San Jose, First Regidor, and Senior Alcalde Viejo (A9-B4-C1-D1), as well as to the political leadership of the community.

Inconsistent performance in the other direction is represented by the Alcalde Shuves for 1961, who was mentioned in Chapter 4. This man began his career as Mayordomo Rosario, served a relatively low second cargo (Alferez Santa Rosa), and was removed from Alferez Divina Cruz in midterm for drinking excessively (A2-B10-ADC). Another man who ended his career with the lowly regarded Alcalde Shuves cargo had begun by serving Mayordomo Rosario and Alferez Rosario (A2-B5). According to one of his sons, drinking also played a part in his downfall, although he never suffered the disgrace of being removed from a cargo. Such highly inconsistent individual careers are rare.

The slightly inconsistent career of Lucas, the rich man of Chapter 7, reveals some of the factors that go into choosing cargos. Lucas began as Mayordomo Santo Domingo, taking the junior of the two posts because the senior one was already occupied when he was ready to serve. He went on to Alferez Trinidad, but then agreed to serve Third Regidor because he thought the waiting list for First Regidor was too long. Finally, he became Senior Alcalde Viejo in 1961 at the age of 55 (A5-B3-C3-D1). He explained that his desire to move quickly to the top of the hierarchy motivated him to compromise by taking cargos of lesser standing than he might have served had he been able to choose.

One of the most interesting stories about Lorenzo Perez concerns his son, Andres, who is now a mature man. As a young boy Andres was sent to San Cristobal to live with a Ladino ice-cream vendor and help the man peddle his wares in the streets. Lorenzo was a rich man and did not need the few pesos Andres earned, but (as Andres tells it) he wanted the boy to learn Spanish and the ways of the Ladino world so that he could benefit from the knowledge as an adult. The period in San Cristobal no doubt did help to make Andres the extremely successful corn farmer and trader he is, and with this success he has launched himself on the most prestigious and expensive cargo career possible.

Families and larger kinship groups present even more interesting cases of inconsistent performance. In the genealogy presented in Figure 3, Antonio, who has already been mentioned in other chapters, is ego, and Lorenzo Perez is his mother's brother. Note that Antonio's career is in sharp contrast with that of his father (who died a young man), his father's brothers, and his own brother. Lorenzo Perez's brother and brother's son have relatively undistinguished careers, but Lorenzo's son has been able to carry on the tradition established by his father.

The single genealogy presented in Figure 4 will give the reader an idea of the consistency with which a family can hold its position over generations. Ego in the genealogy is Shun Vaskis, the Ritual Advisor of the Alferez (5 in the genealogy), who was mentioned in Chapter 6. Besides the family's consistently outstanding performance in the cargo system, two features are notable in the genealogy. The first is the consistently high performance of Shun's sons-

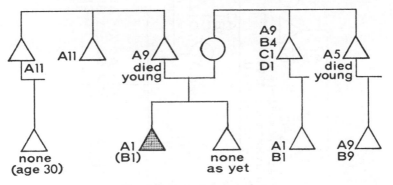

Figure 3. Antonio's genealogy.

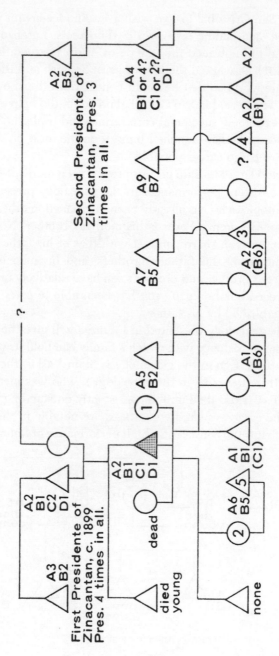

Figure 4. Shun Vaskis's genealogy.

in-law. Shun's dominating personality and his wife's talent for encouraging and maintaining close relations among their daughters are important here. The family, including sons-in-law, is a closely knit unit that offers aid to any member on the occasion of cargo service and curing ceremonies. Ritual kinship ties have been used to reinforce some of the weaker links (for example, between 1 and 2, and between 3 and 4). The workings of family pressure come out dramatically in the case of 4, who is young but should pass a cargo soon if he is to have a distinguished career. When asked if 4 had requested a cargo, Shun replied that he had indeed done so: Mayordomo Rey (A1).[5] In fact, 4 had not requested a cargo, though he is a very enterprising young man who could afford an expensive one. For the present he is more interested in improving and consolidating his economic position. Asked about his father-in-law's report, he replied simply: "That's what *they* say."

The second notable feature in the genealogy is the pattern of declining rank in the projected careers of two of the sons-in-law: A1-(B6) and A2 (B6). Both of these men have compromised in selecting their second cargos because the waiting lists for positions of higher rank are too long.

Finally, consider the case of Domingo at the time he was courting his wife (Figure 5). Though Domingo's father had served as judge in the civil government and was respected in the community, he was a relatively poor man. Domingo lived alone with his mother, for his father had long since been living with a second wife. So this young man with a poor and estranged father was trying to court a girl who was both the daughter of a rich man (whose cargo career had been cut short by an early death) and the sister of a man who had kept the family wealth together and begun a distinguished cargo career. People told Domingo that he would not be able to provide the gifts such a rich family would expect. However, by working for agencies of the national government and for anthropologists, Domingo managed to raise the money to court and marry

[5] Shun later denied that he said this, but I am virtually certain that he did. In any case, it is his son-in-law's reaction to the report that he said it that is crucial here.

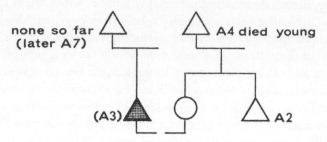

Figure 5. Domingo's genealogy.

the girl in an appropriate style. Now he has requested and been promised Junior Mayordomo Sacramento (A3), a cargo that will enable him, with his limited though growing economic resources, to approach the standing of his wife's family in the community. If my judgment is correct, Domingo probably never will completely overcome his initial social and economic disadvantages, but continuing economic success and a distinguished cargo career might enable him to do so.

Discussion

Most of the discussion and interpretation of the findings of this chapter and those of Chapter 11 are found in Chapter 12. There are, however, two comments that belong here rather than in the more general discussion. The first concerns the difference between the findings based on the Prestige Scale and the findings based on the Cost Scale, and the second concerns the degree of stratification present in Zinacantan.

As has been noted above, the use of the Prestige Scale to order the data consistently yields stronger confirmation of the hypothesis of stratification than does the Cost Scale. This suggests, as did the confirmation of the Prestige Scale through the analysis of informant error in Chapter 8, that the Prestige Scale is the better indicator of the total set of factors that influence Zinacanteco participation in the cargo system.

The success of the Cost Scale alone in ordering the data leads to two conclusions. (1) There is economic stratification in Zinacantan; i.e., individuals and families tend to keep their relative economic standing over time. (2) A man's wealth limits the manner in which he may participate in the cargo system. This second statement is not so much a finding of the present analysis as it is a conclusion drawn from the material presented in Chapters 7 and 8. It bears repeating now, I think, because the evidence presented in this chapter illustrates the importance of the original conclusion.

The success of the Prestige Scale in ordering the data leads to another conclusion. It should be clear, given the fact that much of the Prestige Scale is based on the ranking originally established for the Cost Scale, that much of the success it has in ordering the data is fundamentally the result of the economic element in cargo service. That is, in substantial part, a man's social rank depends upon his economic resources. On the other hand, the superior success of the Prestige Scale clearly indicates that factors other than economic ones influence the estimate made of service in the cargo system by Zinacantecos. The comparison of the ordering of the data by these two scales suggests that, insofar as the Zinacanteco is able to control his cargo career, he tries to increase his prestige within the limits of his economic situation.

The importance of the Prestige Scale as an indicator of the factors influencing personal behavior is further attested to by the fact that it, and not the Cost Scale, most successfully predicts the selection of spouses (see Appendix B, Note 3).

It remains to ask what the findings presented in this chapter reveal about the degree of stratification in Zinacantan. In each of the tests presented above, I have listed the percentage of cases that support the hypothesis. The percentages range from 59 for Test 2, Table 20, to 77 for Test 1, Table 17.[6] Percentages were listed to enable the reader to make a quick evaluation of the strength of the

---

[6] Since the variables are divided to obtain equal marginal totals, the expected percentages for the hypotheses, which might vary substantially from 50 per cent if the marginal totals were uneven, are all close to 50 per cent. For the Tests they vary between 49.8 and 50.3 per cent. For the data presented in Table 22 they are 49.9 and 51.2 per cent.

patterns shown. Higher percentages in support of the hypotheses are obtained when variables are divided with attention to ethnographically significant gaps in the rankings, but it is valuable to see how the data are distributed in these straightforward tests, in which the variables are divided so that an equal number of cases fall on each side of the division.

While there is no question about the statistical confirmation of the hypotheses, the actual distribution of data will strike different readers in different ways. Some will accept the clear statistical confirmation of stratification. Others will be less willing to accept my analysis, in which one case in three is an exception to the stated hypotheses. For the uncommitted reader, I have found a readily accessible body of data that permits a comparison with the United States.[7] Rogoff's study is specifically one of occupational mobility over generations in the Indianapolis area, but the data are comparable. The data were analyzed in the straightforward manner used for my tests presented above. The results are presented in Table 22. In the data for 1910, 63 per cent of the cases support the hypothesis that father and son will have consistent occupational rank. In 1940, 62 per cent of the cases support the same hypothesis.

TABLE 22

Occupational Mobility in Indianapolis, U.S.A.

Father's Occupational Class	Son's Occupational Class		Results
1910 (N = 10,523)	High	Low	
High	3,836	1,247	62% for
Low	2,623	2,547	
1940 (N = 9,892)			
High	3,915	1,697	63% for
Low	1,947	2,333	

NOTE: The data were divided so that equal numbers of cases would fall high and low (within the limits imposed by the original categories). In each case this dividing point made skilled workers and above fall high, and semi-skilled and below fall low.

[7] The original source of the data is Rogoff (1953: 44–45). It is fully reproduced and probably more generally available in Barber (1957: 434–35).

Thus, it would seem that Zinacantan presents a pattern of statifica-tion similar to the one found in Indianapolis. Such a simplistic comparison is, of course, unfair. Indianapolis is a large city and part of a still larger society, while Zinacantan is a community of about 7,650 people. However, the comparison may help the reader to interpret the percentages I present.

And, impressionistically, I would say that stratification in Zina-cantan is not unlike stratification in the United States. Though it is unusual to think of a society of 7,650 people as having classes, I think it would be fair to say that Zinacantan has something close to the open class-system found in the United States. Many indi-viduals and families change their social and economic rank, even though most do not change it significantly. In everyday interaction, social and economic position matters. It does not bind the indi-vidual rigidly as it would in a caste system, but it is seldom com-pletely absent. As I suggested at the beginning of this chapter, stratification is a matter of degree. The stratification in Zinacantan is important to Zinacantecos, and therefore is an important part of the social structure. Exactly how important this degree of social stratification would be on a comparative scale is a question beyond the scope of the present analysis.[8]

[8] Anthropologists sometimes report on societies that seem, on the basis of the evidence they give, to have about the degree of stratification present in Zina-cantan. Yet they often call such societies "socially homogeneous" or "classless." The use of the word "classes" to describe the levels of stratification in many nonliterate societies is perhaps unwarranted. And there is probably no use in getting into the endless controversies and confusions that sociologists have had about the term. However, there would seem to be a great range of socially stratified societies between the ones all investigators would agree to label es-sentially socially homogeneous and the ones in which all would see clear class distinctions. We could benefit greatly, I think, from more attention to the stratification of such societies.

Eleven
Participation in the Cargo System

The cargo system defines the limits of the Zinacantan community. Only insofar as an adult male citizen is a participant in the cargo system, or at least a potential participant, is he a Zinacanteco. Thus the cargo system is important to the maintenance of Zinacantan as an integrated Indian community set apart from the Mexican nation. Below I will review the data on participation and the cases of persons who are marginal members of the community and have had their loyalty tested by the prospect of service in the cargo system.

Full Participation and the Strategy of Participation

At the present time virtually all Zinacanteco adult males participate in the cargo system. Those who do not take cargos are so few that they may be significantly designated as nonparticipants and placed at the bottom of a ladder ranking all others according to the degree of their participation.

The participation of all household heads in the hamlet of Paste is shown in Table 23. For the most part the data speak for themselves, but I will point out some of the more important conclusions that may be drawn from them.

The fact of full participation is the most important feature of the data. In the 50–54 age group and those above it, the average participation is more than 85 per cent. Of those 65 years old and older, 95.8 per cent have participated. Almost every man participates in the cargo system. Below and in later chapters I will refer to this fact as *full* participation—with the understanding that I mean that only about 10 per cent of the men who reach old age have never participated in the cargo system. From the point of view of the

TABLE 23
Participation in the Cargo System: Paste Census

| Age | N | 1 Cargo | | | | 2 Cargos | 3 Cargos | 4 Cargos | Percentage Participating |
		A11	A7-10	A4-6	A1-3				
to 24	11	–	–	–	–	–	–	–	–
25–29	54	1	–	1	2	–	–	–	7.4
30–34	33	3	–	–	1	–	–	–	12.1
35–39	39	2	2	–	5	–	–	–	23.0
40–44	14	1	1	–	2	–	–	–	28.6
45–49	35	3	7	4	7	4	–	–	71.5
50–54	20	3	8	2	2	2	–	–	85.0
55–59	14	–	1	1	1	3	4	–	71.4
60–64	8	2	–	–	–	4	1	–	87.4
65+	24	–	2	1	–	8	3	9	95.8
TOTALS	252	15	21	9	20	21	8	9	

ranking system, the nonparticipants are not an amorphous mass that must be distinguished by other means, but rather a sharply distinguishable category. The first conclusion to be drawn from the data is that although participation in the cargo system does not quite reach 100 per cent, participation in the ranking system is total.

The data in Table 23 show that less than half of all men take their first cargo before the age of 45, but this does not mean that Zinacantecos must wait until a man has passed 45 to estimate the social position he will ultimately achieve through service in the cargo system. This is true for three reasons. First, at each age level the limited number of participants may be distinguished from the non-participants and ranked according to their service. Second, the nonparticipants are not leaving the question of their performance completely open, for, with each passing year, the probability that they will pass more than one cargo diminishes, simply because their active years become numbered. Third, and most important, it is empirically true that those who do not participate when they are young are likely to take lesser cargos when they finally do participate—even if in theory the age of first cargo does not determine which cargo will be taken.

This third statement is supported by the data presented in Table

23. Note that the performance on first cargos is divided into four classes according to prestige. Of the men of less than 45 years of age, seven have passed the low-prestige cargo of Mayor; three have passed cargos of low-middle prestige; one has passed a cargo of high-middle prestige; and ten have passed cargos of high prestige. That is, early in life, those whose behavior does not meet community standards have been selected and appointed as Mayores; and those who are headed for highly prestigious careers have "selected" themselves, or have been selected, and have begun to take first cargos that are highly prestigious. Even at this age, the nonparticipants have already indicated that they are not headed for the top.

As a matter of strategy, a man who hopes to reach the top cargo of Senior Alcalde Viejo must begin when he is young, for he needs the years to pass and pay the debts of four cargos. As was shown in Chapter 10, those who do reach Senior Alcalde Viejo tend to have had very distinguished careers up to that point. Thus, there is a convergence of the patterns present in Table 23 and the patterns of participation reviewed in Chapter 10. Together they strengthen the picture of the social differentiation resulting from service in the cargo system.

In sum, not only are all Zinacantecos included in the ranking system resulting from the hierarchy, but rough estimates of every man's ultimate standing can often be made by his fellows even before he has taken any cargo.

Participation and the Limits of the Community of Zinacantecos

Most nonparticipants are very poor, usually because of sickness, injury, or bad luck in farming. In a few cases the heavy demands made on a curer or a political leader seem to prevent his participation. Eventually most of these men participate to some degree, though the demands of their other roles cut into the resources they can devote to the cargo system.[1] The nonparticipants who are *not* held back by economic limitations or the demands of other roles

---

[1] Of course, their social positions are enhanced by their performance in the other roles, so participation in the cargo system may be less important to them than it is to a man who has no other way of establishing himself in the community.

in public life are very few. They are men whose loyalty is divided between Zinacantan and the Ladino world outside.[2] Their cases offer striking examples of the manner in which the cargo system defines the limits of the community.

In recent years these people with divided loyalties have been, almost without exception, employees of the Instituto Nacional Indigenista (INI). Since INI is committed to educating the Indian and making him part of the larger Mexican society, bilingual Indians who are open to Ladino ideas are especially useful in its programs. Below I will review the cases of two such men, one who has succumbed to the demands of the community and passed a cargo, and another who has permanently defined himself as a Ladino. Two other cases, which will not be discussed, parallel these very closely, and some others are quite similar in important respects.

Antonio, the Senior Mayordomo Rey (A1) in 1960, was pushed out into the Ladino world to earn money when his father died before he was ten years old. He attended school near Mexico City and served in the Mexican army before returning to Zinacantan in the late 1940's. Because of his leadership qualities, his ability to speak Spanish, and his knowledge of things Indian and Ladino, he was hired by INI. He first worked on the promotion of cooperative stores in Indian communities, then became a schoolteacher, and finally was released by INI so that he could become the first Indian Secretario Municipal of Zinacantan. When his political fortunes took a turn for the worse and he was forced to leave the post of Secretario, he was rehired by INI as a schoolteacher.

The high salaries paid by INI (400 to 500 pesos a month) made him a wealthy man. Although Antonio claims that he wanted to pass his cargo, he did not put his name on a waiting list years ahead of time, as others do. He simply took the opening left by the default of a man on the waiting list. Almost certainly there was pressure on him to do this. His comment that he passed a cargo so that he would not lose face in the community (Chapter 9) supports this interpretation.

[2] An undetermined number of Zinacantecos disappear completely into the Ladino world each year, losing all contact with their relatives.

Having made the great investment required by a cargo, he is again firmly entrenched in the community. Not the least of the sacrifices he made in taking the cargo was the loss of his INI job, his principal attachment to the Ladino world. Now Antonio is a corn farmer and a merchant. When in Zinacantan he dresses as a Zinacanteco; when traveling beyond San Cristobal on selling trips he usually dresses as a Ladino.

Shortly after his cargo, Antonio still seemed ambivalent about his commitment to the Indian community. When the pressure to pay the debts from his cargo weighed heavily on him, he talked as if he were considering leaving Zinacantan and enlisting in the Mexican army as a career man. Since his wife also speaks Spanish and has lived in the Ladino world, it was a real possibility. However, as he debated the alternatives his economic situation improved, and he told me that he had decided to stay. Other facts that I learned later indicate that he never seriously considered leaving. Even before the period when he threatened to leave the community because of the pressure of his debts, he had asked for Alferez San Lorenzo (B1), the most expensive and prestigious of the second-level cargos. And, soon after he completed his cargo, his wife became a native curer, cementing her attachment to the community. Clearly, they mean to be Zinacantecos.

Jose, unlike Antonio, decided against taking a cargo when pressure was put on him. A younger man, he rents a room in San Cristobal and alternates between sleeping there and at his house in Zinacantan, where his very Indian wife and mother live with his children. His work on INI educational programs requires that he spend much of his time traveling to various Tzotzil-speaking communities, but he usually spends Wednesday night and the weekend in Zinacantan. Since his wife and mother speak no Spanish, it would be very hard for him to move out of Zinacantan even if he wanted to do so.

Jose was forced into the Ladino world when his father died leaving the debts from a cargo, and he swears that he will never take a cargo. Once the authorities tried to name him Mayordomo Santa Cruz (A6), sending a messenger to his house with the candles that signify appointment to a Mayordomo cargo. Jose promptly set out to return them and refuse the appointment. His description of the incident illuminates the relationship of his type of nonparticipant to the community:

I went to the town hall, but the moletik were not there, for it was Saturday and they had gone to the house of the Senior Alcalde Viejo to change the flowers. The Presidente was there and I asked him to send a Mayor to get the Senior Alcalde Viejo and the rest of the moletik.

The Mayor returned and said they told him that they were too busy to come. They said I should come to the chapel the next morning at nine to settle the matter. The Mayor reported that they said they would offer me another cargo if I wanted it—that if I did not want Mayordomo Santa Cruz, they would give me Mayordomo Rey or Mayordomo Rosario [A1 or A2, both very expensive].

But I didn't wait for the morning to come. I asked where the Senior Alcalde Viejo lived and went right to his house. I told him that I did not accept the appointment and wanted to give the candles back. He said, "Accept. We've appointed you. You must accept. There is no one else to take the cargo. Do us the favor."

I said, "I have no money. I don't accept."

He said, "Accept. You must accept."

I said, "Thank you, thank you; but I don't accept."

Then the others came out of the house and tried to convince me. They tried to give me a drink, but I refused it. They said that I should take the cargo now while I was still young. They said that I always had new clothes and a leather purse, so I must have money.

Then they all started to insult me.

One Regidor said, "Let's put him in jail and then we can settle the thing tomorrow."

Another said, "You don't know God. You're not a Catholic. You're a burner of the saints."

But another one thought about it and said, "We can't put him in jail. He works for INI, and if we put him in jail, they'll put us in jail."

So then they just insisted that I should accept, and they brought drink by the bottle and tried to give it to me; but I didn't accept. They wouldn't accept the candles I was trying to give to them, so finally I just left them by the doorstep of the house and left.

They remained talking about me, but so what.

The next day, Sunday, I went out in the main streets to see if they would try to do something, or try to put me in jail; but they just looked at me and did not put me in jail.

I refused because I have seen what happens when people take cargos. They finish their cargo with a debt, and then their families suffer and their children go without clothes.

The last paragraph of Jose's account is a good summary of the modern philosophy that underlies the positions of several Ladinoized men who continue to live in Zinacantan. It is the philosophy of INI, and most of them have learned it there. Also at INI they have learned to be proud of being Indians—modern Indians. They would like to be the leaders of a new kind of Indian community, one that would adopt Ladino values and not pour its surplus resources into a cargo system which does nothing to improve the living standard. Unfortunately for them, few Zinacantecos see the world in their way.[3]

In sum, then, most nonparticipants are simply poor and unfortunate. However, the cases of Ladinoized men who have stayed in the community illustrate how participation in the cargo system is a crucial part of being a Zinacanteco.

[3] Late in 1964, I was surprised to learn (from Robert Laughlin) that Jose was selected as Presidente of Zinacantan for the term beginning in 1965, and agreed to serve.

Twelve

The Functions of the Cargo System

The cargo system is crucial to the continued existence of Zinacantan as an Indian community, a community separate and distinct from its Ladino environment. Among the functions of the cargo system are: definition of the limits of community membership, reinforcement of commitment to common values, reduction of potential conflict, and support of traditional kinship patterns. After reviewing these functions, I will discuss some differences between my interpretation and the interpretations usually made by students of Middle American Indian communities, and will consider briefly the factors that threaten the continued existence of Zinacantan as an integrated Indian community. (These factors are discussed in detail in Chapters 14–16.)

Any functional analysis is a difficult and dangerous enterprise. In the analysis of a total society this is so simply because the material itself is so complex and intertwined. Any statement assumes a number of others and can usually be alternatively stated from other points of view. Another difficulty results from the complex and distinct uses of the word "function."

I have no solution for either problem, but in the next chapter I will make an attempt to clarify the second, the conceptual-terminological one. In presenting an interpretation of Zinacantan society in this chapter, I will use the word "consequences" ("functions") to denote the results or effects of an institution, and the word "integrative" ("functional") to denote aspects of these consequences that contribute to ensuring the continued existence of the institution. Still another use of "functional"—the one alternatively expressed by the terms "equilibrating system" and "homeostatic system"—will also appear in the last section of this chapter and in succeeding chapters.

Community Integration and the Cargo System[1]

Discussions of the integrative or disintegrative consequences of social institutions seem to me to yield a high proportion of facile arguments, and I am not sure that I will be able to avoid this common fault here. However, I will try to state my conclusions without embellishment and hope that the reader will agree with them on the basis of the evidence that has been presented above.

The most obvious integrative consequence of the cargo system results from the gathering together of people involved in performing ritual duties and in attending fiestas for pleasure. It is especially their cargo roles that bring people from various hamlets into contact with one another. Although the sacred mountains in Hteklum are perhaps the most important reason why Zinacantecos from all hamlets are oriented toward the ceremonial center, it is through the cargo system that they make frequent personal contact with each other there.

The ritual and fiestas of the cargo system bring Zinacantecos together in common religious celebration. This public ritual reaffirms the commitment of each participant to the common religious symbols. Since these symbols are in many ways unique to Zinacantan, the ritual clearly distinguishes Zinacanteco participants from non-Zinacantecos.

Individuals are required to commit themselves to the Indian way of life by service in the cargo system. Some, of course, are lost to the community when they refuse to make the commitment, but the integrity of the community is maintained, for they are defined as nonmembers. Thus, it may be said that the cargo system permits clear definition of the boundaries of the Indian community.

The economic facts of participation in the cargo system require an integrated community and at the same time help to maintain it.

---

[1] Many studies of the cargo system or civil-religious hierarchies in other Middle American Indian communities have been made by anthropologists; and many of the interpretations of the Zinacantan cargo system made below were suggested by their writings. Cancian n.d. is a review of these studies.

Before he spends the great sums required for a cargo, a man must feel assured that his doing so will satisfy at least the majority of his fellows. If only a few of them were to recognize his achievement, the investment would not be adequately repaid. On the other hand, after he has made this tremendous investment in the cargo system, he is required to support the norms of the community that stipulate rewards for such behavior. If he does not, he undermines his investment. And if he enters the Ladino world, his investment is totally lost, and even a detriment to him in some circles.

The cargo system ranks the members of the community into a single social structure. All sectors of the community accord prestige and respect to the incumbent and past cargoholder, and the public nature of cargo service makes it an effective way of ranking all Zinacantecos.

The fact that cargoholders are differentially rewarded according to the type of service done reaffirms the values in terms of which the distinctions are made and on which the ranking is based.

The cargo system provides for what Manning Nash aptly describes as "socially controlled modes of personal display" (1958: 69). That is, it stipulates the rules under which a man may enhance his public image, and thus helps to minimize potentially disruptive innovation and competition.

Because of the advantage in cargo service possessed by a man who has close relations with many kinsmen, the operation of the system encourages the maintenance of traditional kinship patterns.

The expenditure of great amounts of money in the cargo system, especially by the rich, reduces considerably the envy of the rich by the poor. (Envy, because of the attendant danger of witchcraft practiced on the envied by the envious, is a potentially disruptive force in Zinacantan—as it is in many other Middle American communities.) The cargo system assuages this envy very effectively by allowing, and in fact requiring, the rich to make the greatest contribution for community religious observances.

Finally, the consumption of wealth in the service of cargos, in Eric Wolf's terms, "acts to impede the mobilization of capital and wealth within the community in terms of the outside world which employs wealth capitalistically" (1955: 458). That is, the accumulation of capital that might be used for non-Indian types of investment is severely limited. In addition, of course, this enforced expenditure of wealth prohibits many excursions into the Ladino world of consumption that Zinacantecos might otherwise make.

For the most part, then, the economic burden involved in cargo service contributes substantially to the integration of the community. On the other hand, the expenses of cargos also provide great potential for disruption. As long as the traditional norms are held by all Zinacantecos, and the alternatives to being an Indian are unattractive, the cargo system would seem to be a very satisfactory way of converting economic surplus into social position. However, if and when the norms weaken and the non-Indian environment becomes more attractive, the expenses of cargos may only add to individual motivation to reject the traditional system.

In sum, many aspects of the cargo system are crucial to the maintenance of Zinacantan as an integrated Indian community. Breakdown of the system would mean more than simple disappearance of cargo service as an aspect of being a Zinacanteco. It would have ramifications throughout the complex of characteristics and conditions that keeps the Zinacantan community separate from the outside world. As Adams has pointed out in a review of change in Guatemalan Indian communities, with change in the sociopolitical structure "the Indian's resistance to culture change began to disintegrate. His insulation was gone." (1957: 48.) In Zinacantan too, the cargo system provides substantial insulation against the pressures for change that exist in the environment.

Stratification and Leveling

Though most of the interpretations of consequences offered above are commonly found in analyses of the cargo system made by students of other Maya communities, the list does reflect an unusual emphasis. In this section I will contrast my own emphasis on the stratifying consequences of the cargo system with the more usual emphasis on its leveling consequences.

I have emphasized the fact that, through the operation of the cargo system, individuals establish their social rank in the community. (In the process they may show their economic rank.) The cargo system thus acts to separate the community into multiple social statuses. Insofar as the attainment of high social position involves the expenditure of great amounts of money, the system rewards achievement according to two values basic to the Maya: productive agricultural work and community service. The positive evaluation of manual work reflected in this system is in strong contrast with the values of Ladino society, where manual work is not so highly valued. Thus the operation of the cargo system rewards and reinforces behavior appropriate to the Indian value system. In addition, of course, the differential distribution of social rewards represented by the cargo system reflects the high value placed on ability to handle certain positions of authority.

Many writers on Middle American Indian communities have emphasized the fact that the expenditures required for service in the cargo system tend to homogenize the population with respect to wealth.[2] They reason that since the rich spend more than the poor, in the end "the rich" and "the poor" are not greatly different in level of wealth. That is, the community is economically leveled. "By using the income and resources of individuals and the community, the hierarchy keeps any one family from accumulating very much surplus cash or property." (Nash 1958: 69.)

The supporters of this interpretation usually note that: (1) the level of wealth and of production technology is low to begin with; (2) the system of bilateral inheritance tends to fragment estates; and (3) potentially productive time is devoted to serving in communal offices, both civil and religious (Wolf 1955; Nash 1964).

While the importance of these factors in Zinacantan and in other communities is undeniable, the evidence for Zinacantan clearly

[2] Especially important are: Tax 1953; Wolf 1955 and 1957; Nash 1958; and Carrasco 1961. I quote Nash because his statements often provide the sharpest picture of the leveling position. Wolf's article (1955), already well known for its definition of the term "peasant," provides the subtlest picture of all the complexities involved in any interpretation of the consequences of the cargo system. Cancian n.d. provides a detailed review of the positions of these authors.

indicates that some degree of economic stratification exists despite their operation. Evidence from other communities is fragmentary. The weight of it probably supports the leveling interpretations that the students of these communities make, but most reports also contain evidence that can be read as support for the stratifying interpretation. Unfortunately, because reports on most other Maya groups are communities studies that cover a much broader range of information than I do in this book, there is no detail on patterns of participation that may be compared with the data from Zinacantan (Cancian n.d.). It might be noted, however, that an earlier study of Zinacantan, done without extensive sampling of patterns of participation, interpreted the cargo system as primarily a leveling mechanism (Zabala 1961a).

Clearly, both the stratifying and the leveling tendencies exist. Those who emphasize the leveling consequences of the cargo system do not deny that it results in social stratification, any more than I deny that it produces economic leveling.

The supporters of each interpretation, however, represent the consequences that they emphasize as being the ones that are crucial to maintaining the integration of the community. The contrast between the positions becomes more important and more interesting, I think, when viewed in the light of the theoretical orientations behind them. Interpretations that emphasize the leveling consequences proceed on the theory that differentiation is disruptive. Interpretations that emphasize the stratifying consequences proceed on the theory that differentiation is integrating.

The supporters of the economic-leveling interpretation espouse what might be labeled a conflict theory of society. If people were not uniformly poor, they argue, conflict would develop in the community. Thus the leveling consequences of the cargo system lead to suppression of potential conflict and greater community integration.

This interpretation seems reasonable, especially given the belief-system described in Chapter 9. There is no doubt that Zinacantecos believe it proper for individuals to be made poor by cargo service. And in listing the reduction of potential envy and witchcraft as an integrating consequence of the cargo system, I have assumed that the reduction of conflict is important to community integration.

The stratifying interpretation of the cargo system rests on what might be termed a consensus theory of society.[3] That is, I would argue that, given the shared values in support of cargo service, the system continually reinforces and reaffirms these values for the community and the individual. Differential distribution of respect and deference is determined by performance in the cargo system. I do not pretend to explain the origin of the particular relative values of the different roles. Rather, I am concerned with the manner in which the cargo system, in both its social and economic aspects, continually reinforces these values by rewarding most the people who meet them best. Since the system extracts service and consequent commitment to the normative system from virtually all adult males in the community, it is a particularly effective creator of community integration. This is all the more true because the values and norms to which each man commits himself through cargo service are distinct from and often in conflict with those of the Ladino environment.

In sum, then, the conflict theory postulates potential conflict and interprets the consequences of the cargo system so as to explain the avoidance of this conflict—yielding a relatively neutral, integrated state. The consensus theory postulates a relatively neutral state and interprets the consequences of the cargo system so as to explain the presence of a positive state of community integration. Both throw some light on the operation of the cargo system.

However, in terms of the observed behavioral patterns in Zinacantan, the stratifying interpretation makes much more sense than the leveling interpretation. For if the leveling interpretation were the more appropriate one, the economic stratification that exists in Zinacantan should result in substantial disruption in the com-

[3] I do not always think in terms of this theory, nor do I mean to imply that the supporters of the leveling interpretations always work in terms of the conflict theory. These statements about the general theories behind the interpretations are post hoc constructions intended only to illuminate the difference between the positions.

munity—and this internal conflict is not at present apparent. In fact, I think, service in the cargo system legitimizes the wealth differences that do exist and thus prevents disruptive envy. There is, in effect, sufficient leveling (the result of differential economic contribution to cargo service) to satisfy normative prescriptions, but not enough to produce an economically homogeneous community. The economic stratification that exists is condoned and even encouraged by the fact that greater social rewards are given to the rich. As long as Zinacantan society is analyzed as a stable, integrated system, the stratifying interpretation contributes more to the understanding of that integration than does the leveling interpretation.

The Cargo System Through Time

The empirical chapters that follow offer a diachronic analysis of the cargo system in the period from the beginning of this century to about 1980. In them I will show that the synchronic analysis made above will not be applicable to Zinacantan in the near future. The integrative consequences of the cargo system cannot be maintained in the future.

The two major forces threatening the integration of the community are population growth and economic expansion. An expanding population means that more and more adult males become available for cargo service; and insofar as the number of cargos does not expand to meet this growing population of potential cargoholders, it is impossible to maintain the full participation described in Chapter 11. Those who cannot participate because of the scarcity of cargos cannot be integrated into the community in the ways described above. And, as the exclusion of adult males increases, it becomes less and less possible to see the cargo system as the basis of a single, community-wide ranking system. The universal prestige and the universal reinforcement of community values is weakened to the degree that scarcity of cargos prohibits universal participation in the system.

The threat posed by economic expansion has two aspects. First, insofar as increased wealth means that the expensive cargos could be served by more men than actually can be accepted into the available positions, the respect for the unique achievement formerly accorded to those who could manage such cargos tends to be lost. Second, insofar as the traditionally defined cargo system does not consume the increasing wealth of the community, this wealth is available to individuals for other uses—uses that may very well be found in the Ladino rather than the Indian way of living.

If these forces of population growth and economic expansion had operated unopposed against the integrating consequences of the system as described above, the integration of the community based on the cargo system would have long since disappeared. In fact, however, there have been compensating or equilibrating forces that have helped to maintain the balance described in the synchronic analysis presented above. That is, the history of the cargo system since the turn of the century is best seen as a history of changes tending to compensate for population growth and economic expansion.

An increase in the number of cargos has offset to some degree the expansion of population. In Chapter 14 the degree to which this increase in the number of cargos has contributed to maintaining equilibrium is analyzed. In Chapter 15 the history of the cargo system since 1900 is reviewed, and it is shown that the waiting lists have consequences that may be considered functional equivalents of increasing the number of cargos. However, the effect of the waiting lists as equilibrating variables is shown to be limited.

Economic expansion that seriously threatens the integrating consequences of the cargo system is a more recent phenomenon. Clearly, the increasing number of cargos available for service has compensated somewhat for the increase in community resources. However, compensation for increasing individual wealth, which might be expected to take the form of higher cost for already existing cargos, has not appeared. A number of voluntary groups whose members spend relatively small amounts of money on ritual have appeared as wealth has increased, but membership neither demands the resources nor confers the prestige that the cargo system does.

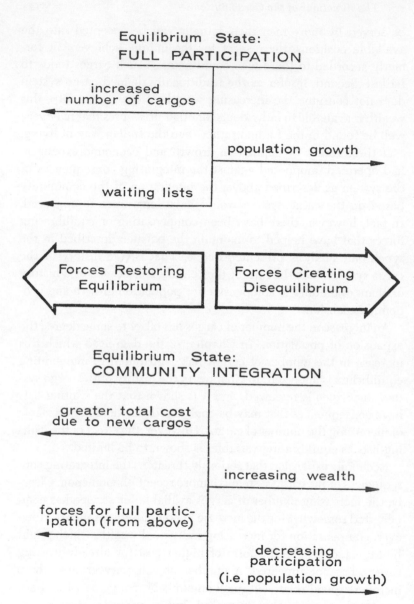

Figure 6. Variables and systems in the diachronic analysis.

In sum, the major threat to the integrating consequences of the cargo system has been population growth, and the more important compensations have been those relevant to this threat. That is, the threat has been to the aspects of community integration that depend on full participation in the cargo system. For this reason, Chapters 14 and 15 take full participation, not integration of the community, as the stable state that is being directly threatened. This limitation of the discussion to a subsystem of the whole facilitates analysis. In Chapter 16 community integration is taken as the stable state that is threatened, and the disequilibrating effects of both lower participation and increased wealth are considered. That is, degree of participation, which in Chapters 14 and 15 is the most general state of the subsystem under study, becomes in Chapter 16 simply a variable in the larger system in which community integration is the most general state. Figure 6 presents this outline in diagrammatic form.

Thirteen

Functional Analysis and the Single Society

Anthropologists have frequently used functional analysis to interpret the information they have collected on a given society, yet
little effort has been spent in examining the logic of confirming
their interpretations. In this chapter I will present some of the
ideas on the problems of testing and confirming a functional analysis of a single society that have concerned me during the analysis
of my material on the cargo system. The chapter is not crucial to
the descriptive purpose of the book, and is not needed to understand the ethnographic material on change presented in Chapters
14 through 16. However, the discussion should throw some light on
the choices I have made in analyzing that material, and will, I hope,
clarify the logic of functional analysis as it is used here.

My purpose is to extract from the quagmire called "functional
analysis" a set of concepts and uses that: (1) retains a substantial
part of current usage; (2) shows internal logical consistency without at the same time being empirically sterile; (3) distinguishes
functional analysis from other types of analysis, especially the type
sometimes denoted by the mathematical sense of the word "function"; and, (4) permits statement of functional analyses so that
they may be scientifically tested.

I shall begin by exploring the meanings, implications, and interrelationships of three concepts that are commonly used to refer to
various aspects of "functional analysis." They are: consequences,
equilibrium, and integration.

Consequences

In ordinary language, a consequence of an institution is often
called an effect, a result or a consequence. This term can be used

to denote two types of statements, one useless for functional analysis as a distinctive type of analysis, and the other crucial to it. Contrasting these types will help to make clear the characteristics of the useful one.

The first or "useless" meaning might be called "direct consequence" that is, a simple effect that has not been clearly stated in the description of the institution. For example: A direct consequence of the operation of the cargo system is the gathering together of many Zinacantecos in the ceremonial center. From this, a simple and obvious generalization might be made: "The operation of the cargo system involves the gathering together in the ceremonial center of Zinacantecos from many hamlets." This follows directly from the descriptions of the various ceremonial occasions, and is acceptable without reference to any general theories or broader empirical generalizations about similar events. The fact that it is a generalization that need not have been stated in a full description of the operation of the cargo system does not give it any special status once it is stated.

A somewhat less obvious generalization that should also be classified as a direct consequence is this: "Cargo service involves significant amounts of money for most cargoholders; it is an economic burden." Given the cost of cargos, the typical earnings of corn farmers, the large debts most cargoholders have after their service, the years of work required to repay the debts, and the expressed desire to be out of debt, the generalization can again stand without the support of a theory. These kinds of direct consequences or simple generalizations are important in the description of the operation of institutions, but they hardly deserve a special term or extensive discussion.

An indirect consequence[1] is one that follows from the operation and structure of an institution seen in relation to an underlying theory of some sort. The same aspect of the cargo system described above as a direct consequence might be described as an indirect consequence in this way: "The gathering together of Zinacantecos for common ritual tends to reinforce the bonds of interdependence

---

[1] This distinction is in no way parallel to the distinction between manifest (intended and conscious) and latent (unintended and unconscious) consequences.

of the participants and to strengthen their commitment to common symbols." Clearly, this generalization does not follow directly from the description of the various ceremonies. It is an interpretation of the gatherings in terms of a theory of communal ritual observances. The obvious source of the interpretation is Durkheim, but it finds support in various other writings, such as the reports of social psychologists on conformity experiments. In making the connection with more general statements, I have classified the gatherings of the cargo system as similar to other group activities that have the consequence of increasing the interdependence and common commitment of the participants—that is, the integration of the group.

The second direct consequence stated above, "Cargo service is an economic burden," may be interpreted to have the following integrating indirect consequence: "The size of the economic investment is so great that the individual is committed to the Zinacantan community, where he will be rewarded for his investment (as opposed to the Ladino environment, where he will not be rewarded); and he is committed to the system of norms that stipulate such reward." This generalization clearly does not follow directly from the description of the economic facts of participation in cargo service. It is an interpretation with complex underlying theory. And the relevant general theories in this case are much more diverse and less clear than they are in the case of the indirect consequence stated immediately above.[2] However, the interpretation seems to me a reasonable one, and I would guess that most readers accepted it without too many reservations when it appeared in the preceding chapter.

The kinds of statements of indirect consequences an analyst makes when trying to give a holistic account of the operation of a total society or institution become even more complex than the examples given above. The underlying theory is often even more obscure. In any case, however, the analyst immersed in the details of a single society or institution is usually concerned with how it operates rather than with general theoretical principles. He states

[2] It has been suggested that Homans's (1961) most recent work provides relatively simple theoretical background for this interpretation.

the interrelationships and consequences in terms of the ethnographic material. Although knowledge of established theories will, in fact, influence the interpretations he makes, my impression is that the conscious connections are generally made in terms of the empirical material at hand.

Whatever the analyst's actual mode of procedure, making a precise statement of the theoretical underpinnings of his interpretations involves a number of problems. First, confirmed general theories are neither plentiful enough nor clearly enough codified to permit them to be used with any facility. Second, given the complexity of many of the analyses that are undertaken, the exposition would become impossibly extended and cumbersome if their theoretical bases were fully articulated. The massive intellectual effort might increase the care with which statements were made, but it would be unlikely to contribute to their confirmation. In addition, since each complex institution is (on the level of empirical materials at least) a unique or almost unique configuration of variables, the effort to classify in terms of general principles might result in the loss of "richness" of detail. Concern about richness per se is ascientific, but when the same concern is presented as a concern with appropriate classification of empirically complex material, it becomes a proper scientific problem.

In sum, while it is clearly important to make statements of indirect consequences, their confirmation presents very complex and difficult problems because of the paucity of confirmed general theory on the one hand, and the complexity of the holistic study of institutions on the other. Yet if such statements of indirect consequences are to be included in the repertoire of scientifically testable statements that can be made about a particular institution or a single society, some kind of solution to the problems must be found.

The problems are real ones, and they cannot be completely eliminated; but there is a way around them. First, it is essential to recognize the analysis of indirect consequences in the society for what it is: a "little theory" tailored to the single case of the institution being analyzed. Such an analysis is a theory about the interrelations of various aspects of the institution under study. It is a little theory rather than a general theory because it makes no claim to the generality of the postulated relationships. In fact, such a little theory is stated without any attempt to phrase its component hypotheses in terms that make the case available for comparison. Thus, the statement that participation in the cargo system strengthens commitment to the Zinacantan community and Maya work values becomes a theory of the local relation of communal rituals and commitment to the community, not an interpretation of local events in terms of general principles.[3] This reconceptualization consolidates the problem of testing and confirming the interpretive statements into one that can be handled in terms of additional data about the institution under study, and only in those terms.

The little or local theory is subject to the rules of testing that apply to any theory. New cases that are not included in the data used in the inductive formulation of the theory are needed to test it. However, since the theory is by definition limited to a single institution in a single society, the appearance of a new case in the usual sense is impossible. Thus the logic of testing such a little theory is more complex than that normally encountered in testing theories formulated in general terms. The testing and confirmation must depend on internal variation in the system under study—on the local creation of what would count as essentially new cases. That is, it must depend on change in the institution under study.

Since the present section must conclude by leaving open the problem of testing, it may be useful to restate briefly what has been said about the confirmation of statements of indirect consequences. This statement will also summarize briefly what is to come.

The available logics of confirmation are essentially two. One shows that statements made about the case at hand are merely instances of more general theories that already have independent support. The other shows, through internal variation in the system under study, that the postulated relationships do hold.

The first might draw on the literature of the social sciences to

---

[3] As noted above, this is not to say that the idea behind the interpretation does not have roots in general theory or knowledge of other cases.

find general confirmation for the statements made in the interpretation of a particular society. Alternatively, the logic of using more general findings that support the particular interpretation of one society may look to the findings of cross-cultural research of the kind done with the Human Relations Area Files. Even when it is available, however, this kind of support goes against the character of functional analysis insofar as it is conceived of as a little theory uniquely explaining the particular happenings in a particular society; and it exposes the analysis to the dangers of incorrect identification and classification of specific materials. My purpose is not to deny the value of the kind of confirmation procedure just described. It is rather to explore the possibilities for the alternative one, which limits itself to data about the single institution or society.

This second logic may be characterized by its dependence on the equilibrating properties implied by functional analysis as I interpret it. It depends on the idea that an appropriate or correct analysis will permit prediction of the equilibration that will take place when one or more of the variables in the system change. Successful prediction of compensations for such changes will be taken as confirmation of the little theory.

Equilibration

An equilibrium system is one in which several variables interact so as to maintain some other property of the system. In other words, it is a homeostatic, self-maintaining, or directively organized system.[4] Figure 6 (Chapter 12) diagrams such a system: the number of cargos and the population size compensate for each other's variation so as to maintain the property of the system called "full participation."

The distinctiveness of an equilibrium system is based on the fact

---

[4] This definition of an equilibrium system draws heavily on Nagel's formalization of functionalism (1956), and on Francesca Cancian's discussion of the ways in which functional analysis so defined can be used to analyze change (1960). Both these papers should be valuable to those interested in the metatheoretical aspects of the problems being discussed here. Though they will be recognized quickly enough, I should mention that I have many other intellectual debts to many previous writers on the subjects covered in this chapter.

that the property being maintained may be defined independently of the variables maintaining it. If the property being maintained were defined by the interaction of the variables maintaining it and by nothing else, there would be no equilibrium system, but rather a simple one involving "function" in the mathematical sense. The property being maintained must be independently measurable, and it should be maintainable by variables other than the specific ones found maintaining it in a particular empirical situation. If the property being maintained always varies with the variables maintaining it, and disappears when they disappear, it is then only a tautological restatement of the relationship among the variables. Such usage gives no distinctive meaning to the terms "equilibrium system" or "equilibration."

This definition may be illustrated in terms of the example of an equilibrium system mentioned above. Full participation is the stated "property that is being maintained." Taken in its general sense—namely, degree of participation—it is simply a restatement of the relation of population level and the supply of cargos (assuming a continued high motivation to participate in the cargo system). Full participation, as opposed to degree of participation, is something more than a simple tautological restatement of the relationship of the variables of population level and supply of cargos, but it is still definable only in terms of those variables.

However, in its more complex sense, full participation may be understood as clearly independent of the variables that maintain it. That is, while it may be maintained by the proper relationship of those variables, it does not become meaningless without this proper relationship. As I suggest above, and show in detail below, it may be understood as "full degree of commitment to the community through participation in the cargo system." In the face of population growth this property is maintained by variables other than simple increase in the number of cargos. A section of Chapter 15 is devoted to showing how the waiting lists for cargo positions help to maintain "full degree of commitment to the community through participation in the cargo system" without an actual increase in the number of available cargos. Thus the property is not simply defined by the variables most important in the system originally described.

In essence, this means that functional equivalents are admitted, and, in fact, that a system defined so that functional equivalents cannot be admitted cannot be an equilibrium system if the idea of equilibrium system is to have any distinctive meaning.

This short characterization of equilibration is elaborated below in the discussion of integration.

It might also be emphasized here that the applicability of this formal model to the analysis of any case is an empirical issue, not a theoretical or metatheoretical one. To state the model is not to imply that it will be useful in the analysis of data—in other words, that "the world is really this way." Whether or not the model applies is entirely an empirical question to be answered in terms of its usefulness in unraveling the complexities of a given case. This must be emphasized because it is this fact of scientific procedure that disposes of the common criticisms that equilibrium analysis is teleological and conservative. It is neither. In some cases it may be appropriate to criticize an analyst for distorting the data because of teleological thinking or conservative bias. However, if his distortion happens to be associated with application of the equilibrium model, it is the man, not the abstraction, that is to blame.

Integration

Integration is the most complex of the concepts under discussion. Its ordinary-language meanings are more diverse than those of the other two concepts. And the meaning it will be given here seems to salvage less of this diversity than has been the case with the other two concepts.

I cannot find a way to make the concept meaningful and at the same time eliminate the complexity introduced by its implication that strain or conflict are absent. To handle this problem by refusing to face it would reduce any practical utility this discussion may have. In discussing the problem of strain or conflict, however, I try to separate it from the balance of the argument—from the part about which it is possible to be a little more clear.

Above I equated integration of a group with "the interdependence and common commitment of the participants," and, if there must be a simple definition, this is the one that I would adopt. It might be better, however, to pursue a more detailed definition—even if it must be a looser one. To begin with, some kind of system that can be distinguished from its environment must be assumed. In this case it is the Zinacantan community. In the preceding chapter it was suggested that several consequences of the cargo system contribute to the integration of the community. Among them are the following:

(1) Clear definition of the boundary of the community through participation in the cargo system.

(2) Reinforcement of distinctive common values and norms because of: participation in common ritual, the advantages of large kin groups in cargo service, and the sizable economic investment required by cargo service.

(3) Reduction of forces that lead to boundary crossing, especially through the reduction of "discretionary" income that might otherwise be spent in the Ladino world.

(4) Reduction of internal conflict through legitimizing of wealth by cargo service and through actual reduction of wealth differences.

The first three of these characteristics lend themselves easily to abstract formulation: (1) the boundary of the system should be clear; (2) its distinctive internal features should be maximized; and (3) its internal features that necessitate exchange with the environment should be minimized. These characteristics can be stated abstractly and therefore may be readily used in a formal definition of the concept of integration. But if empirical sterility is to be avoided, something must be said about conflict or strain (in what follows I will use "strain" to imply both).

The problem of strain is double-edged. First, there is the idea, expressed in (4) above, that integration is greater insofar as internal strain is reduced. I think this, in its simplest sense, must be accepted as part of the definition of integration. Second, there is the empirical fact that the presence of strain often indicates that a system is integrated. As I will argue later, the very fact that a system can endure strain is part of what is meant by integration, and often the very aspects of a system that seem to contribute to integration also involve a counterforce, which may be identified as strain-producing. In Zinacantan, for example, the expense of cargos creates strain between officials appointing cargoholders and prospective appointees (or strain between opposing motivations in the appointee); but this expense is at the same time the key to the reinforcement of commitment to the community that results from cargo service. It is often true that strain appears to result in increased integration over the long run.[5] Given this empirical tendency, it is still possible to define an integrated system as maximally integrated when internal strain is at a minimum, but this should be done with the realization that strain may never be completely absent in a genuinely integrated system.

Given these empirical characteristics of systems that are to be called integrated, we must still ask: In what sense is saying that a system is integrated a scientifically meaningful and productive statement in the study of single societies? If the only thing meant by saying that a system is integrated is that it permanently displays the four characteristics listed above (or any other set of characteristics, for that matter), then we have not come very far. If "integration" is to be more than a summary term for a set of characteristics identified before the fact of labeling, some sort of commitment

[5] Under the headline "A High-Level Excuse for Slugging Your Wife," the *San Francisco Chronicle*, August 8, 1964, pp. 1 and 10, carried the following summary of a study published by John E. Snell, Richard J. Rosewald, and Ames Robey (1964) in the then-current *Archives of General Psychiatry*: "A wife [who has dominated a passive husband] feels the need to be punished, the report said. And the husband was said to require an occasional chance to reestablish his masculine identity. This condition can go on for years to the mutual satisfaction of husband and wife, the researchers found. But the delicate balance becomes upset when a third party—generally the oldest son who reaches the age of adolescence—starts interfering. At this stage, the wife may turn to the law for help."

In the cases studied, the periodic wife-beating apparently helped maintain the integration of this precariously integrated system, until the son grew up and forced the integration-maintaining conflict to stop.

must be made. I think the following metatheoretical commitment makes the most sense: *An integrated system will tend to be self-maintaining to the degree that it is integrated. That is, integration implies equilibration.* Later I will also want to assume that equilibration is a sign of an integrated system.

This commitment is a metatheoretical rather than a theoretical one because it involves no testable proposition about the empirical world.[6] I am arguing that integration meaningfully defined implies equilibration, and where I think I see integration but find that equilibration does not appear under the appropriate conditions, I must decide that my original identification of integration was incorrect, not that the definition should be rejected.

My reasons for making this commitment are as follows. To say that a system is integrated and at the same time imply nothing about change (or management of strain) is to say that there is a near-perfect balance or fit at present, but that if any change appears, all the postulated interrelationships may no longer hold. That is, the analyst using such a definition of integration makes no prediction at all about the system. If "integration" means only that things are as they are, if it has no implications for the dynamics of the system, then it means little that is useful.[7] Moreover, if "integration" means only this, then there is no way to test the statements of relationship (or consequences) made in interpreting the empirical characteristics of the single society; and insofar as this is true

[6] A theoretical commitment (a hypothesis) linking integration (as identified by the empirical characteristics it summarizes) with other states of such a system could be made; and such a theoretical proposition about connections in the empirical world might then be tested. However, I think that, given the difficulty of identifying the empirical characteristics of an integrated system on a general level, a metatheoretical commitment may be more productive. And I think it probably approximates more closely much of the thinking about "functional" systems. Such a metatheoretical commitment links integration to other states or characteristics of the system by definition.

[7] Francesca Cancian has pointed out that "integration" is commonly used to refer to that state of a society in which there are low strain and high commitment to common values; and that, if the problems of measuring strain and commitment can be solved in a synchronic analysis, there is no reason why this meaning should not be used—even without any implications for the dynamics of the system. This is of course true, but I think the use of "integration" in the present discussion is a more productive one.

the statements are meaningless, for a proposition that admits no test or contradiction is meaningless in empirical science.

The metatheoretical linking of integration and equilibration, of course, offers no empirically testable proposition either, but it does suggest a testable proposition in which any set of empirical conditions identifying integration in a static analysis implies equilibration in the face of change. Thus, the scientifically productive contingency is entirely subsumed under the various meanings of "integration."

Although to say a system is integrated must mean that the system will tend to preserve itself by compensating for changes internal and external to it (by equilibration), totally successful compensation is, of course, not implied. A breakdown of the system may occur.

Plasticity is another characteristic that must be included in the definition of an integrated system. Plasticity means that the system will not break down immediately if change brings about disequilibrium, but instead will be able to contain some measure of strain without breakdown. In some senses plasticity is a better measure of the degree of integration of a system than is equilibration. This ambiguity, produced by the parallel status of equilibrating capacities and strain-containing capacities, is at the base of the problem of defining integration so as to conserve a substantial proportion of the current meanings. These current meanings are worth preserving, I think, because they come out of the extensive experience of scientists with the type of system that is of concern here. To reject either aspect for the sake of rigor would be to devalue the ultimate goal: productive study of empirical cases.

Testing Functional Analyses of the Single Society

This definition of integration has complex implications for the testing of a functional analysis of a single society—that is, for the testing of the statement that a system is integrated (or, on a more specific level, that a consequence is integrating). If an analyst has made a synchronic functional analysis of a system and has said that it is integrated, he has in effect made a hypothesis (a little theory) about its behavior in the face of change. That is, he has stated something about the dynamics of the system. This hypothesis may be tested against data on change of the system (assuming we adopt the single-case logic described above).

Given such a hypothesis or little theory, and a change that threatens the hypothesized integration of the system, there are the four following possibilities for the interpretation of the response to the change.

(1) If the system breaks down, the hypothesis can be neither confirmed nor rejected. That is, the change may have been so great that the system could neither equilibrate nor contain the strain. Though it might still (after breakdown) be desirable to say that the system had been integrated, this statement is an untestable one, for the breakdown points to the essentially tautological conclusion that the change was too great to be equilibrated or the strain too great to be contained.[8]

(2) If strain appears at the appropriate points and is contained, there is evidence for the hypothesis that the system is integrated. However, because strain is so difficult to identify and evaluate, this kind of evidence is not the best possible.

(3) If equilibration takes place at the appropriate points and compensates for the change, then there is substantial evidence confirming the hypothesis that the system is integrated.

(4) If none of the three alternatives listed above occurs, then it must be concluded that the analysis and the hypothesis did not identify the factors of the system crucial to its integration. That is, the hypothesis or little theory must be rejected.

A simple example may clarify these four possibilities and point up problems in my formulation. Suppose a social scientist studies a college fraternity and concludes that, as a social system separate from other fraternities and the social environment, the fraternity is integrated by the fact that the members share in the performance

---

[8] Of course, if the analyst has been able to specify the limits within which equilibration is possible, he might want to claim that the change went beyond these limits and brought about breakdown. (The problem of defining such limits in the study of a single society is discussed below.) Here, however, I am referring to a case for which such limits are not specified and for which little detail about the breakdown process is available.

of three types of ritual: hazing, the saying of a special grace before dinner, and weekly ceremonies in a room closed to nonmembers.

If he means that the fraternity will stay together as a separate social system as long as exactly the same rituals are performed, but that it will disband completely if the rituals are changed the least bit, he has not said anything that requires special terminology. He has merely said that the fraternity exists when the rituals exist, and does not exist when the rituals do not exist. This is a simple hypothesis of covariance.

On the other hand, the social scientist might have the hypothesis that the social system (the fraternity) will tend to persist and that the rituals or a functional equivalent will be maintained in the face of change. That is, he may accept the assertion that integration meaningfully defined implies equilibration. And, insofar as his hypothesis is correct, the rituals should tend to be maintained if threatened.

With this hypothesis he may take a meaningful look at the system if change occurs.

(1) If the fraternity suddenly disbands, no information relevant to testing the hypothesis is produced.

(2) If the college administration suddenly orders abandonment of an important part of the rituals (for example, the hazing) and the social scientist finds that subsequently the members are less faithful in attending meetings and more apt to disagree with each other in public where the reputation of the fraternity is at stake, it may be concluded a) that the ritual is important to the maintenance of the fraternity as a separate social system, and b) that the system has some plasticity that allows it to continue when it is not in perfect equilibrium.

(3) If the college administration suddenly orders abandonment of the hazing, and the members develop more elaborate dining-room rituals, it may be concluded that the rituals are important to the maintenance of the fraternity as a separate social system.

(4) If the college administration suddenly orders abandonment of the hazing and nothing happens (i.e., there is no sign of decreased loyalty to the fraternity and no sign of compensations for

the lost ritual) then the hypothesis or little theory that the hazing is important to the integration of the fraternity must be rejected.

Thus, of the four types of response to change that would threaten the hypothetical integration of the system, only two provide clear tests of the hypothesis or little theory. If there is no response to the threat, the hypothesis must be rejected. Equilibration in face of the threat confirms the hypothesis. Appearance of strain that is successfully contained also provides confirmation of the hypothesis within the limits imposed by the difficulties of identifying and evaluating strain. And breakdown of the system leaves the analyst without any evidence about the appropriateness of his hypothesis.

Something more should be said about interpreting the breakdown of the system. This alternative (number 1 above) refers to the case in which breakdown occurs without a preliminary period of contained strain or equilibration (numbers 2 and 3 above). If contained strain or equilibration is observed, and the system later breaks down, there is, of course, no problem: the integration of the system is confirmed and the subsequent changes that produced breakdown may be interpreted as having gone beyond the limits within which compensation had been possible.

Simple breakdown may be grounds for rejection of the hypothesis that the system is integrated, if the analyst is willing to say that there was ample opportunity for equilibration and none occurred; but to define "ample" would of course be a difficult undertaking in many cases.

The identification of the limits beyond which compensation is impossible, and the rigorous definition of breakdown are problems beyond the scope of the present effort. It is true, of course, that the equilibrium or homeostatic model as it is used in other kinds of research—research on the human organism, for example—is usually combined with some definition of the limits beyond which equilibration is impossible. For example, it is known that there are certain compensations for rise in body temperature, and that when the temperature goes beyond a certain limit these compensations no longer suffice and the system breaks down—the person dies. These limits have been established by research on a large sample of similar systems (human organisms), and while it would be desirable to know the parallel limits in the equilibration of social institutions and societies that are interpreted as integrated systems, acquiring this knowledge presents a problem apart from those treated here. The present effort is devoted to analysis of the single case, and it is aimed at avoiding the complications of cross-case analysis.

In some single-case analyses, the analyst may use general theory or structural features of the system to make predictions about the limits of compensation in the system under study.[9] These predictions, of course, constitute a further little theory about the system, and may be tested and confirmed if and when the system equilibrates or contains strain up to these limits and breaks down when the disequilibrating changes pass them.

Though the appearance of equilibration has been treated as a clear confirmation of the hypothesis of system integration, there is a complication that should be mentioned. This is the problem of functional equivalents. The logic used must allow for the appearance of functional equivalents as compensations for changes in the system under analysis, but this necessity introduces the problem of interpretation of what is and what is not a functional equivalent; and this problem in turn complicates the interpretation of the equilibrating system. This is not a contradiction in the logic, but it is a real danger in practical analysis.

Consequences, Equilibrium, and Integration

The above view of functional analysis provides a way of seeing the relations among some of the various meanings of "function";

---

[9] For instance, in the chapters that follow, in discussing the limits of compensation for population growth through increase in the number of cargos, I argue that some kind of ceiling is put on the number of cargos by the limited number of conceivable locations for new chapels and saints that the cargoholders might serve. And in discussing the limits of compensation possible through the waiting lists, I point out that it is unlikely that men will be willing to wait more than twenty years for a cargo. A further argument could be made that since adulthood seldom lasts more than 40 years in Zinacantan (because life expectancy is low), waiting lists that disposed of the cargos for more than the next forty years would be an ineffectual compensation.

and, more important, it gives some empirically testable substance to the statement that a society is integrated.

In brief, my argument has been as follows. The only kind of consequences worth distinguishing by a separate concept ("consequences") are the indirect ones that are interpretations of the effects of institutions in terms of theoretical underpinnings. Among them, only those interpreted as effecting the integration of the system under study are of concern in functional analysis.

Because of the difficulties inherent in studying complex social institutions and because of the lack of codified theory, the analyst concerned with testing or supporting his interpretation of the integrating consequences of a particular institution may be hard-pressed. Yet insofar as he cannot frame a test, insofar as he cannot specify what would cause him to reject his statements, they are weaker and the analysis is less useful—even though his knowledge may be immense and his understanding perfect.

An alternative to testing his interpretation of a particular institution, his little theory, by deductive or cross-cultural logic is to test it by internal variation in the institution. If his statements about integration are meaningful ones, he should expect integration-maintaining equilibration to take place when changes threatening that integration appear internally or in the environment. If equilibrating compensations do appear, he can properly consider them as confirmation of his interpretation. If they do not appear, and there is no sign of strain in the system or breakdown of the system, he should reject his interpretation.

It is this logic that enables me to consider the chapters that follow as something of a confirmation of the synchronic analysis made in preceding chapters.

Fourteen

Population Growth and Full Participation

The rapid growth of population in Zinacantan is creating a situation in which there are more adult men than the cargo system can accommodate. Since the stratifying and integrating consequences of the cargo system depend on full participation, this situation threatens the equilibrium of the entire social system. In this chapter data on population growth and on the increasing number of cargos available on the first level are presented. Then two idealized models of the cargo system that show the manner and degree of the disequilibrating effect of growing population are constructed.

The Population of Zinacantan

Population data from Zinacantan are available from censuses taken at various intervals since the turn of the century. These data are presented in Table 24. During the most disrupted period of the Mexican Revolution the population was seriously underenumerated and the census figures are almost useless for the purposes of this analysis. The population totals for 1900 and 1940 are probably accurate enough to be of considerable use; and the totals for 1950 and 1960 give every indication of being quite accurate, though they might be a little low because of the difficulties of doing a census in Zinacantan. Since I am concerned with the future as well as the past, I make projections to estimated population in 1970 and 1980. (The method of making the projections is described in the note to Table 24.) Of most concern here, of course, is the number of adult males present in Zinacantan and eligible for cargo service at any given time. These figures are presented in Table 25.

It should be noted that although the rate of population growth

TABLE 24

Population of Zinacantan

Year	Population	Year	Population
1900	3,114	1950	6,312
1910	2,556	1960	7,650
1921	1,551	1970	9,257
1930	2,129	1980	11,201
1940	4,509		

NOTE: The figures for the censuses of 1900, 1921, 1930, 1940, 1950, and 1960 are from the official census publications of the Mexican government. I am grateful to Franz Blom of San Cristobal for aid in gathering the figures through 1950, and to George Collier for similar aid with the 1960 figure. The figure for 1910 is from Tax 1944.

The figures for 1970 and 1980 are projections that I have made. They are based on the rate of increase (1.21) shown in the figures for 1950 and 1960.

The figures from 1910 to 1940 are all too low. This is obvious from internal evidence in the censuses as well as from the growth rates that may be calculated from the data presented here. The growth from 1930 to 1940 represents 112% of the 1930 population (rate: 2.12), and the growth from 1940 to 1950 represents 40% of the 1940 population. The later rate of 1.40 is possible, but unlikely.

The rate of 1.21 based on the 1950 and 1960 figures is certainly not a gross overestimate; it may even be an underestimate, for populations similar to Zinacantan are growing at higher rates.

in Zinacantan is substantial, it is not as high as those found at present in many other parts of Latin America. Health programs of the Instituto Nacional Indigenista and of agencies of the United Nations have probably contributed greatly to recent spurts in the growth rate, and these programs will probably have an even stronger effect in the years to come.

The Cargos

The increasing number of first-level cargos has compensated somewhat for the growth in population. At the turn of the century only 21 first-level cargos had to be filled each year.[1] Although the eight Mayor positions existed, those who passed them were still expected to take a Mayordomo position or some other first-level cargo before moving up the hierarchy. In effect, Mayor did not count as cargo service. At that time it was possible, but not easy, to fill all the cargos from the population available.

[1] These were the 34 positions listed in Chapter 4 minus the eight Mayores, one Mayordomo of San Sebastian, the two cargos served in Navenchauc and the two cargos served in Apas.

TABLE 25

Zinacantan Male Population

(by ten-year cohorts)

Year	Age			
	25–34	35–44	45–54	55–64
1900	190	208	38	28
1930	*219*	128	*66*	42
1940	340	*277*	112	*82*
1950	545	324	182	108
1960	595	397	206	130
1970	720	481	250	157
1980	872	582	303	190

Year	Age			
	20–29	30–39	40–49	50–59
1900	264	236	58	32
1930	*225*	*151*	95	51
1940	*360*	*323*	*183*	83
1950	582	*433*	224	121
1960	604	518	282	152
1970	731	627	342	184
1980	885	759	414	223

NOTE: All figures from 1960 and before are from government censuses. Italicized figures show internal inconsistencies that indicate that the censuses were underenumerated. Figures for 1970 and 1980 were calculated from the projections in Table 24 using the 1960 age-sex distribution as a standard.

As the population grew in the second quarter of the century, men were allowed to insist that they had done their first-level service by passing Mayor. Mayor is now so firmly entrenched as a first-level cargo that most middle-aged informants do not know that it once did not count as the equivalent of Mayordomo. One man who had passed Mayor as a youth in the 1930's asked for Senior Mayordomo San Antonio (A9S) for 1964, simply because he chose to do so. He wanted to start in a "proper" way, not as a low-prestige Mayor. Most others who pass Mayor go directly to an Alferez cargo if they continue in the system. Thus, the 21 first-level cargos at the turn of the century had increased to 29 by the 1930's.

About 1940 a second Mayordomo San Sebastian (A8) was added

to the single one that had served with the other ten Mayordomos until that time. Thus, the number of first-level cargos was raised to 30.

The two Mayordomo cargos served in Navenchauc were instituted about 1954. The image of the saint that they serve was given to the hamlet by the Catholic priest in 1952.[2] A short time later the men of Navenchauc decided to build a chapel to house it, and the creation of two cargos to serve the saint and the chapel followed. These entirely new positions raised the total of first-level cargos to 32.

The cargos and the chapel in Apas are even newer than those in Navenchauc. The chapel was built in 1962. Since it is dedicated to the Señor de Esquipulas, the cargos established were Mayordomo Rey and Mesonero, like those of the similarly dedicated chapel in Hteklum. During the summer of 1962, there was one temporary incumbent in each of the two cargos. However, it was understood that their service would not count toward progress in the hierarchy. In 1963 and 1964 there were regular senior and junior incumbents in each of the cargos, making a total of four new positions. This raised the total of first-level cargos in Zinacantan to 36, the figure used in the calculations made below.[3]

[2] Protestant missionaries worked in Navenchauc in the years before 1952. They did considerable linguistic work, but found the Zinacantecos very hard—indeed, impossible—to convert. They have commented that the old were too stubborn and the young too weak in the face of the older authorities. We have never found a single person among many acquaintances in Navenchauc who remembers them as missionaries, but all remember them as people who spoke the language well. Though I can find no records bearing on the matter, I have been told that the Catholic priest donated the image and encouraged the building of a church in Navenchauc in order to show that the missionaries had had no success.

[3] Note that in Chapter 4 I have listed two cargos for Apas, keeping to the 1962 ethnographic present. The total of four is based on information gathered on a short field trip in the summer of 1964. I am not sure that this figure will remain stable. In 1962 there were those who wanted four cargos, making the Apas chapel similar to the one for the Señor de Esquipulas in Hteklum, and those who argued that the hamlet was too small to provide four men each year. At that time, I happened to visit one of the leaders of Apas (Lucas) in his home a few hours after a meeting in which it had been decided that the hamlet could provide only two cargoholders per year for its chapel. Sometime between that meeting in the summer and the installation of the first regular incumbents at the end of December, this decision was reversed, and four men entered service.

A rough calculation of the age cohort 30–39 for 1960 indicates that it in-

The chapel (and indirectly the cargos) in Apas came into being as the result of a dream of one of the residents. He dreamt that an image—a "saint"—of the Señor de Esquipulas, which now resides on a plantation in the hot country below Apas, wanted to come to Apas to be worshiped, and that this saint would not come until a proper chapel had been erected to house it. When he succeeded in convincing the other residents of the hamlet of the inspired character of his dream, they contributed the labor and money necessary to construct the chapel. It has been provided with an altar and pictures of the Señor de Esquipulas purchased in San Cristobal, but the saint itself has not yet appeared. Zinacantecos believe myths that tell of such travels of saints, but some of the more sophisticated residents of Hteklum have made remarks indicating that they do not believe the saint will appear in Apas.

Although the circumstances that produced the additional cargos in Navenchauc may not repeat themselves, the circumstances that produced the Apas cargos are likely to occur again.[4] To provide for such further expansion in the period from 1970 to 1980, I have added four more cargos.[5] Thus the following calculations are based on these numbers of cargos: 21 in 1900, 21 in 1930, 29 in 1940, 30 in 1950, 32 in 1960, 36 in 1970, and 40 in 1980.

cluded 39 men in Apas. Since there are 40 cargos to be filled in the corresponding 10-year period, the fit is tight. Even with the backlog probably present because of the shortage of cargos in Hteklum, and the anticipated future expansion of population, this balance means that virtually all Apas men will have to serve their first cargo at home if the four cargos are to be kept filled. I suspect that many men will continue to go to Hteklum, and that the elders will have to draw on younger men to keep the cargos filled. The shortage of willing incumbents may become so acute that the cargos will again have to be limited to two, but this seems unlikely.

[4] It was rumored that Paste was offered a saint at the same time that Navenchauc was, but that the people did not want to spend the money to build a chapel. This story may be true, or it may simply be part of the characterization of Paste people as frugal that is often made by people of other hamlets.

[5] Three factors limit the possibility of increasing the number of first-level cargos. (1) The number of hamlet units that could build chapels following the recent pattern of expansion is limited. (2) There is, I think, a limit to how much change the traditional structure can take—though recent innovations seem to have solid acceptance already. (3) New first-level cargos, if they are to provide real opportunities for service in the cargo system, must be accompanied by some increase in the number of second-level cargos. There have been no indications of how this might be accomplished, nor is there a ready example for it—such as the example Salinas provided for Navenchauc and Apas.

This compensation for population growth will be built into the models that follow. Thus, the models represent the gain of the growth in population over the increase in available cargos.

The columns labeled "no compensation" in Tables 26 and 27 show that the situation would have been much more serious if there were no increase in the number of cargos. The columns will be best understood after reading the sections that follow.

Model 1: The Changing Age of Perfect Fit

Suppose the following conditions govern the behavior of persons taking cargos:

Condition 1A: All men take cargos, or

Condition 1B: Ninety per cent of all men take cargos. (See Chapter 11 for the empirical reasons for assuming the 90 per cent figure.)

Condition 2: Cargos are distributed according to the following principle: no man takes a cargo until all cargo-taking men older than he have had their first cargo.

Condition 3: At some point in the past this system was in perfect balance so that all men had cargos as they reached a given age and all cargos could be filled by men of that given age.

If these conditions obtained, the increase in population and the consequent decrease in the number of cargos available per capita would tend to raise the age at which a man takes his first cargo. Full participation would be maintained, but, in requiring all cargo-taking men in a given age group to pass their first cargos before any men from a younger age group pass theirs, the model forces upward the age of taking a first cargo. People grow older while waiting for those older than they to finish serving. In effect, the model slides the age of cargo-taking up the narrowing population pyramid to a point where it is so narrow that there are enough cargos for all men of that age. Hence the label "the changing age of perfect fit"—perfect fit being the parity between the supply of cargos and the demand for cargos of a given age group.

The ages at which first cargos would be taken if this model were the fact of behavior in Zinacantan are listed in Table 26 for conditions 1A and 1B of the model. Condition 1A represents an idealized situation in which all men take cargos. Condition 1B represents the situation in which ten per cent of men do not take cargos. As shown in Chapter 11, this latter condition allows as full stratification as the former one, and it is closer to the reality of the situation in Zinacantan.

Under the more realistic Condition 1B, the age of perfect fit is 35.2 in 1940, 41.7 in 1960, and 44.2 in 1980. This rapid increase in the age of perfect fit threatens full participation in two ways. Neither of them are direct threats, of course, because by definition, full participation is maintained by the model. Rather, the first threat makes full participation meaningless and the second one makes it impractical.

First, under the assumptions of this model, the age of perfect fit rapidly becomes so high that the cargo system no longer has the consequences discussed in Chapter 12. Especially because life expectancy in Zinacantan is relatively short, delay of first participa-

TABLE 26

Model 1: Ages of Perfect Fit

Year	Age under Condition 1A (100% Participation)	Age under Condition 1B (90% Participation)	Age if No Compensation (90% Participation)
1900	29.2	26.6	26.6
1930	30.6	below 25	below 25
1940	38.5	35.2	42.3
1950	41.2	39.5	44.5
1960	43.3	41.7	48.5
1970	44.4	42.9	51.2
1980	45.8	44.2	54.5

NOTE: For condition 1A these figures were obtained by plotting the population figures for 10-year age groups given in Table 25 and cutting the curve with the number of cargos available for the appropriate 10-year period. For example, for 1980, the figure 414 for the 40–49 age group was plotted at age 45 and the figure 303 for the 45–54 age group was plotted at age 50. The points were connected with a straight line. Then a line representing 400 cargos (40 per year from 1975 through 1984) was drawn and the point of intersection of the lines read as the age of perfect fit. Thus the figures given above for tenths of a year are approximations.

For condition 1B the same procedure was used, but the population figures used in each case represented 90% of those given in Table 25.

The no compensation calculation was made in the same manner, but the number of cargos was not adjusted for the date. It remained at 21, the number available at the turn of the century.

tion in the cargo system until age 45 would leave most of the men of the community unable to express their self-image and unable to gain prestige in the community during most of their adult lives. Thus, while the model does not lead to the destruction of full participation strictly defined, it rather rapidly reaches the point where the integrative consequences of full participation no longer operate.

Second, the very high age of first cargo is impractical from the point of view of the cargo system as a whole. If service in a first cargo were delayed until age 45, few men would live long enough to go on to the higher-level cargos. From the point of view of the individual, those who had hopes of reaching Senior Alcalde Viejo would not tolerate such a delay. Model 2, which follows, explores the results of abandoning the principle of full participation so that some men at least enter the cargo system early enough to avoid the disadvantages of Model 1, the Changing Age of Perfect Fit.

Model 2: The Constant Age of First Cargo

Suppose the following conditions govern the behavior of persons taking cargos:

Condition 1A: All men who take first cargos take them at age 35. Those who do not take a first cargo at age 35 are bypassed and never take a first cargo, or

Condition 1B: All men who take first cargos take them at age 40. Those who do not take a first cargo at age 40 are bypassed and never take a first cargo.

Condition 2: At some point in the past this system was in perfect balance so that the number of men of cargo-taking age (35 or 40) was exactly equal to the number of cargos available at that time.

If these conditions obtain, the increase in population and the consequent decrease in the number of cargos available per capita would tend to increase the proportion of men who are bypassed and never take a first cargo.

The percentage of men who would be bypassed if this model were the fact of behavior in Zinacantan is noted in Table 27. It is

TABLE 27

Model 2: Percentages Bypassed at Constant Age of First Cargo

Year	Condition 1A (age 35)	Condition 1B (age 40)	No Compensation (age 35)
1900	11.0%	0.0%	11.0%
1930	0.0	0.0	0.0
1940	10.2	0.0	35.0
1950	30.7	7.4	51.5
1960	38.2	19.4	59.4
1970	42.6	25.1	66.5
1980	47.3	31.3	72.3

NOTE: These figures were obtained by subtracting the number of cargos available for a 10-year period around a given date from the number of men in the appropriate 10-year age group, then calculating the percentage of the total that would be bypassed. For example, for Condition 1A for the year 1980, the number of cargos available for the 10-year period 1975 through 1984 (400) was subtracted from the number of men in the 30–39 age group in 1980 (759). The result of the subtraction (359) was then taken as a percentage of the total (759), yielding a percentage bypassed (47.3%). For the no compensation column, the number of cargos available was held at 21.

difficult to decide whether condition 1A or condition 1B would be more appropriate for application in Zinacantan. Condition 1A is probably closer to the ideals of Zinacantecos, and it certainly does more to avoid the problems reviewed in the discussion of Model 1 above. Thus, I will use it for illustration in the discussion below.

Under condition 1A, about ten per cent of 35-year-old men would be excluded from cargo service in 1900 and 1940. As noted in Chapter 11, this situation may be defined as full participation, and in some sense it may be considered ideal, for it allows men with special problems to avoid cargo service. Given the population listed for 1930, the model shows that there would not be enough 35-year-olds to fill the existing cargos, and presumably men would have to be drawn from younger age groups. (The influenza epidemic of 1918 caused many deaths in Zinacantan, and the Mexican Revolution resulted in a few more, but there is no doubt that the 1930 census is seriously underenumerated.)

By 1960, 38.2 per cent of the 35-year-old men would be excluded from the cargo system; and by 1980 the figure would reach 47.3 per cent.

These facts directly threaten full participation; and in turn they threaten the integration of the society that is based on the cargo system. Insofar as there is less than full participation, the integration of the society would be weakened, for the part of the population that would be left out of the cargo system would not be committed to the community in the ways discussed in Chapter 12. Even the position of those who would participate is weakened, for they could no longer look to the entire community for respect. Presumably, those who would not participate would look elsewhere for sources of prestige, and would further weaken community integration by introducing alternative prestige symbols, which would compete with the cargo system's. I do not think that it is possible to specify the point at which equilibrium would break down; but, certainly, when the cargo system can accommodate only half of the adult men, the community as a system will be in a serious state of disequilibrium.

The Models and the Reality in Zinacantan

Both of the models presented above point to eventual serious disequilibrium in the system being examined here. Moreover, both models make predictions concerning observable facts about participation in the cargo system. Model 1, The Changing Age of Perfect Fit, predicts that the average age of taking a first cargo will be 41.7 in 1960. Model 2, The Constant Age of First Cargo, predicts that 38.2 per cent of men of 35 years will be bypassed by the system in 1960.

Both of these predictions depend on the assumption that none of the conditions of the models have been violated since the point of perfect balance. If the conditions were violated, the models would, in effect, fall behind; and the predictions for the year 1960 would be more extreme than they are under the conditions listed. That is, the numbers shown in Tables 26 and 27 would be underestimates. The models would fall behind for the reasons explained in the next two paragraphs.

For Model 1, if condition 2 is violated by a young man's taking a cargo before his elders, then a further adjustment upward in the age of perfect fit must be made to allow for the participation of all cargo-takers. If such violations continue, the age of perfect fit is pushed up drastically. It is no significant "relief" of the problem that the violator has already passed a cargo when he and his age group reach the age of perfect fit, because the age cohort of young men who are violating condition 2 is constantly growing with the population. The effect of the violations multiplies even if the proportion of the younger group that violates the condition remains fixed. Thus, if condition 2 of Model 1 were violated, we would predict that the age of taking the first cargo will be higher than the age of perfect fit predicted by the model.

For Model 2, if condition 1A is violated and men take their first cargos at ages other than 35, the proportion of those bypassed by the system will be higher than predicted. If men take cargos before they are 35, they contribute to the displacement of men of 35 in a manner similar to the displacement of men at the age of perfect fit in Model 1, aggravating the problem because the age groups following are continually growing. If men take cargos after the age of 35, they also displace a man in the 35-year-old group, though they reduce the displacement in their own age group. Since the absolute number of men bypassed at age 35 even under ideal conditions increases, the number of men of more than 35 years who have the opportunity to violate condition 1A of the model grows. Thus, if condition 1A of Model 2 were violated, we would predict that the proportion of men not passing a cargo at age 35 will be greater than the model predicts.

The data presented in Table 23 (p. 123) are directly comparable with the predictions made by the models. They indicate that the conditions of both models have been violated in the past to such an extent that the cumulative effect makes the predictions of both models gross underestimates of the present disequilibrium.

Stated in terms that make it testable with the data presented in Table 23, the prediction of Model 1 is that one-half of the cargo-takers—45 per cent of the total male population—will have passed a first cargo by age 41.7. Table 23 shows that (for Paste), only 4 out of the 14 men (28.6 per cent) between 40 and 44 years of age have passed a cargo. Thus it may be concluded, though the sample is too small to give certainty, that the median age of taking the first cargo is more than the 41.7 years predicted by Model 1. Note that the same data show that 71.5 per cent of men between 45 and 49 years of age have passed at least one cargo. Thus, the median age of first cargo is less than 49 years.

Stated in terms that make it testable with the data presented in Table 23, the prediction of Model 2 is that 61.8 per cent of the men between 30 and 39 years of age will have passed at least one cargo (condition 1A); or alternatively, that 80.6 per cent of the men between 35 and 44 years of age will have passed at least one cargo (condition 1B). Table 23 shows less than 30 per cent participation for all age groups through that of 40–44 years of age. Thus, it may be concluded that more people than predicted by the model are being bypassed at the ages stated in the conditions of the model.

Exactly how the conditions of the models may have been violated in Zinacantan in the past is impossible to tell from the data available in Table 23. It is clear from these data, which were collected in 1960, that many men have violated condition 2 of Model 1 by taking cargos before the age of perfect fit. It is probably true also that the conditions of Model 2 are being violated by persons older than, as well as younger than, the constant age of first cargo. It is impossible to be certain, however, because the data in Table 23 do not include the actual age at which men older than 35 (or 40) in 1960 passed their first cargos.

Summary

Examination of population data has revealed that full participation is being seriously threatened by population growth in Zinacantan, and that the expanding number of first cargos available has not been an adequate compensation for the growth in population. Model 1 showed that maintaining full participation by raising the age of first cargo would bring the age of first cargo to 44.2 by 1980, thus making full participation meaningless and impractical. Model 2 showed that bypassing a portion of the adult men at a given age (35)—and thus maintaining the cargo system as an effective integrating force for some adult men—would reduce the number of men included in the system in 1980 to 52.7 per cent of those eligible. This means that the cargo system would lose its effectiveness as a stratifying and integrating force in the society because it would not include enough of the population.

A review of actual data on participation in the cargo system as of 1960 indicates that both models make gross underestimates of the degree of disequilibrium. This is true because the system has been in disequilibrium for some time and the predicted effects have been compounded by past violations of the conditions of the models.

On the other hand, examining the state of disequilibrium that would have existed had there been no increase in the number of first cargos (Tables 26 and 27, "no compensation" column) indicates that the increase in the number of cargos has been a substantial compensation for the disequilibrating effects of population growth. The second equilibrating force, the cargo waiting lists, has further delayed the onset of serious disequilibration of the system.

Fifteen

The Waiting Lists

This chapter describes the adjustments made by Zinacantecos as cargos have become scarcer. The most important of these adjustments is the creation of waiting lists. Before discussing the lists in detail I will review the changes in recruitment procedures that have taken place since the turn of the century.

Recruitment Since 1900

In 1900 all cargoholders were appointed by the moletik, who were responsible for finding incumbents for all cargos. They were able to enforce their appointments by sending a man to jail if his explanation of his inability to pass a cargo did not satisfy them. Both the responsibility and the power of the moletik, though in theory persisting to the present, have in actuality been reduced by the abundance of volunteers. In their roles as chief executives of the entire cargo system, the moletik are not as influential as they were in 1900.

Older informants report that in the first quarter of the century the fear of being appointed to a cargo often kept young men out of the ceremonial center. A young man did not dare remind the moletik of his existence by appearing near them at a fiesta. And all men had to be cautious when buying a horse or a mule, for the moletik could reasonably demand that they fill a cargo if they seemed to have surplus money.

The practice of requesting cargos—a practice that eventually led to the establishment of the waiting lists—began slowly. An old man who passed Senior Alcalde Viejo (D1) in 1947 tells a convincing story about his father, who had also passed Senior Alcalde Viejo.

About 1902, when his father wanted to be Senior Mayordomo Rosario (A2S), no one requested cargos—the moletik always sought out their appointees. His father, however, took a bottle of drink to the moletik and requested that he be allowed to serve the very expensive Senior Mayordomo Rosario. The man's manner of retelling the story clearly indicated that his father had been proud of his own initiative, and had emphasized that few followed his lead. There is no evidence that many men asked for cargos in the next two or three decades.

Another old informant tells of being named to Senior Mayordomo Rosario (A2S) about 1920. He refused the appointment and was jailed, but for only three days. Three years later he returned to tell the moletik that he was ready, that he would take Senior Pasionero (A4S) if it was available. When the man they had appointed became sick just before entering, the moletik immediately notified my informant and he entered. To his mind, his declaring his availability did not amount to asking for the cargo, nor did he know of other people who directly asked for cargos at that time.

By the early 1930's the situation was changing. Shun Vaskis, one of the oldest men in Zinacantan and Senior Alcalde Viejo (D1) in 1933, reports that in that year only a few people requested cargos. Those who did so wanted to enter in the next term. If the cargo they desired was already filled, and the moletik could not persuade them to take some other cargo, they simply came back again the next year. The cargos requested in 1933 were the most prestigious ones: Senior Mayordomo Rey (A1S), Junior Mayordomo Rey (A1J), Senior Mayordomo Rosario (A2S), Senior Mayordomo Sacramento (A3S), Senior Pasionero (A4S), and Senior Mayordomo Santo Domingo (A5S). Some of the same cargos had also been requested five or six years earlier, when Shun had been First Regidor (C1).

By the middle of the 1930's, then, the practice of requesting cargos was well established, but there were no waiting lists. I was never able to determine exactly when or how the lists came into being, for most of the men who served as Senior Alcalde Viejo (D1) between Shun Vaskis in 1933 and my other informant in 1947 have long since died. Certainly the lists had not been established by 1937 or 1938, for the Senior Scribe for those years cannot remember keeping them. In 1940, the man who passed Senior Mayordomo Rey (A1S) did not have to wait, and he remembers nothing about lists. The man who passed Junior Mayordomo Santo Domingo (A5J) in 1942 claims that he did so because the senior post was filled, but he does not remember any lists. However, this man requested Alferez San Antonio in 1944 and had to wait six years for the cargo; and the son of the man who passed Alferez Divina Cruz in 1945 says that his father had to wait two years for the cargo. Thus, it seems that some sort of lists were established by the early 1940's. The Senior Alcalde Viejo for 1947 distinctly remembers that there were lists in a book, but says that they were short. He points out that he even had to seek a Senior Mayordomo Rosario (A2S) that year.

From his point of view the waiting lists are an unfortunate thing. It gives less pleasure, he thinks, to have to wait years for a cargo that one could enjoy and pay for at present. His attitude is perhaps that of many Zinacantecos, but since 1947, when he passed his final cargo, many of the lists have become so long that men must come forward to ask for a cargo many years before they can actually consider themselves financially ready to serve. As will be discussed in detail below, the waiting lists have become part of the thinking about the cargo system, and requesting a cargo when one is still young has become part of the preparation for serving it.

The Waiting Lists

The lists are kept in hard-cover notebooks, and a page or more is devoted to each year in the future up to the last year for which there is a cargo requested.[1] When a man requests a cargo, the Scribes write down his name, the cargo he has requested, and the hamlet in which he lives. Before the fiesta of San Lorenzo each year, the Scribes who will serve the coming year make new copies of the lists. On August 8, at the fiesta, they sit by the side of the

[1] The waiting lists for the cargos served outside Hteklum (in Salinas, Navenchauc, and Apas) are in the hands of the elders (not a formal group) of each hamlet. At the appropriate time these men notify the Scribes in Hteklum, who send the appointee his formal notification of appointment.

church of San Lorenzo and read the lists to a crowd of men who want to make sure that their names remain on the list or to ask for a cargo. All those who are on the list present a bottle of drink to the moletik at this time. If a man fails to appear with his bottle (and has not made some special arrangement with the moletik previously), it is assumed that he no longer wants the cargo he asked for. After notifying him of his delinquency, the moletik and Scribes are free to drop his name from the list and insert another.

Like many other waiting lists for scarce commodities, the cargo waiting lists are subject to a certain amount of tampering when their keepers (the moletik and the Scribes) are men open to bribery. The actual cases of important changes in the lists are very few, and I think that the moletik and Scribes for 1961 were telling the truth when they said that they deplored the tampering with the books that had occurred in the past years, and that they never did such things themselves. Few men report having ever had their names lowered, that is, having had their service put off to a more distant time. However, the moletik may favor certain individuals over others, or force reluctant individuals (like Antonio) to serve when someone else drops out and his position has to be filled in the near future. The practice of giving written receipts to men who requested cargos was instituted by the moletik in 1957, but it was short-lived.

The history of the cargo system since 1952 is perhaps best seen directly in the waiting lists. Of the lists made since the 1940's I was able to copy only three.[2] Tables 28–30 summarize the information

[2] Getting access to even three of the lists was a very delicate and time-consuming task. The lists are kept in the house of the Senior Alcalde Viejo (D1) during the year of their use, and are retained by him after they have been superseded by newer lists and he has left his position. I first saw the lists for 1961 in the house of the Alcalde with the help of the Senior Scribe, who was hired as an informant with this objective in mind. Later the Alcalde became a good friend, and he allowed me to make microfilm copies of the lists in the summer of 1962. In order to see and copy the lists for 1958, I had to make a heavy demand on the friendship of Domingo and his father by asking them to present me to the family of the deceased Alcalde for 1958. They did so late in 1961. Also late in 1961 I began to seek out the lists for 1952 with the aid of Antonio, who had been Junior Scribe in 1952. In the summer of 1962 he arranged to have the Senior Scribe for 1952 borrow the lists from the Alcalde and attend them while I made a copy in my own notebook.

TABLE 28

The Cargo Waiting Lists, 1952

	1953	1954	1955	1956	1957	1958	1959	1960	1961	1962
A1S	×		×	×	×	×	×	×		
J	×		×							
A2S										
J										
A3S	×	×	×	×	×		×	×	×	×
J	×	×	×	×	×	×	×	×	×	
A4S	×	×	×	×	×	×	×			
J	×	×	×	×	×		×			
A5S	×	×		×	×	×	×			
J	×	×						×		
A6S	×	×	×							
J										
A7S	×									
J	×									
A8S										
J										
A9S										
J										
A10S	×									
J	×									
A11S										
J										

	1953	1954	1955	1956	1957	1958	1959	1960	1961	1962
B1	O	×		×	×	×	×	×	×	×
B2	×	×	×	×	×	×	×	×	×	×
B3	×	×		×	×	×	×			
B4	×	×	×	×	×	×	×			
B5	×	×	×	×						
B6	×									
B7	×						×			
B8										
B9										
B10										
B11										
B12										
ASD	×									
ADC	×	×	×	×	×	×	×	×		
C1	×	×	×	×	×	×	×			
C2	×	×	×	×	×	×	×			
C3										
C4										
D1										
D2										

NOTE: This table and the two that follow present the cargo waiting lists as of the years 1952, 1958, and 1961. The information was taken from the notebooks of the Scribes who served with the moletik in each of those years. An × indicates that the cargo has been asked for. A zero indicates that the Scribes mistakenly listed two men for the same cargo in the same year. Note that in 1952 the longest waiting period was 10 years. In 1958 it was 16 years; and in 1961 it was 20 years.

In many cases a cargo is filled for many years in the future, but there are still openings near the present. For example, in the 1952 lists A3S has no candidate listed for 1958, but is requested for 1959, 1960, 1961, and 1962. This was probably the result of the recent death or default of the person scheduled to fill the cargo in 1958. The moletik may close such a gap by moving the other candidates down one year, or they may insert a new name if someone presents himself. Many Zinacantecos are on the watch for the latter type of situation so that they may get into the cargo system sooner than would be possible if they placed themselves at the end of the list. I think that some of the gaps are the result of men asking for a junior-senior pair of cargos because they want to serve together. They must of course both request their cargo for the first year available to the senior. I do not know how to explain oddities like the B7 for 1959 (1952 lists), or the A8J for 1974 (1961 lists).

TABLE 29

The Cargo Waiting Lists, 1958

	1959	1960	1961	1962	1963	1964	1965	1966	1967	1968	1969	1970	1971	1972	1973	1974
A1S	×	×	×	×	×	×	×	×	×	×	×	×	×	×	×	×
J	×	×	×	×	×	×	×	×	×	×	×	×	×	×		
A2		×	×	×	×	×	×	×	×	×	×		×	×		
J			×	×												
A3S	×	×	×	×	×	×	×	×	×	×	×	×	×	×		×
J	×	×	×	×	×	×	×	×	×	×		×		×		
A4S		×	×	×	×	×	×	×	×	×	×					
J	×	×		×	×	×	×	×								
A5S	×	×	×	×	×	×	×	×	×	×	×	×				
J	×	×	×	×	×											
A6S	×	×		×	×	×										
J																
A7S	×	×	×	×	×	×	×	×	×	×						
J	×	×	×	×	×	×	×	×								
A8S	×		×	×	×	×										
J																
A9S	×	×	×	×	×	×										
J																
A10S	×	×														
J																
A11S																
J																
B1	×	×	×	×	×	×	×	×	×	×	×		×	×	×	
B2	×	×	×	×	×	×	×	×	×	×	×	×	×			
B3	×	×	×	×	×	×	×	×	×	×	×					
B4	×	×	×	×	×	×	×	×	×	×						
B5	×	×	×	×	×	×	×	×								
B6	×	×	×													
B7	×	×	×		×	×										
B8	×	×	×	×	×											
B9																
B10																
B11	×															
B12																
ASD	×	×	×	×	O		×									
ADC	×	×	×	×	×	×	×	×	×	×	×	×	×			
C1	×	×	×	×	×	×	×	×	×							
C2	×	×	×	×	×	×	×	×								
C3		×	×		×											
C4	×															
D1	×	×	×	×	×											
D2																

TABLE 30
The Cargo Waiting Lists, 1961

	1962	1963	1964	1965	1966	1967	1968	1969	1970	1971	1972	1973	1974	1975	1976	1977	1978	1979	1980	1981
A1S		×	×	×	×	×	×	×	×	×	×	×	×	×	×	×	×	×	×	×
J	×	×	×	×	×	×	×	×	×	×	×	×	○	×		×	×	×		
A2S	×	×	×	×	×	×	×	×	×	×	×	×	○	×		×		×		
J	×	×	×	×	×	×	×				×	×				×				
A3S	×	×	×	×	×	×	×	×	×	×	×	×	×	×		×	×			
J	×	×	×	×	×	×					×	×								
A4S	×	×			×	×	×	×	×	×										
J	×	×	×		×	×		×	×											
A5S	×	×	×	×	×	×	×	×	×	×	×	×	×	×						
J	×		×	×																
A6S	×	×	×	×	×	×	×	×												
J	×		×	×	×	×	×	×												
A7S	×	×	×	×	×	×	×	×	×	×	×	×	×							
J	×	×	×	×		×		×	×											
A8S	×		×	×	×	×	×	×												
J	×		×									×								
A9S	×	×	×	×	×	×	×	×	×	×	×	×	×							
J																				
A10S	×	○	×																	
J																				
A11S																				
J																				
B1	×	×	×	×	×	×	×	×	×	×	×	×	×	×						
B2	×	×	×	×	×	×	×	×	×	×	×	×	×	×						
B3	×	×	×	×	×	×	×	×			×		×							
B4	×	×	×	×	×			×	×	×	×									
B5	×	×	×	×	×	×	×	×	×	×										
B6	×	×	×	×	×	×	×	×	○											
B7		×	×	×		×														
B8	×	×	×			×	×	×			×	×	×	×						
B9	×																			
B10																				
B11		×	×																	
B12	×	×	×																	
ASD	×	×	×	×	×	×	×	×	×											
ADC	×	×	×	×	×	×	×				×	×	×	×	×	×	×	×		
C1	×	×	×	×	○	×														
C2	×	×	×	×	×	×	×													
C3	×	×																		
C4																				
D1	×	×	×	×	×	×														
D2																				

from these lists. In 1952, there were 57 men waiting for first-level cargos and 40 waiting for second-level cargos. By 1958, these figures had grown to 137 and 67 respectively; and 1961 found them at 182 and 87. In terms of rates, the lists for first-level cargos grew at 13.33 names per year between 1952 and 1958, and at 15 names per year between 1958 and 1961. For second-level cargos the comparable figures are 4.5 and 6.67 names per year. These rates indicate the degree to which the cargo system is falling behind in meeting the requests of persons who *want* to take cargos—leaving aside for the moment those who will serve only if appointed.

A revealing, though somewhat artificial, calculation is that of the rate at which the lists are falling behind the total capacity of the cargo system—that is, the capacity of the system viewed under the false assumption that the people who request specific cargos would take *any* cargo at all. This rate is calculated by dividing the increase per year by the number of cargos available (excluding Mayor). The results are as follows: Between 1952 and 1958 the system fell behind 0.67 years per year for the first-level cargos, and 0.38 years for second-level cargos. For the years 1958 to 1961 these rates of falling behind increased to 0.75 and 0.56 respectively. By 1961 the moletik had enough "orders" to fill all cargos on the first level for 9.1 years and all cargos on the second level for 7.25 years. Since the most prestigious cargos are the ones requested, and the people who ask for such cargos would serve in others only under very great pressure, the cargo system is in fact much further behind than this calculation indicates.

Table 31 shows a very close correspondence between the prestige of a cargo and the number of men waiting to serve it. For the cargos of the second level, the correspondence is perfect for the highest eight of the twelve ranks in the Prestige Scale. For the first-level cargos the correspondence is only approximate, but the points where correspondence is lacking suggest interesting ad hoc speculations about the reasons for the lack of correspondence. Mayordomo Rosario (A2) lacked a long list of candidates until recently, suggesting that the number of persons so wealthy that they could request such an expensive cargo was small enough to

TABLE 31
Preference for Cargos

Cargo	1952 Rank	1958 Rank	1961 Rank	Sum of Ranks	Mean Ranking
FIRST LEVEL					
A1	4	1	1	6	1.5
A2	9	6	2	17	6
A3	1	2	3	6	1.5
A4	2	4	6	12	3.5
A5	3	4	5	12	3.5
A6	5	8.5	7	20.5	7
A7	6.5	4	4	14.5	5
A8	9	8.5	9	26.5	9.5
A9	9	7	8	24	8
A10	6.5	10	10	26.5	9.5
SECOND LEVEL					
B1	1.5	1	1.5	4	1
B2	1.5	2	1.5	5	2
B3	4	3	4.5	11.5	3
B4	3	4	7	14	4
B5	5	5	4.5	14.5	5
B6	7	8	4.5	19.5	6
B7	6	6.5	8	20.5	7
B8	10	6.5	4.5	21	8
B9	10	11	11	32	11
B10	10	11	12	33	12
B11	10	9	10	29	9
B12	10	11	9	30	10

NOTE: The ranks for individual years are simply an ordering according to the number of registered requests for the cargo (both senior and junior) found in the Scribe's books for that year. Thus in 1952, A3 was first with 17 requests, A4 was second with 13 requests, etc., and A2, A8 and A9 were tied for ninth place with no requests.

The sum of ranks is simply a summing of the positions in the three columns at the left of the table. The mean ranking, which is discussed in the text, is based on the sum of ranks. Thus, A1 and A3 are tied for first and second with a sum of ranks of 6; A4 and A5 are tied for third and fourth with a sum of ranks of 12, etc.

be satisfied by the more prestigious Mayordomo Rey (A1). Recently the length of the waiting list for Mayordomo Rey seems to have made Mayordomo Rosario more desirable, even though a bit of prestige must be sacrificed by the man who takes it instead of waiting for Mayordomo Rey. Another interesting exception to the general correspondence is Mesonero (A7). As the most prestigious of the lower-cost first-level cargos, it is a good prestige bargain.

Of course, as noted in Chapter 8 in the discussion of the Prestige Scale, Mayordomo Sacramento (A3) is by far the best bargain of all, and this is reflected in the fact that it was very much desired even in 1952.

Consequences of the Waiting Lists

Quite clearly the waiting lists offer no permanent solution to the problem of satisfying the increasing demand for cargos. They delay individual participation, but do not allow the system to handle any more participants in a direct way. However, they have had some consequences that have delayed the day of reckoning for the cargo system.

It should be noted that the waiting lists may be interpreted in terms of their consequences for the community, even though their creation was anything but a community effort. The creation itself resulted from the desire of individuals to ensure that they would be able to pass the cargo they wanted. From the point of view of the individual the lists have ensured orderly access to the cargo of his choice. Furthermore, they have allowed men to prepare properly for the service, for usually they know the date of their service years in advance. In addition, from the point of view of those who are not motivated to serve in the system, the great demand for cargos, and the lists this demand has created, have reduced considerably the possibility that they will be appointed without warning. These consequences are helpful to the individual, but, while they may explain in part individual motivation to create and maintain the lists, they do not reduce the threat to community integration posed by the overdemand for cargos.

It is other consequences of the waiting lists that may be seen as "functional equivalents" of participation—as equilibrating variables that help to offset the scarcity of cargos that results from population growth. The most important of these is what may be labeled the "surplus value" of being on the cargo waiting list. An individual may define himself as a person of a certain category simply by being on the waiting list for a certain cargo. The community cannot blame him for the fact that there is a long waiting list. Certainly being on the list is less satisfactory than actually passing the cargo; he has only demonstrated intention and has not accomplished anything. However, though the knowledge of who is on the waiting list for a given cargo is not nearly as widespread as the knowledge of who has passed it, it is sufficiently widespread in the neighborhood and hamlet of a prospective cargoholder to compensate somewhat for his lack of actual achievement.

For example, the waiting lists have given Domingo, the principal informant of Harvard anthropologists working in Zinacantan, a great advantage. The community's ambivalence about his job and his own ambivalence about his position in the community could not have been resolved had it not been for the lists. He is too poor to pass a cargo immediately, but his salary assures him a good surplus for a number of years to come. Thus, he has been able to request Junior Mayordomo Sacramento (A3J) for some eight years hence—with the hope that the man who is listed for the senior post will default, leaving Domingo as Senior Mayordomo Sacramento (A3S).[3] Ever since he requested the cargo early in 1962, Domingo's life as a Zinacanteco has taken on new meaning. He is struggling to save enough to build a new house, for his present house is not large enough to accommodate the group of Mayordomos who will arrive for ritual during the cargo. When he has extra money he considers buying a large pot or some other household object that will be useful for the cargo. He has built himself a whole set of economic worries based on the fact that he must pass a cargo eight years from now, and has thus reduced tremendously the anxiety that other Zinacantecos will envy him for the money he earns working for the anthropologists. And, indeed, he has a powerful argument with which to meet any direct confrontation on the issue, as well as a clear proof of his intentions, which

[3] The ethnographic present is 1962. In 1963, the man listed for the senior position in Domingo's year defaulted, and his place on the list was given to Domingo. By the summer of 1964 Domingo had completed his new house and was struggling to pay off the debts incurred during its construction. He had contracted for the weaving of the expensive black robe the Mayordomos wear during ritual and was making plans to meet further expenses of his cargo—still six years away.

will slowly spread through the group of people most interested in his position in the community of Zinacantecos.

The waiting lists have served Domingo well, and they have at the same time ensured his continued commitment to the Zinacanteco way of life. Without such an opportunity for early commitment, Domingo and people like him would have to endure years of uncertainty, which might end in Ladinoization.

From the point of view of the community, then, this surplus value of the lists is integrating. People are committed to a certain level of service before they can actually pass the cargo. This commitment may substitute for actual performance when Zinacantecos make an estimate of their fellows. Moreover, the lists allow the moletik to identify people who are not requesting cargos commensurate with their position and wealth. Were it not for the lists, a man's failure to serve an appropriate cargo could be explained by the fact that the cargo was not available. With the lists, however, he may show his good intentions—if he has any.

An appointment to one of the lower cargos is often used to force the hands of men who are very rich but refuse to request a cargo or who are leaning toward Ladino society. Such men are usually named for immediate service as Mayores, but they seldom accept the position to which they are appointed. Rather than accept a poor showing, they place their names on the lists for a cargo appropriate to their position and wealth. In short, they are shamed into taking the appropriate action.

Because of this surplus value, the cargo waiting lists have effectively dampened the disequilibrium caused by population growth in Zinacantan. They directly reduce the disequilibrating effects seen in both models presented in Chapter 14. By making people wait for cargos they have the same effect as Condition 2 of Model 1 —they push upward the age of first cargo, thus allowing more people into the system. And, by extracting a commitment before actual service, they compensate for the loss of early ranking, thus solving the problem that made Model 1 result in a "meaningless" sort of full participation. Similarly, the statement of intended participation they allow permits the "inclusion" of more men in the

30 to 39-year-old age cohort that was the focus of attention in Model 2.

The waiting lists are only a temporary solution, however. The cargo system is not providing enough positions for the growing population. For more than a decade the waiting lists have absorbed the surplus, but it is improbable that men will be satisfied with a situation in which they must wait more than twenty years for a cargo. In a few years the waiting lists as well as the cargo system will be full to capacity, and there will be no way to handle the demands of men seeking to establish their position in the community.

Sixteen

Disequilibrium and the Future

The integration of Zinacantan society that has been a consequence of the cargo system will inevitably break down. This is both the prediction and the conclusion of this study. This final chapter includes: (1) a review of the equilibrating system described in Chapters 14 and 15, and of the problems of precisely defining the state of disequilibrium towards which the system is tending; (2) a discussion of the economic situation in Zinacantan, and its contribution to increasing the disequilibrium of the system; (3) an evaluation of the likelihood of some of the alternative adaptations that might be made in Zinacantan when the cargo system is no longer capable of integrating the society.

The Equilibrating System

In Chapters 14 and 15 three variables have been viewed as an equilibrating system tending to maintain full participation in the Zinacantan cargo system, and through this the integration of the society. The increasing population is the disequilibrating variable that threatens full participation, for the increased number of adult men cannot be accommodated by the cargo system. The increase in the number of first-level cargos is an equilibrating variable that has tended to compensate for the disequilibrating effects of increasing population. The cargo waiting lists, especially because of the surplus value they provide for individuals awaiting cargos, have also tended to compensate for the disequilibrating effects of increasing population. However, the lists are only a temporary compensation that has been particularly effective during the last

decade. Unlike the number of cargos, which in theory could increase tremendously, the lists have a limited effective capacity,
which is rapidly being reached.

The equilibrating variables have not been compensating fully
for the disequilibrating effects of population growth in recent
years, and the system is already in disequilibrium. The present
disequilibrium of the system is a fact, and its continued worsening
is all but certain. However, the speed with which this disequilibrium will weaken the integration of the society is much less certain.
The weakening of this integration, with its effects on the lives of
Zinacantecos, will be determined principally by factors in the
environment—or rather the environments. Both Zinacantan as the
environment of the system and Mexican society as the environment of Zinacantan must be seen as potential sources of the alternatives that may replace the cargo system, wholly or in part,
as the predominant community-wide social institution in the society.

A comprehensive discussion of the future of Zinacantan and the
cargo system would involve, at the very least, a detailed analysis
of the belief and value system of the Zinacantecos, an evaluation
of the present and potential effects of the Mexican government's
INI programs to acculturate the Chiapas Indians, and a set of
thoroughly grounded predictions about the economic future of
Chiapas and Mexico as a whole. My closing comments on the
future of the cargo system must be on a much smaller scale. In the
following section I will discuss some of the economic problems that
have intensified the disequilibrium, and argue that the economic
factor will be crucial in the future of Zinacantan.

The Economic Factor

The economic factor was not considered in the analysis of the
equilibrating system presented above because it does not bear
directly on the maintenance of full participation.[1] In the subsystem
in which full participation is the system property being main-

[1] A diagram of relationships described in the remainder of this paragraph is
given in Figure 6, p. 142.

tained, the economic variable may be seen simply as part of the environment. In the larger system—the system in which integration of the Zinacantan community is the property being maintained— the economic variable may be seen as a strong disequilibrating force. It has been more convenient to discuss population growth, the increasing number of first cargos, and the cargo waiting lists with reference to the subsystem property of full participation, but they may also be seen as variables in the super-system in which integration is the property being maintained (see Figure 6). In this super-system the variables have the same effects, but the disequilibrating effects of the expanding economy are added to the disequilibrating effects of population growth.

The improvement of the economic situation of most Zinacantecos has its roots in the Mexican Revolution. As early as 1914, the Ley de Obreros (Worker's Law) legally freed the Indian population of Chiapas from economic attachments to large landowners that often approximated slavery (Moscoso 1960: 18ff.) By the time these laws were put into practice, land reform had begun, and by the late 1930's many Zinacantecos had acquired plots of land under the Ejido land reform system (Edel 1962). It appears that the laws protecting labor, combined with the expropriation of parts of the enormous *fincas* (plantations), had the effect of opening large areas of land to rental by Zinacantecos. Edel (1962) has come to approximately the same conclusion in his study of the history of land reform in Zinacantan and its environs. The change is illustrated by the history of various middle- and upper-class families in San Cristobal who now rent land to Zinacantecos. The men of these families usually enter a profession today, but, before reform took away the cheap labor and the immense holdings that made agriculture very profitable, many of their ancestors devoted themselves to the management of farmlands.

The expansion of economic opportunities for Zinacantecos has more than met the growth in population. That is, not only are greater numbers able to earn a living, but in general they are able to earn a better living than their fathers were. Older informants report that there used to be many more poor people, and there is nothing but support for their statements in the history of Chiapas as far as I know it. This economic expansion may be seen as having a double effect on the cargo system and the demand for cargos in Zinacantan. First, the expansion necessary simply to maintain the past standard of living in Zinacantan would have produced more people capable of passing expensive cargos. That is, the absolute number of the rich, taken as a fixed proportion of the total society, grows with the expansion of population, even if the standard of living only remains stable. Second, the improvement in the earning power of the average person has increased his capacities with respect to the cargo system. There is, then, a growing surplus of economic capacity that cannot be absorbed by the cargo system.

The existence of this economic surplus has already affected the patterns of religious celebrations and participation in the cargo system. Some examples follow.

The Castilleros and the Voluntarios are groups of young adult men (and some older men) who support fiesta activity that is independent of the cargo system. In the late 1930's the Castilleros began as a single small group specifically devoted to providing fireworks for the major fiesta. By 1961 there were three much larger groups, and they paid for a number of fiestas themselves, without the normal taxes on the entire township. The calendar in Appendix D lists the fiestas that are principally supported by these voluntary groups. The men contribute 5 to 20 pesos apiece for each fiesta, part of the money going for candles that they publicly carry into the church at the height of the fiesta. In this way they are able to demonstrate their interest in the religious celebrations, but neither in the amount contributed nor in the impression made on observers is this activity comparable to passing a cargo, which is what they would probably prefer to do.

The effect of the surplus of wealth and the relative scarcity of cargos is much more telling when seen in specific cargo careers. Three cases of men from the hamlet of Navenchauc show dramatically how wealthy men are compromising in order to pass cargos fast enough to make possible a complete cargo career ending with Senior Alcalde Viejo (D1). The three have recently passed the first-level cargos A2S, A1J, and A1S. Their wealth, their capacities, and their past performance would make each a candidate for any of the three most prestigious and costly Alferez positions: B1, B2, or B3. All, however, have asked for B6, a much lesser, though respectable, Alferez position. Two of them (those shown in Figure 7) have indicated that they did so because the wait for B1, the most costly and prestigious Alferez position, was too long. The third requested B6 before he had completed A1S in 1961, indicating that he was very concerned about getting a second cargo soon enough, and that the expenses did not frighten him. All these men are compromising by taking lesser cargos in order to save time. The cargo system can neither challenge their economic capabilities nor satisfy their desires for prestige.

A very dramatic series of events in 1962 illustrates this frustration even more clearly. A man appeared before the moletik to request A1S, even though the wait is 20 years. They insisted that he should take a cargo immediately, for they needed someone to fill the relatively modest post of A9. The man retorted that if the moletik forced him to take A9, the request was theirs and not his. The bottle of drink he presented to request A1S should be considered as his request for Alferez, he argued—this despite the fact that it is unheard of to ask for a second-level cargo before entering a first-level cargo. In the end, he accepted the post of A9 and was put on the waiting list for one of the lesser Alferez positions in the near future. In April he began to serve A9 as agreed, but apparently made it clear that he considered this cargo beneath his capacities. During the summer of 1962 his house burned down, and Zinacantecos immediately interpreted this to mean that he was being punished for serving his position with an unhappy heart (see Chapter 9). Affluence, which made this man feel that A9 was beneath his dignity, was very disruptive indeed in this case.

The whole of the Zinacantan community also shows a prosperity that was uncommon in the past. Zinacantecos normally contribute labor for community projects, as is the custom throughout the Maya region. However, when it was decided in late 1961 to build a new chapel for the Señor de Esquipulas because the existing one was considered too small, the general meeting decided that it would be too much trouble if the project were organized on the traditional basis and the chapel built of adobe. It decided to tax every family about 20 pesos and give the contract for construction of a brick chapel to a Ladino contractor from San Cristobal. Any Zinacanteco who cared to work on the project would be paid like any other laborer if the contractor wanted to hire him. In 1963 Robert Laughlin reported on a meeting held to decide on the materials to be used in construction of the altar for the new chapel. The consensus was that the best (the most expensive) should be used, and no objections were raised to this plan.

In sum, there is a growing surplus of cash in Zinacantan. And there is a growing number of men who cannot buy prestige and demonstrate their economic success through the traditional patterns of participation in the cargo system. Besides frustrating the ambitions of countless Zinacantecos, this situation leaves growing financial surpluses that cannot be disposed of in the socially controlled ways common in the past. Perhaps more than anything else, the manner in which these new surpluses find an outlet will determine the direction that life in Zinacantan will take.

The Future of the Zinacantan Community

Disequilibrium is a matter of degree, and so is community integration. While it is possible to predict with confidence that radical change will take place in Zinacantan in the next decade or two, it is impossible to specify the time or manner of the changes. The community is becoming ever more open to innovation as its insulation disappears. What takes place will depend in large part on what alternatives the environment offers. Below I will review some of the possibilities that would make for essentially conservative adjustments. However, I think the future will bring a more complex and radical adjustment than can be foreseen at this time.

It is very unlikely, but possible, that some extreme change might reestablish and maintain full participation in the cargo system. New cargos may be created at a much faster rate than they have been in the last decade, thus allowing fuller participation. This is highly unlikely, I think, especially because Zinacantecos do not think in terms of the balance of the total population and the total number of cargos available.

An alternative possibility for radical adjustment that could maintain full participation would be the division of Zinacantan into two complete townships, each with a cargo system. This is suggested by the fact that there is a small *political* movement to separate the hamlets distant from the ceremonial center and establish a civil government for them in Navenchauc. At present this movement is proceeding completely within Zinacantan. It probably would meet insuperable opposition at the state level, which is controlled by Ladinos. Moreover, the present cargo system is supported by the belief that it was established by the gods in the earliest days of Zinacantan. I do not think that such a firm footing could be quickly established for a completely new cargo system, or that the alternative has much chance of occurring. Moreover, it seems unlikely that any expansion of the cargo system, however radical, could absorb the expanding economic surplus of the average Zinacanteco.

A second alternative would be a reintegration of the community along *Indian* lines not so heavily dependent on the cargo system. One possibility that immediately presents itself is that of an expansion in the ranks of the curers, which would provide more prestige-conferring alternatives to service in the cargo system. However, it does not seem likely that this adaptation could be a long-term solution because it does not readily offer an outlet for socially controlled modes of personal display, as the cargo system does. The economic surplus would still remain uncontrolled; and given the increase in curers (who are potential witches), the path toward increasing witchcraft and disintegration described by Redfield in *The Folk Culture of Yucatan* (1941) suggests itself.

I cannot imagine any integration based on Indian principles that would overcome the problems created by the growing economic surplus.[2]

The third alternative is a breakdown of Zinacantan as a tightly

---

[2] As I stated in Chapter 11, no tendency to increase the cost of already established cargos was noted in the period 1960–62.

integrated Indian community. An elite of cargoholders could develop, but the drive of others to gain the prestige their economic status should command would inevitably force them into the Ladino world. It is possible to imagine the importation of alternative prestige symbols by persons who consider themselves Zinacantecos, but it is very hard to see how participation in the cargo system and any new set of symbols of achievement could be reconciled into a single standard by which all members of the society could be evaluated, as they have been in the past. The owner of a small truck will certainly have proved himself, but what will he and the man who has spent an equal amount on passing A1S and B1 have to say to each other?

As the cargos become less and less of an economic burden on the community, and other outlets for income become more important, the prestige that comes from passing cargos must diminish. Whatever the future of Zinacantan, the increasing population and the improving economic conditions will destroy the importance of the cargo system as the social institution through which the community of Zinacantecos is integrated.

Appendixes

Appendix A
The Fieldwork

The approach used in this study has been influenced by the nature of the subject matter as well as by the intent of the investigator. I hope these notes on the field situation, data-gathering, and informants will help the reader to reconstruct the manner in which the study was made. The last section of this appendix describes the samples on which the tests in Chapters 9 and 10 are based.

Fieldwork and the Field Situation

The fieldwork was done between September 1960 and August 1962. During this period, 18 months were spent in the field. My wife and I first arrived in San Cristobal Las Casas in late August of 1960, and were introduced to Zinacantan by Robert Laughlin, who was completing his own research there. April and May of 1961 were spent in Cambridge working on the material gathered during the first field trip. We returned to Mexico for the period June 1961 to January 1962; and I made a final trip in the summer of 1962. The main lines of the study were set in Cambridge in the spring of 1961, and the last two trips to the field were devoted to gathering data to answer specific questions.

Throughout the 15 months of the first two trips we maintained a house in San Cristobal and rented an Indian house in Hteklum. For the first few months we lived in Hteklum a good part of the time. However, as we became better known in the community, casual visitors made formal work in the Hteklum house impossible, especially because many informants did not want to be seen working with me on a formal basis. Because of this we began to use the Hteklum house as similar houses are used by Zinacantecos who live in the outlying hamlets—as a place to live during fiestas.

The 12-kilometer ride from San Cristobal to Hteklum takes between twenty minutes and an hour, depending on one's willingness to pay for tires slashed by the sharp rocks on the road. Thus frequent trips were possible, and, on the rare occasions when it was the only way to convince an old informant to come to San Cristobal, I made the round trip twice in one day to pick up the informant and return him to his home. Later in the fieldwork we developed many contacts in the hamlet of Navenchauc on the Pan American Highway. By this time we were exchanging hospitality with a number of families and could always find a place to sleep and eat if our stays in the hamlets had to be longer than a few hours.

Interviewing was the principal source of information. Information obtained in this manner was cross-checked among informants, and, especially in the case of ritual description, was rechecked by observation. Although participant observation was important in acquiring general knowledge about Zinacantan—and especially in learning about Zinacantecos' attitudes about cargos—participant observation in the ritual of the hierarchy presented a difficult problem. It is often not appropriate for a man who has no formal role in the ritual to be present. Seeing the ritual is not prohibited; but, for example, an adult man who stands gawking at a small group of cargoholders eating a meal is invited to eat—with the shameful implication that he does not have food of his own. Except at the larger fiestas, one simply does not stand around in the vicinity of cargoholders.

On rare occasions I participated as a helper of cargoholders, but full participation in such a role involves much work and little observation. My most valuable observation was done in the latter part of the second field trip. The moletik for 1961 were particularly kind in allowing me free access to their group. I was able to sit with, eat with, and talk with officials in a way that no one not holding a cargo could.

All of my interviewing was done in Spanish, and I learned barely enough of the native language to be polite in ritual situations and to discuss the whereabouts of Spanish-speaking informants with their Tzotzil-speaking families. I regretted my decision to work in Spanish only when language difficulties limited my participation in social and ceremonial situations. Though the decision limited my choice of informants somewhat, it enabled me to obtain information that otherwise would have gone ungathered, for the months I would have spent learning Tzotzil were spent gathering data. The disadvantages of this situation were largely offset by my wife, Francesca, who learned Tzotzil for her own research. She devoted the better part of a year to the language, and after the first few months her ability to speak it greatly expanded our social horizons.

As is no doubt common in fieldwork, especially in the early stages, gathering of data was sporadic and interspersed with periods of personal irresolution, social activity, and unsuccessful efforts to open new avenues of information. Zinacantecos solidify social relations, resolve tensions about unsure social relations, mark the intervals of ceremonies, and close formal and semiformal agreements with alcoholic drinks. The fledgling in Zinacantan spends a good deal of time and effort wondering when to accept and when to refuse a drink—and the puzzlement usually ends in drunkenness. In the months before I learned to use drink to express my own attitudes and to serve my own ends, a substantial part of my time was spent recovering from the effects of my ignorance.

Gathering the Data

The data gathered may be divided into three types: (1) gossip and observations, (2) interview material, and (3) censuses. The first type was collected in a wide range of situations—from completely social visits with friends in their homes to very contrived meetings with specific individuals with whom I wanted to talk; and from casual observations made in the course of stays in Zinacantan to special trips made to observe a specific segment of ritual.

Formal interviewing of informants provided systematic reviews of ritual activity and relatively detailed discussions of many other questions about the cargo system. Most of the interviewing was done at our house in San Cristobal. Informants (who were often so elusive that it took several days to track them down and make arrangements) usually arrived about 9 A.M. and worked until 3 or 4 P.M., stopping to have lunch with us. More than 100 formal interviews were recorded in about as many days of interviewing. I usually spent a substantial amount of time reviewing notes and writing out questions in preparation for an interview. The interviews were conversational in style, and the questions were used only when the conversation lagged. I took notes while interviewing and typed them and my comments later in the same day.

The gathering of the third type of data, census materials, is discussed after the following review of informants.

Informants for Formal Interviews

Twenty informants were interviewed. One, Domingo de la Torre Perez, who is permanently employed by the Harvard Chiapas Project, was interviewed most intensively. Four others—Juan de la Cruz Akov, Manuel Perez con Dios, Antonio Lopez Tsintan, and Mariano Gomez Tantiv—worked with me for more than six or eight day-long sessions each. The remaining 15 were interviewed for one or two days each on special topics. In only three cases were interpreters needed: the sons-in-law of the two oldest informants helped me with those interviews, and Domingo helped me to interview his brother-in-law.

All but four of the informants were paid for their work. Zinacantecos are able to accept this situation without difficulty, and the pay made it possible to demand a more efficient working schedule than would have been possible had all the questioning been done on an informal basis. Of the four who were not paid, two are my ritual kinsmen. This relation, by custom, involves exchange of favors. The only pay offered them was the liquor we drank together. Two others refused pay. One was a Ladinoized man working for good pay with the Instituto Nacional Indigenista; the other was the Senior Alcalde Viejo for 1961, who, interviewed toward the end of his term, could afford to emphasize the grandeur of his position by magnanimously refusing to accept pay.

Of the 20 informants, one was a Ladino and one a woman. Of the remaining 18, 12 had passed cargos in the religious hierarchy, five were young men and anticipated passing cargos, and one was very Ladinoized and had refused to accept a cargo. Of the 12 who had already passed cargos, two had completed four cargos, one three cargos, one two cargos, and the remainder a single cargo. The oldest had passed his first cargo before 1920. Five of the men had also passed Presidente Municipal, the oldest in 1918.

In their ability to speak Spanish, of course, the majority of the informants were not representative of the community as a whole, but I do not think this factor introduces any great bias, for many of them were very traditional people despite their unusual ability to speak Spanish. Twelve of the 20 informants came from the ceremonial center and the immediately adjacent areas, a part of the township which includes about one-fifth of the total population. The nature of our contacts and the subject of the study made this desirable. I was careful to check with the eight informants from distant hamlets for bias that this factor might have introduced. Finally, I interviewed a greater proportion of rich persons than the population as a whole includes. In large part this was dictated by the fact that only the rich pass the upper-level cargos and have detailed knowledge of the activities on those levels. Three or four persons who could be called poor and a number of "middle-class" persons were included among the informants, so I do not think that the oversized group of rich informants distorted my picture of the hierarchy. The poorer persons worked with me for the longest periods, the very rich being too busy to sacrifice more than a day or two for the wages I paid. More detail on the five principal informants follows.

Domingo is a resident of the ceremonial center. Although he is only in his middle twenties, he served for many years as a Sacristan and was an invaluable teacher of ritual patterns. In the years since he was first employed as an informant by B. N. Colby in 1958, he has acquired a great deal of knowledge about anthropological research. Because of this he made an excellent advisor on the practical aspects of research problems, such as the recruitment of informants with specialized knowledge or the phrasing of particular questions.

Manuel, a man of 60, was especially helpful because of his extraordinary knowledge of the cargos passed by others in the community. His special talent in this direction seems to be explained by a number of factors. First, he is a resident of the ceremonial center and has seen many people pass cargos. Second, he was a Scribe and a Sacristan for many years and thus was in close contact with cargoholders. Third, and perhaps most important, he is a very intelligent man who never managed to participate fully in the hierarchy himself. He passed only one cargo. Zinacantecos who have been very successful in the cargo system tend to know considerably less about the performance of people who have had less impressive careers.

Juan, a 40-year-old resident of Paste, is a past Presidente Municipal and a very important political leader who has not yet passed a religious cargo. He has exceptional knowledge about people and a talent for making lists of things, but his ability to respond to open-ended questions is limited.

Antonio is a Ladinoized man of 40 who lives on the outskirts of the ceremonial center. He was Secretario Municipal of Zinacantan in 1954 and 1955, the only Zinacanteco who has ever held the post. In 1960 he passed the most expensive cargo on the first level (A1S) and kept detailed accounts of the expenses. Though he had committed himself to the Zinacanteco way of life by passing the cargo, his detached attitude and keen and imaginative mind made him an excellent source of insights into the operation of the cargo system. Unfortunately, his desire to please sometimes made him try to stretch his knowledge beyond its limits.

Mariano, a 55-year-old resident of Hteklum, has passed three cargos. In a sense, he was the most limited of the five major informants, but his extensive experience and his willingness to see social activities in terms of conflicting positions made him an invaluable source of case materials on the activities of the cargoholders.

The Censuses and Samples

The problems of taking a sample of individuals from a large preliterate population can be difficult ones. First, population lists from which a random sample might be drawn are often not available. Second, the resistance a census-taker encounters in a modern Western society may be increased several times over in a preliterate society not accustomed to such procedures. And those preliterate societies that are in contact with a dominant western culture are often especially suspicious of census-takers, for to them writing and papers often mean trouble and some form of exploitation.

In Zinacantan both of these problems are present. The voting lists taken for the Mexican government by native census-takers record individuals by Spanish surnames, which are assigned according to a set of rules that reduce quite different Indian names to the same Spanish surname. Hence the voting lists are completely useless for distinguishing individuals. Lists kept by the native scribes include the names of all adult males of tax-paying age and generally record Indian names. However, they were not available to me until the very end of the field period.

Even if good lists were available early in the field period, the problems of actually doing a door-to-door survey of a random sample of households are so great that it would have been impractical. Houses are far apart in many of the hamlets, and their exact location is known only by residents of the hamlet or neighborhood. Men are often absent. And, most important, Zinacantecos would be upset and antagonized by direct questions about their family connections. These facts are not secret in Zinacantan, but it would be very hard to explain to Zinacantecos how they could be useful to the anthropologist in a way that would not harm the people of the hamlet.

This latter problem was overcome to some degree by taking censuses and other data indirectly—from a limited number of informants in interviews in San Cristobal. The informants were trusting friends who had associated with anthropologists long enough to know that they would not use the information to the detriment of the population. Nevertheless, all the censuses had to be taken under the promise that no one in the community would be told that the informant gave such information.

The problem of getting a representative sample remained. Random sampling was impossible for the reasons mentioned above; and the size of Zinacantan is so great that a total survey was also impossible. The problem of sampling had to be solved in another way. Fortunately, the very clear division into hamlets made it possible to take complete lists of the population of some of these subdivisions of the township. The possibility of biased selection of individual cases was eliminated by including everyone in the hamlet.

Three such hamlet censuses were taken: one for Hteklum, the ceremonial center, one for Paste, and one for Apas. There is no systematic way of demonstrating that these three sample populations are representative of the entire township. However, they include more than 25 per cent of the total population and are distributed over the area rather well. There is no reason to think that the samples taken are not representative.

In addition to the material collected in the three censuses mentioned above, a certain amount of information was recorded in less systematic ways. Below the various censuses and "samples" are discussed, along with the manner in which they were combined to make the samples actually used to test the hypotheses presented in Chapters 9 and 10.

The Paste Census. The Paste Census includes some 252 households and more than 1,250 people. Juan served as the informant for all the work on the census. Professor Evon Z. Vogt did the principal task of compilation with Juan, recording each household, its approximate location, the names of the head and his spouse, the other people living in the house and their relation to the head, and the most recent cargo passed by the head of the household, if any. For my own purposes I added the following with the same informant: the names of all brothers and sons of the household heads and their location in the census, and the residence pattern. The residence was considered patrilocal if the couple lived on land adjacent to the husband's family and matrilocal if the couple lived on land adjacent to the wife's family. There were a small number of neolocal couples who had purchased or inherited land situated away from both family units. Perhaps because he is the political leader of the hamlet, Juan's knowledge of these facts was amazingly good—if it can be judged by his consistency with himself over a period of months. His knowledge did not include facts about the earlier cargo careers of older men, however.

The Hteklum Census. The Hteklum Census was first done with Domingo and then reviewed with Manuel, who, being older, knew more about deceased relatives of the individuals listed. The information recorded was the same as that recorded for Paste, plus complete cargo careers of all heads of households. The census includes 78 households and 384 individuals.

The Apas Census. The Apas Census was done with Lucas, the leader of Apas, and his son in law, who had been a Principal and knew each household. Since I did not know the geography of the hamlet at the time, there is no information on location of households. The households were recorded simply in the order they come on the tax-collecting route of the Principal. Otherwise the information recorded was identical with that in the Hteklum census. Because of Lucas's age (about 55) and knowledge of family histories, it was possible to learn what cargos had been passed by the deceased fathers of many household heads. In addition, the natal household of the wife was recorded. The census includes 85 households and 413 individuals.

The Paste Economic Sample. The Paste Economic Sample was taken from a survey made by two informants under the direction of B. N. Colby and Professor Vogt. The work was done in Paste, but it was impossible for them to cover the entire hamlet both because of the immense effort required to do a complete house-to-house survey and because of the problems of rapport such a survey would have caused. The sample as I use it includes all cases that have the following information complete: amount of corn seeded in the previous year by the head of the household, and cargos of the head of the household.

The Total Career Sample. The Total Career Sample includes all recorded cases of men who have passed more than one cargo. Only name, hamlet of residence, and cargos passed are included. These cases were taken from several sources. All the cases from the Hteklum and Apas Censuses and the Paste Economic Sample are included. In addition there are several cases that Juan was able to remember in the course of doing the Paste Census. All the cases recorded in interviews on diverse subjects and in casual conversations are also included. A major source of information about cargo careers was the responses of informants to open-ended questions like: "Name all the people you know who have passed an Alferez cargo." Manuel produced the overwhelming proportion of the answers elicited by this method. This method of questioning produced more information on people who had passed prestigious cargos than on people who had passed lesser cargos. This is a defect in the sampling, but I have no reason to believe that this defect significantly affects the results of the analysis of the total sample. The patterns revealed by the total sample are not different from those revealed by the smaller samples that were systematically taken, i.e., the censuses. The combined Hteklum and Apas Censuses, which are used in Table 16, give an even stronger confirmation of the hypotheses than do some of the tests made on the total samples. Almost all cases were checked more than once with the original informant, and were cross-checked with other informants.

The Total Generation Sample. The Total Generation Sample includes all cases for which there is information about the cargo careers of a son and his father. It was gathered in various ways, as was the Total Career Sample. Much of the information included was gathered by asking informants about the fathers of individuals already included in the Total Career Sample.

The Apas Marriage Sample. The Apas Marriage Sample was taken from the Apas Census. It includes all couples for whom the cargo-career history of each spouse's father was available.

A Note on Subsamples

The hypotheses presented in Chapters 9 and 10 were tested against data from the subsamples (e.g., the hamlet censuses) as well as against the four samples discussed directly above. To simplify presentation, I do not include tests based on the subsamples. It should be noted that the subsamples yield the same results as the total samples. In some cases the subsamples are too small to yield statistically significant results, but the distributions are in the direction predicted by the hypotheses.

Analysis of Samples Given in Chapter 10

Note 1: Statistical Tests

All the two-by-two tables shown in Chapter 10 are constructed by dividing the distributions in half on each variable. This system of division of the variables ensures against idiosyncratic manipulation of the data so as to support the hypotheses, but it may sometimes make too little of the patterns that can be seen in the full distribution. Original distributions (or data from which they can be reconstructed) are found in the tables presented below.

All the reported probabilities for chi-squares in Chapters 9 and 10 are one-tailed. One-tailed probabilities are appropriate because the hypotheses predict direction (Siegel 1956: 108). In addition, the decision to use one-tailed probabilities is supported by the fact that the hypotheses in Chapter 10 are interlocking—all predict related phenomena and all predict in the same direction. An inverse relation in any of the distributions would call for serious questioning of the entire set.

The formula used to calculate the chi-squares incorporates a correction for continuity (Siegel 1956: 107).

Note 2: Calculations for Tables 18 and 19

To calculate the numbers presented in the Prestige Scale column of Table 18 from the data presented in Table B. 2 the procedure described below was used. Other procedures might be utilized and their results might be slightly different, but the difference would not affect the conclusions drawn. The following procedure seems to be the most straightforward.

The 28 first-level cargos ranked in the Prestige Scale were taken as 14 groups of two, e.g., A1S and A1J occupied the highest-ranked group and the eight Mayores (A11) occupied the four lowest-ranked groups. Each of the 12 cargos of the second level was taken as a "group." One might imagine a fourteen-by-twelve table similar to the eleven-by-twelve Table B. 1 below.

Then the highest groups in each ranking (the upper left of the table) were taken to constitute the highest-ranking "X" percentage of paths. The three top-ranking first cargos combined with the three top-ranking second cargos (any combination of A1, A2, or A3 with B1, B2, or B3) make up approximately five per cent of the paths: $3/14 \times 3/12 = 9/168$ = (approx.) $5/100$. Similarly, $6/14 \times 6/12 = 36/168 =$ (approx.) $20/100$; and $9/14 \times 9/12 = 81/168 =$ (approx.) $50/100$.

The cases of individuals reaching third-level cargos by each of the groups of paths were then taken as a percentage of the total number reaching a third cargo ($N = 82$), and that percentage was entered in the appropriate place.

For the Cost Scale column of Table 18 the data were rearranged by the Cost Scale and the same procedure was followed.

In calculating paths to D1 (Table 19) a similar procedure was followed. The possible paths through third cargos were divided into three groups. For these purposes C1 was considered equivalent to ASD (this equivalence was not used in the calculation for Table 19, for there are no cases of a D1 who had taken ASD third cargo, but it was used in another calculation referred to in the text). C2 was taken as equivalent to ADC (which was used as a third cargo for one case). C3 and C4 were taken as equivalent to each other.

Thus there are three possible paths through the third cargo to be combined with the already established paths through first and second cargos. Approximations to 5, 20, and 50 per cent were reached in the following way:

$$5/14 \times 5/12 \times 1/3 = 25/504 = \text{(approx.)} \; 5/100$$
$$7/14 \times 7/12 \times 2/3 = 98/504 = \text{(approx.)} \; 20/100$$
$$9/14 \times 9/12 \times 3/3 = 243/504 = \text{(approx.)} \; 50/100$$

Percentages of recorded cases were then calculated as they were for Table 18.

The last four cases of careers leading to D1 (all 22 cases are listed on p. 208) obviously present problems for analysis by this simple procedure. For the summary statement presented in Table 19 I resolved them in the following ways:

(1)　MRSal-4-1 was rated as $7/14 \times 4/12 \times 1/3 = 1/18 = $ upper 20%
(2)　1-ASD-4 was rated as $1/14 \times 1/12 \times 3/3 = 1/168 = $ upper 5%
(3)　6-6 was rated as $6/14 \times 6/12 = 3/14 = $ upper 50%
(4)　MySal-12 was rated as $3/14 \times 12/12 = 3/14 = $ upper 50%

My impressions of their standings were used to rank the Salinas cargos. I made conservative, i.e., low, estimates of their rank. Dropping these cases altogether yields slightly stronger confirmation of the hypothesis.

Note 3: Calculations for Table 21

Table B.4 presents the data on which Table 21 is based. Note that two cargos are taken as better than one of any kind. This seems a fair procedure since all the fathers of spouses shown in Table B.4 should be old enough to have had the opportunity to pass two cargos, since they have married children. To insure that low performance of some fathers was not simply an artifact of age, two tests were made. (1) Mean age of the spouses was taken in cases where both fathers had passed two cargos and in cases where both fathers had passed A11 only or no cargos. For the former, mean age of spouses was less than 30; for the latter, more than 30. (2) For some unknown reason, when these 21 cases were laid out in a two-by-two table and analyzed there appeared an inverse relation (chi-square 2.31) between age of spouses and cargo performance of fathers. In 8 of 11 cases with spouses under 30, fathers had had two cargos. In 7 of 10 cases with spouses 30 or more, fathers had had A11 only or no cargos.

Table B.4 rearranged by the Cost Scale does not produce a significant distribution (chi-square < 1) if the variables are halved.

It should be noted, however, that a matrix showing first cargos only of fathers (arranged by either the Prestige or the Cost Scale) does not produce a significant distribution (chi-square < 1) if the variables are halved. It does yield a significant distribution (chi-squares both 4.48) if the variables are divided between A10 and A11.

In effect, then, the very lowest-ranking individuals tend to marry the other lowest-ranking individuals, and among the higher ranks there is considerable interchange. This is not surprising given the very small size of the population and the fact that there is a strong tendency to hamlet endogamy.

The Tables

All the data on which statistical analyses in Chapter 10 are based are presented below.

Table B.1 presents all the cases (N = 145) used for Tests 3 and 4, Table 17. Since it is arranged by the Prestige Scale it is the distribution on which Test 3, Table 17, is based. To arrive at the equivalent distribution for Test 4, Table 17, the cases must be rearranged by the Cost Scale.

The first two cargos of the 82 cases presented in Table B.2 are also listed in Table B.1, so that producing a distribution recording all cases of careers limited to two cargos at the time the data were collected would require substracting Table B.2 from Table B.1.

Likewise, the first three cargos of the first 18 cases leading to D1 (listed on p. 208) are found in Table B.2 (and, of course, their first two cargos are to be found in Table B.1). Except for those leading to D1, the cases listed in the section on additional cases were not used in the statistical analyses.

Table B.3 is self-explanatory. It is shown arranged by the Prestige Scale (Test 1, Table 20) and must be rearranged by the Cost Scale to produce the matrix used for Test 2, Table 20.

Table B.4 is self-explanatory.

TABLE B.1

Total Career Sample: Two Cargos (A and B)

(Prestige Scale)

		First Cargo										
		A1	A2	A3	A4	A5	A6	A7	A8	A9	A10	A11 TOTALS
	B1	15	7	2	2	–	–	–	–	–	–	– 26
	B2	7	3	6	2	3	1	1	–	1	1	– 25
	B3	–	2	–	–	4	–	–	–	–	–	– 6
	B4	1	2	3	3	4	1	1	–	2	–	– 17
Second Cargo	B5	3	6	5	2	2	2	2	–	1	–	– 23
	B6	–	1	2	2	1	6	1	1	–	–	3 17
	B7	–	–	1	2	–	–	–	–	–	1	– 4
	B8	–	–	–	–	–	–	–	2	–	–	– 2
	B9	–	–	1	1	–	–	2	–	1	1	2 8
	B10	1	1	–	1	–	–	3	1	1	–	1 9
	B11	–	–	–	–	–	–	–	–	1	–	1 2
	B12	1	–	–	–	–	–	–	–	2	1	2 6
	TOTALS	28	22	20	15	14	10	10	4	9	4	9 145

Total Career Sample: Additional Cases

The sample includes 22 careers ending with D1. The first three cargos of
18 of these are as follows (ABC): 111, 111, 111, 122, 211, 213, 221,
241, 311, 351, 412, 523, 562, 621, 862, 921, 941, and 54ADC. Two additional cases present problems of notation and analysis given the simplified system used, but follow the rules of progression in the cargo system
perfectly. One began with the Mayordomo Rosario in Salinas (MRSal-
4-1). The other took the seldom-used option of Alferez Santo Domingo
as a second cargo (1-ASD-4). According to the best information I could
obtain, two other cases involve men who reached a D1 cargo after only
two previous cargos. One apparently passed A6, B6 and then D1. The
other began as Mayor of Salinas, then passed B12, then D1.

The sample includes nine cases of men who passed D2. Five of them
passed three previous cargos, and four of them only two previous cargos
(see Chapter 4). The cases are as follows (ABC): 222, 463, 662,
35ADC, 88ADC, 32, 35, and 88. The fourth individual who reached
D2 after only two previous cargos began with Mayor of Salinas and
then passed B6.

The sample includes six cases of ASD as a fourth cargo. They are as
follows (ABC): 111, 112, 112, 312, 362, and ?11. An additional case
of ASD not listed elsewhere involves a man who passed the cargo twice.
He began as A11, and then passed ASD twice. Another case of ASD as
a second cargo is listed above with the careers leading to D1.

As mentioned in Chapter 4, in Zinacanteco theory ADC may be
passed as a second or a third cargo. In fact there are no recorded cases
of service in it as a second cargo.

TABLE B.2

Total Career Sample: Three Cargos (A, B, and C)
(N = 82)

A	B	C	A	B	C	A	B	C	A	B	C	A	B	C	A	B	C	A	B	C	A	B	(C)	A	B	(C)
1	1	1	2	1	1	4	2	1	1	1	3	4	1	2	2	1	3	2	5	4	1	1	ASD	2	5	ADC
1	1	1	2	1	1	4	7	1	1	1	3	4	7	2	4	6	3	3	4	4	1	1	ASD	2	10	ADC
1	1	1	2	2	1	6	2	1	1	2	2	6	5	2	5	2	3				1	10	ASD	3	5	ADC
1	1	1	2	4	1	6	6	1	1	4	2	6	6	2	5	3	3				2	2	ASD	3	7	ADC
1	1	1	2	4	1	9	2	1	1	5	2	7	4	2	5	4	3				2	3	ASD	3	9	ADC
1	1	1	2	5	1	9	4	1	2	1	2	7	9	2	7	5	3				2	3	ASD	4	4	ADC
1	1	1	2	5	1	11	6	1	2	2	2	7	10	2	7	9	3				2	6	ASD	4	5	ADC
1	2	1	3	1	1	11	6	1	3	1	2	8	6	2	7	10	3				4	2	ASD	5	4	ADC
1	2	1	3	4	1				3	4	2				9	11	3				4	4	ASD	5	4	ADC
1	5	1	3	5	1				3	5	2										6	5	ASD	6	6	ADC
									3	6	2													8	8	ADC
																								8	10	ADC
																								11	12	ADC

NOTE: Alferez Santo Domingo (ASD) and Alferez Divina Cruz (ADC), though in theory second-level cargos, are in practice usually served as third or fourth cargos.

TABLE B.3

Total Generation Sample

(Prestige Scale)

		Son's First Cargo											
		A1	A2	A3	A4	A5	A6	A7	A8	A9	A10	A11	TOTALS
	A1	8	1	1	1	–	–	2	–	–	–	2	15
	A2	2	4	–	3	–	–	1	1	–	–	2	13
	A3	2	2	1	1	1	2	1	1	–	–	2	13
Father's First Cargo	A4	1	3	1	1	1	–	–	1	–	–	1	9
	A5	3	–	1	1	2	–	1	1	1	–	2	12
	A6	–	–	–	1	1	1	–	4	1	–	–	8
	A7	–	1	–	–	–	–	1	1	–	–	–	3
	A8	–	–	–	–	–	–	–	–	–	–	–	–
	A9	3	–	–	–	1	–	–	–	1	1	–	6
	A10	–	–	–	–	–	–	–	–	–	–	1	1
	A11	–	1	–	1	1	–	–	–	–	–	2	5
	none	3	2	1	1	2	–	3	2	–	1	3	18
	TOTALS	22	14	5	10	9	3	9	11	3	2	15	103

TABLE B.4

Apas Marriage Sample

(Prestige Scale)

		Husband's Father												
		Two cargos	A1	A2	A3	A4	A5	A6	A7	A8	A9	A10	A11	none	TOTALS
	Two cargos	11	1	1	4	–	2	1	–	–	1	–	–	5	26
	A1	–	–	–	–	–	–	–	–	–	–	–	–	1	1
	A2	1	–	–	–	–	–	–	–	–	–	–	–	–	1
	A3	–	1	–	–	–	–	–	–	–	–	–	–	1	2
Wife's Father	A4	–	–	–	–	–	–	–	–	–	–	–	–	–	–
	A5	2	–	–	–	–	–	–	–	–	–	–	1	–	3
	A6	–	–	–	–	–	–	–	–	–	–	–	–	1	1
	A7	2	–	–	–	–	–	–	–	–	–	–	–	–	2
	A8	–	1	–	–	–	1	–	–	–	–	–	–	–	2
	A9	1	–	–	–	–	–	–	–	–	–	–	–	–	1
	A10	–	–	–	–	–	–	–	–	–	–	–	–	–	–
	A11	1	–	–	–	–	–	–	–	–	–	–	–	2	3
	none	2	–	–	1	–	2	1	1	–	–	–	3	5	15
	TOTALS	20	3	1	5	–	5	2	1	–	1	–	4	15	57

Appendix C

Auxiliary Personnel of the
Senior Mayordomo Rey (A1S), 1960

Except for the Musicians and the Women's Advisor, who were unaccompanied, all the auxiliary personnel who came to help the Senior Mayordomo Rey (A1S) for 1960 brought along their wives and young children. The Mayordomo Rey said that it would be most correct to say that the family, not just the man, is recruited to help, for the women help with the kitchen work.

Each helper is listed below, along with the following information about him: his age, his relationship to A1S, the cargos he had passed, and the people who accompanied him to the house of the Mayordomo Rey.

Ritual Advisor. The Ritual Advisor directs all the activity of the year and must be recruited first, for he tells the cargoholder how to begin. He was age 60 and no relation to A1S, had passed A6S and B4, and was accompanied by his wife only.

He served only on the following occasions: ceremonies of entering the cargo; Fiesta of San Sebastian; Semana Santa; the meal at San Juan; three visits to Salinas; Fiesta of the Virgen del Rosario; Christmas; ceremonies of leaving the cargo.

Special Helpers and General Helpers. The Mayordomo Rey has Special Helpers and General Helpers. The Special Helpers are two in number, and they appear every time the cargoholder has duties to perform. (They are responsible for finding their own replacements if they cannot appear.) The General Helpers come only at the big fiestas (listed below). For the Special Helpers the cargoholder goes to the Presidente Municipal and asks that they be freed from any communal work for the period of the cargo. For the General Helpers and other auxiliary personnel he makes no such request.

The Special Helpers, who happened to be brothers, were: (1) age 40, no relation to A1S, had passed A10S, and was accompanied by his wife and a child of 11 or 12 years; (2) age 28, no relation to A1S, had passed no cargos, and was accompanied by his wife, an infant, and a walking child.

The General Helpers were: (3) age 21, no relation to A1S, had passed no cargos, and was accompanied by his wife and a small child; (4) age 42, ritual kinsman of A1S, had passed A2S, and was accompanied by his wife (he has no children); (5) age 19, husband of A1S's wife's sister, had passed no cargos, and was accompanied by his wife (no children yet); (6) age 35, ritual kinsman to A1S, had passed no cargos, and was accompanied by his wife and two sons, ages 11 and 9; (7) age 44, ritual kinsman to A1S, had passed A11, and was accompanied by his wife (brought no children with them); (8) age 38, ritual kinsman to A1S, had passed A11, and was accompanied by his wife and a girl of 2 or 3 years.

All eight helpers helped with such things as the preparation of the firewood before the cargo began. They also appeared on the following occasions: ceremonies of entering the cargo; Fiesta of the Señor de Esquipulas; Fiesta of San Sebastian; Fiesta of the Virgen del Rosario; ceremonies of leaving the cargo; Fiesta of San Sebastian after leaving the cargo. On Jueves Santo only numbers 1, 2, 3, and 5 appeared.

The number of helpers was set by the Ritual Advisor, who told the Mayordomo Rey to recruit two Special Helpers and six General Helpers.

The helpers were given a bottle of drink when first asked to help for the year, and another bottle when asked to appear for the first time. For other occasions, no drink is obligatory, nor did the cargoholder himself have to go to notify them to appear. The Special Helpers came each week without being asked. However, often the Mayordomo Rey's wife or another person in the household took a small bottle of drink to the General Helpers to remind them that they were to appear on a given day.

In seeking helpers the Mayordomo Rey went to friends and ritual kinsmen. He had no refusals; the first eight he asked accepted.

Cannoneer. The Cannoneer was: age 39, no relation to A1S, had passed no cargos, and was accompanied by his wife and an infant. He served only on the following occasions: ceremonies of entering the cargo; three visits to Salinas; Fiesta of the Virgen del Rosario; Fiesta of San Sebastian; ceremonies of leaving the cargo.

Musicians. Besides the original gift of drink when they are recruited, the Musicians are given a small bottle of drink each week to remind them to appear for the weekend ritual. Number 3 below served only until March, and was replaced by number 4, who completed the year.

(1) The violinist was: age 25, a ritual kinsman of A1S, and had passed no cargos. (2) The harpist was: age 36, a ritual kinsman of A1S, and had passed no cargos. (3) One guitarist was: age 25, a relative of A1S's mother, and had passed no cargos. (4) The other guitarist was: age 45, no relation to A1S, and had passed no cargos.

Women's Advisor. This is the woman who directs all the work of the kitchen. She appeared for every occasion that involved kitchen work—including every weekend that the Mayordomo Rey was on duty. She was: age 46, and the daughter of A1S's mother's brother.

Substitute for Times when the Mayordomo Rey Is Drunk or Tired. For the Fiesta of the Virgen del Rosario in Salinas and the Fiesta of San Sebastian after leaving the cargo, the Mayordomo Rey must have a man to fill in for him when he is too tired or too drunk to go on with the ritual. This man must be a past Mayordomo Rey so that he will know exactly what to do. The substitute was: age 40, no relation to A1S, had passed A1S, and was accompanied by his wife and an infant.

Horse Rider for San Sebastian. For the Fiesta of San Sebastian after leaving the cargo, the Mayordomo must provide a horse and rider to be entered in the "races." The Mayordomo Rey owned a riding horse and helper number 6 did the riding.

The Ritual Calendar

Three calendars determine the specific dates of ritual activity in Zinacantan. The first is based on the fixed annual occurrence of saints' days as they are found in the church calendar.[1] The second is based on the Easter calendar, which changes from year to year. The third is simply tied to the days of the week, especially Sunday. The first calendar is principally that of the Mayordomos and Alfereces (B). The second involves all the cargoholders, but is especially that of the Pasioneros (A4) and Alcalde Shuves. The third is that of the Mayordomo Reyes (A1), the Mesoneros (A7), and the moletik (C and D). I will present the three calendars separately as the Saints' Calendar, the Easter Calendar, and the Sunday Calendar.

The manner in which the calendars overlap in any given year sometimes makes special arrangements necessary. For example, if the fiesta of the Sagrado Corazon (Easter Calendar) should fall on the day of San Juan (June 24 on the Saints' Calendar), compromises are made so that the cargoholders may attend to both sets of duties, or else one of the fiestas is celebrated on another day. Such conflicts do not occur frequently, and I have not considered them in the following exposition.

The Saints' Calendar

Many fiestas involve ritual patterns that are repeated at various times during the year. These will be called *standard ritual patterns,* and where possible I will describe the ritual performed on a given date in terms

[1] The calendar that is used by Zinacantecos, and many other people in Mexico, to determine the dates of fiestas is the *Calendario del más Antiguo Galvan* (Librería y Ediciónes Murguia, S. A., Mexico, D. F.). It is a small booklet of about 125 pages, published annually and sold in shops and by street vendors toward the end of each year. The 1962 calendar is the 136th to appear. The Sacristans and the Scribes, as well as many other Zinacantecos, purchase the calendar each year. Except for a few cases where Zinacantecos use slightly different names for fiestas, it is my source for the spelling of Spanish names for fiestas.

of them. Where a fiesta cannot be completely described as one of these standard types or a combination of them, special note is made of the fact.

The basic fiesta pattern is seen by Zinacantecos as being three days long, the last of the three days being the saint's day according to the Catholic calendar. The first day is called *chuk nichim,* "tying the flowers in bunches." The second day is *ishperesh,* a name apparently borrowed from the Spanish *vispera,* "vespers." The third day is *sba k'el k'in,* "look at the fiesta."

(1) The *changing of the flowers* on altars in the houses of the Mayordomos and at the two churches in Hteklum, San Lorenzo and San Sebastian, is a standard ritual pattern. It is normally done at the churches on the first day of the fiesta and in the houses of the Mayordomos on the night before the first day.

(2) The activity of the second and third days has many variations. In the standard pattern that I will label *simple fiesta,* the second day is a day of no activity, except for the sponsor of the fiesta, who is responsible for seeing that skyrockets are purchased in San Cristobal and that a Ladino woman from Hteklum who knows special prayers is recruited to pray in the church on the third day. On the third day of a simple fiesta the Mayordomos gather at the church of San Lorenzo before dawn. They dance inside the church, going outside to drink at the beginning, middle, and end of their dancing. Their helpers shoot off skyrockets to mark intervals in the dancing and the praying. At the end of the dance they retire to the house of the sponsor and are served a meal. This ends their formal duties, though they sometimes return to the church in the afternoon to continue celebrating, especially if the Ladino woman (who happens to know many prayers) has agreed to pray in the afternoon as well as the morning.

(3) The *taking out of the rosaries* is a standard addition to the basic pattern described above. When this is done, the rosaries are counted in the houses of the Mayordomos on the night of the second day. They are taken to the church before dawn on the third day and are placed around the necks of the saints. After the dancing they are returned to the houses of the Mayordomos. Besides the Mayordomos, this pattern involves the Sacristans, who attend the Mayordomos at their various houses while the rosaries are being taken out and counted, and who eat a special meal as guests of the Mayordomos.

(4) Another standard pattern is that of the *change of Mayordomos,* which takes place when a new Mayordomo is to enter office. In this case the old incumbents are not present at the flower-changing in the churches on the first day, for they are busy preparing for the events that will take place at their own houses. The second day is filled with

ritual at the houses of the old incumbents. Ritual Advisors are present and a meal is served. The major activity is the washing of the chest and the clothes of the saint, in preparation for their transfer to the new incumbents. The Sacristans, who know special prayers for the occasion and the proper procedures for washing, have important roles in this ritual. On the third day the chest and the small image that are kept in the house of the Mayordomo are transferred to the house of the new incumbent, and he offers the assembled group a meal.[2] The moletik are present to witness the final counting of the rosaries at the house of the old incumbent. At all changes of Mayordomos, the rosaries are taken to the church according to the procedure described above.

(5) The last of the standard patterns of the Mayordomos is the *celebration of the chest*. This small celebration is held on the first day of the fiesta. The Senior Mayordomo whose chest is being celebrated goes to the church as usual for the flower-change. For this occasion he is accompanied by his Ritual Advisor and his Cannoneer, who shoots off blasts during the flower-change. After the Mayordomos have finished changing the flowers in the second church, San Sebastian, the Ritual Advisor invites them to the house for a special meal and dance. The Sacristans come and say special prayers, and the Mayordomos light candles for the chest.

(6) The Alfereces have a single standard ritual pattern, which I will call the *Alferez round*. It involves a "round" during which the group goes from the house of one member to that of another, picking up each man at his home in a specified order. This begins on the first day of the fiesta. On the second day the Alfereces end the round at the church, having been on visits all through the night, and participate in ritual with the Mayordomos. On the third day they are again active at the church. During this three-day period a new incumbent is sworn in. For each of three days before a fiesta in which Alfereces are involved a flutist and two drummers walk all the major streets of the ceremonial center playing tunes that announce the fiesta. One the day after the fiesta the Alfereces as a group visit their Musicians to thank them for their service.

The sponsors. The pair of Mayordomos who are sponsors of a fiesta have varied additional duties, depending on the types of ritual involved. At the very least, they provide a larger share of the flowers and pine

---

[2] Each of the six pairs of Mayordomos has a sacred chest and a small image of their saint, which are their responsibility during their year in service. The chest is always kept on an altar in the house of the senior of the pair. Three of the seniors, A5S, A2S, and A8S, also keep the saints. In the other three cases, A3, A6, and A9, the juniors provide altars for the saints in their houses. If the chest and the saint are in separate houses, the ritual is performed twice, first at the senior's house and then at the junior's.

needles needed for the flower-change in the churches. Usually they also provide a meal for all of the Mayordomos at the house of the senior member of the pair. (In general, the senior member bears the greater part of the sponsoring responsibilities.) If the Alfereces are involved in the fiesta, they provide skyrockets and get a cannoneer to serve on the third day of fiesta at the church. If the Alfereces are not involved, the sponsors provide the skyrockets.

The volunteers. The volunteers are groups of men, usually young, who make regular contributions for the celebration of fiestas. They include the Castilleros and Voluntarios mentioned in Chapter 16. The money they contribute goes for candles, extra skyrockets, and elaborate fireworks. Sometimes they hire a band. In 1962 there were three such groups, each headed by a committee that administers the contributions. Membership in the groups is voluntary. The organizations themselves are relatively new, and their activities change from year to year.

The Saints' Calendar is as follows:

December 14 through January 6: Very elaborate special ritual activities during the entire period. The A2 pair is sponsor of all the special activity.

December 15: Flower-change, A2 pair sponsor.

January 6, Epifania, Adoración de los Santos Reyes: Flower-change (January 4), A6 pair sponsor. Alferez round with change of ADC and B7. Volunteers add to the fiesta.

January 13: Change of A8 pair. No other activity.

January 15, Señor de Esquipulas: Entirely a fiesta of the volunteers.

January 20, San Sebastian: Flower-change, A8 pair sponsor. Alferez round with change of B8 and B11. All cargoholders in office at the time are very active. Many who have completed cargos the year before have special roles (see Chapter 4). Attendance reaches three to five thousand. One of the two largest fiestas of the year. Unique pattern of ritual from January 18 to January 22. Volunteers very active.

February 2, Virgen de Candelaria: Flower-change and simple fiesta, A2 pair sponsor. Activity of volunteers. [3]

April 22: Change of A6 pair and A9 pair. No other activity.

April 29, San Pedro Martir: Flower-change, A6 pair sponsor. Alferez round with change of B4 and B12. Special distribution of palms.

---

[3] This fiesta, less than a decade old, was formerly celebrated mostly by Ladinos. It is promoted by the volunteer group whose leader dreamt that it should be celebrated. This man persuaded the Mayordomos to take out rosaries in order to make the fiesta more important, but after doing so for one year, they refused to continue the practice because of the extra expense involved.

May 3, Santa Cruz: A6 pair sponsor of special decoration of all crosses. Celebration of the chest of A6 pair.

June 13, San Antonio: Flower-change and simple fiesta, A9 pair sponsor.

June 24, San Juan: Flower-change, A5 pair sponsor. Special "middle-of-the-year" observances by many cargoholders.

Special flower-change: In most years (depending on the Easter Calendar) there is no fiesta between San Juan and Santo Domingo, which occurs in August. The Mayordomos make a special flower-change in the interim because the flowers in the church will not last out the six-week period.

August 4, Santo Domingo: Flower-change, A5 pair sponsor. Change of A5 pair. Alferez round.

August 10, San Lorenzo: A3 pair Sponsor for Mayordomos. Alferez round with change of Alferez de Santo Domingo and B1. Most cargoholders very active. The Capitanes (A10 pair) serve their entire cargos. Attendance reaches three to five thousand. One of the two largest fiestas of the year. Unique pattern of ritual from August 8 to August 11 (and beyond for those cargoholders who take Santo Domingo to the fiesta of August 15 in Ixtapa). Volunteers very active.

August 30, Santa Rosa: Flower-change, A2 pair sponsor. Change of A2 pair. Special activities of Mayordomos, with Ritual Advisors present. Ritual of "Killing of the Saints," at which Cannoneers are especially active.

September 8, Virgen de Natividad: Flower-change, A2 pair sponsor. Alferez round with change of B6 and B10.

September 21, San Mateo: Flower-change and simple fiesta, A6 pair sponsor.

October 7, Virgen del Rosario: Flower-change, A2 pair sponsor. Alferez round with change of B5 and B9. Special activities of A1 pair and moletik in Salinas (see Sunday Calendar).

October 18, San Lucas: Special trip of Santo Domingo to fiesta in town of San Lucas Zapotal, A6 pair sponsor. No activity in Zinacantan.

November 1, Todos Santos: Flower-change, A9 pair sponsor. Celebration of the chest of A9 pair. Special activities of the Mayordomos and Sacristans at the cemetery.

November 25, Santa Catalina: Flower-change and simple fiesta, A8 pair sponsor. Celebration of the chest of the A8 pair.

December 8, Purísima Concepción de María Santísima: Mostly a Ladino fiesta in which Ladinos change the flowers in the church. Sponsoring A2 pair responsible only for providing two bags of pine needles.

December 12, Virgen de Guadalupe: Special trip to Santo Domingo to fiesta in Navenchauc. (Sponsor not known.)

The Easter Calendar

The dates of most of the ritual activity that takes place between the end of January and the beginning of June each year in Zinacantan are set by the Catholic church calendar, which revolves around the observance of Easter. Since the day of the year on which Easter occurs varies from year to year, the dates of the fiestas also vary. The series of fiestas set by this calendar begins with Carnaval and ends with the Sagrado Corazon de Jesus.[4] In presenting the calendar I will include the dates as they were in 1962.

The Pasioneros (A4) serve their entire cargos during the period covered by this calendar. The Alcalde Shuves serves his cargo during Carnaval.

The Easter Calendar is as follows:

Carnaval (March 3 to March 6): Saturday through Tuesday. Very intense ritual activity involving the Mayordomos, Alfereces, and moletik, as well as the Pasioneros and Alcalde Shuves, who may be considered the sponsors.

Miércoles de Cenisa (March 7): A priest comes to say Mass and distribute ashes. The Mayordomos are invited to dance at the house of the Senior Pasionero after Mass.

Los Viernes: The Fridays of Lent are observed.

Primer Viernes (March 9): The Mayordomos and the Pasioneros change the flowers on the platforms that are used to carry the saints in procession. There is a procession of the Pasioneros, Mayordomos, Alfereces, and moletik through the church and the churchyard.

Segundo Viernes (March 16): The ritual is the same as on Primer Viernes, but only the senior cargoholders are present.

Tercer Viernes (March 23): The ritual is the same as on Primer Viernes, but only the junior cargoholders are present.

Cuarto Viernes (March 30): This is a large fiesta involving special ritual. Flower-change, A6 pair sponsor.

Quinto Viernes (April 6): The ritual is exactly like Primer Viernes.

Sexto Viernes (April 13): The ritual is exactly like Primer Viernes.

Flower-change (April 14): On the day following Sexto Viernes there is a flower-change, A9 pair sponsor.

Domingo de Ramos (April 15): On the Sunday following Sexto Viernes a Mass is said and palms are distributed.

---

[4] The periods involved for the years 1959 to 1962 are as follows (the first date is that of the Saturday of Carnaval, and the second is that of the Sagrado Corazon de Jesus, which always falls on a Friday): 1959: February 7 to June 5; 1960: February 27 to June 24; 1961: February 11 to June 9; 1962: March 3 to June 29.

Semana Santa: The week between Domingo de Ramos and Pascua de Resurrección has the following activities:

Lunes Santo (April 16): No formal activities. Mayordomos making preparations.

Martes Santo (April 17): A small procession.

Miercoles Santo (April 18): The holy elders[G] wash the Santisimo.[5]

Jueves Santo (April 19): Mass. Ritual reenactment of the Last Supper in which the priest takes the role of Christ and the Mayordomos take the roles of the Apostles.

Viernes Santo (April 20). Reenactment of the Crucifixion in the church of San Lorenzo. Holy elders have the principal roles. Large attendance.

Pascua de Resurreccion (April 21): Easter. Mass. The B2 and B3 invite all for sweet gruel after Mass.

Letanías Menores: On the sixth Monday after Easter begin the Letanias Menores.

Lunes de Letanias (May 28): A small procession.

Martes de Letanias (May 29): Celebration of the chest of the A5 pair.

Ascensión del Señor (May 31): Special ritual with the A2 Senior in a major role. Celebration of the chest of the A2 pair. Always falls on the Thursday after the Martes de Letanias.

Venida del Espíritu Santo (June 10): Special ritual with the B1 in a major role. The Alferez Santo Domingo and B1 give sweet gruel. Always falls on Sunday, the tenth day after Ascension del Señor.

Santísima Trinidad (June 17): Alferez round with change of B2 and B3. Special ritual.

Corpus Christi (June 21): Celebration of the chest of the A3 pair. Always falls on the Thursday after La Santisima Trinidad.

Sagrado Corazón de Jesús (June 29): Flower-change and simple fiesta, A3 pair sponsor. Special activities.

The Sunday Calendar

The Sunday Calendar involves the Mayordomo Reyes (A1) and the Mesoneros (A7) almost exclusively. Most of their ritual activity takes place on Sunday. As noted in Chapter 4, the moletik perform many of their administrative functions on Sunday also, but their ritual activity is spread over all three calendars.

The cargos of Mayordomo Rey and Mesonero last for the calendar

---

[5] The holy elders are six in number. They are usually men who have passed four cargos, or at least have passed Alferez Santo Domingo as a third cargo. They have important roles in the ritual of Semana Santa. The Santisimo is a life-sized image of Christ that is attached to a large cross during a reenactment of the Crucifixion on Viernes Santo.

year. The ritual described in detail in Chapter 6 is the basis of most of their activity. This pattern, which I will call a *simple Sunday*, is varied in two ways. The first is that of the *Mayor Sunday*, on which the Mayor de Salinas visits them in the chapel with his gift of salt. Such a visit involves a few added embellishments on the simple Sunday. The second is that of the *change-of-duty Sunday*. This takes place when the Senior Mayordomo Rey and the Senior Mesonero are replaced for a month of duty by the Junior Mayordomo Rey and the Junior Mesonero, or vice versa. The ritual at the chapel does not change, except that the incoming Mayordomo Rey and Mesonero are present while the outgoing ones perform the duties of their last weekend. After the ritual at the chapel, there is a formal transfer of the rosaries of the saint from the house of the outgoing Mayordomo Rey to the house of the incoming one.

Since all the swearing-in ceremonies are held in the chapel of the Señor de Esquipulas, the Mayordomo Rey and the Mesonero who are on duty at the time must attend.[6] For these occasions they take out the rosaries of the saint. The other ritual commitments of the Mayordomo Reyes and the Mesoneros, which are few, are listed in the calendar which is presented immediately below.

The Sunday calendar is as follows:

December 30: Starting in the evening and continuing all through the night, the following new officials are inaugurated: all the moletik (C and D), the A1 pair, and the A7 pair.

All Sundays in January before the fiesta of San Sebastian: All these Sundays (through January 20) are simple Sundays. All four cargoholders (A1 pair and A7 pair) are present.

First Sunday after the fiesta of San Sebastian: The pattern of service that holds through the entire year begins this Sunday. The Senior Mayordomo Rey and the Senior Mesonero serve the next four Sundays in the following rituals: First Sunday, Mayor; Second Sunday, simple; Third Sunday, Mayor; Fourth Sunday, change-of-duty. With the change-of-duty Sunday, the juniors take the duty for four weeks, following the same pattern. Then they are replaced by the seniors again, and so on. Each serves six such terms.

The remaining Sundays of the year: There may be one or two Sundays left in the year after the seniors and the juniors have each served six terms. They are served by both seniors and juniors. The Mayor de Salinas comes in his regular turn.

Other fiestas: The Mayordomos Reyes and Mesoneros are also involved

---

[6] All the cargoholders except the Mayordomos and the Capitanes are sworn in. That is, all second-, third-, and fourth-level cargoholders are sworn in, and, among the first-level cargoholders, the Mayordomos Reyes, Mesoneros, Pasioneros, and Mayores are sworn in.

in the following fiestas: Señor de Esquipulas, San Sebastian, Cuarto Viernes, Semana Santa, Corpus Christi, San Juan, San Lorenzo, Virgen del Rosario, and Navidad (Christmas). The Mayordomos Reyes make an elaborate and expensive trip to Salinas alone for the fiesta of the Virgen del Rosario.

Visits to Salinas: Besides their trip for the fiesta of the Virgen del Rosario, the Mayordomos Reyes make three visits to Salinas to bring gifts to the Mayor de Salinas. The visits are made after the fiestas of San Sebastian, San Juan, and Navidad, which represent the beginning, middle, and end of the year.

Oath of Office for Senior Alcalde Viejo

The following text was recorded in Tzotzil and translated into English by Robert Laughlin. I am grateful to him for permission to use it here. This oath is also used for the swearing-in of the Junior Alcalde Viejo, the Regidores, and the Mayores.

The outgoing Senior Alcalde Viejo addresses his replacement:

Ah beloved ancient father,
has your earth arrived,
has your mud arrived,
here beneath the foot,
here beneath the hand,
of Señor Esquipula,
beloved ancient father?
What else should we do?
What else would we do?
The sun has risen,
the hour has arrived.
Here you will receive,
here you will possess,
the lord, the divine holy oath,
beneath the foot,
beneath the hand,
of Señor Esquipula,
beloved ancient father.
You will receive your humble name,
you will receive your humble
    nomination,
for twelve months,
for twelve days.
Will you serve
Will you witness?
Will you sin,
will you do evil,
beneath the foot,
beneath the hand,
of Señor Esquipula,
beloved ancient father?

Will you be a worthy servant?
Will you be a worthy witness?
Have you seen,
have you looked,
as I have seen,
as I have looked?
Is your father not alien,
is your mother not alien?
You give them their burden,
you give them their overburden,
beloved ancient father.
So it enters your foot,
so it enters your hand,
the divine holy oath.
Beneath the foot,
beneath the hand,
of Señor Esquipula,
beloved ancient father.
For this we talk together,
for this we move our lips.
Will you remember your lowly
    incense,
will you remember your lowly
    smoke,
beneath his foot,
beneath his hand?
Your lowly pine,
your lowly candles,
beneath the feet,
beneath the hands
of Señor Esquipula,

beloved ancient father,
and the holy martyr,
the holy creditor,
beloved ancient father.

Let us be one,
let us be two.
You are my father,
you are my mother.

The incoming Senior Alcalde Viejo replies:

Ah beloved ancient father,
do you wait for my humble earth,
do you wait for my humble mud,
with Señor Esquipula,
beloved ancient father?
I have entered beneath the foot,
I have entered beneath the hand,
of Señor Esquipula,
beloved ancient father.
I have come to possess
the divine holy oath,
beloved ancient father.
Will I be a worthy servant,
will I be a worthy witness,
for twelve months,
for twelve days?
If my father is not alien,
if my mother is not alien.
I give them their humble burden,
I give them their humble overburden.
If I have seen,
if I have looked,

as you have seen,
as you have looked,
as you have served,
as you have witnessed,
beloved ancient father.
For this we will talk together,
for this we will move our lips.
If I remember my humble incense,
if I remember my humble smoke,
in one evening,
at one dawn,
on one Saturday,
on one Sunday,
beloved ancient father.
For this it enters my foot,
for this it enters my hand,
the divine holy oath,
beloved ancient father,
We are one,
we are two.
You are my father,
you are my mother.

Glossary: English, Spanish, and Tzotzil Words

ENGLISH GLOSSES USED IN TEXT FOR TZOTZIL WORDS

English Gloss	Tzotzil Word (some loans)	Spanish Gloss
cannoneer	hten kamaro	
curer	hʔilol	curandero
drink	poš	aguardiente
elder	mol	anciano
hamlet	parahel	paraje
holy elder	čʼul mol	
general helper	hčʼomil	ayudante
junior	ʔiȼʼinal	menor
musician	hvabahom	musico
musicians of the	ya hvabahom	musicos de los
alfereces	ʔalperesetik	alfereces
ritual advisor	totil meʔil	
ritual kinsman	kumpare	compadre
sacristan	piškal	sacristán
scribe	ʔiškirvano	escribano
senior	bankilal	mayor
special helper	hmakbalal	
special musicians	ya hvabahom mukʼtik htoykʼin	
swearing in	huramentu	juramento
sweet gruel	ʔul	atole
jaguar	bolom	
town hall	kavilto	cabildo
women's advisor	meʔel	viejita

ENGLISH GLOSSES USED IN TEXT FOR SPANISH WORDS

English Gloss	Spanish Word
civil government	ayuntamiento constitutional
cold country	tierra fría
hot country	tierra caliente
new incumbent	entrante
old incumbent	saliente
sponsor	encargado
temperate country	tierra templada
township	municipio

TZOTZIL NAMES FOR CARGOS

The Tzotzil phrase *martomo —— bankilal (ʔiȼ'inal)* is equivalent to "mayordomo —— senior (junior)" as I use it in the text. The Tzotzil phrase *ʔalperes* —— is equivalent to "alferez ——" as I use it in the text.

All the Spanish names listed in Table 2, Chapter 4, and all the Tzotzil names listed immediately below are in common usage except those for the Alferez Divina Cruz. It is called *kahvaltik rioš* in ordinary conversation. The name Alferez Divina Cruz is known only by the very Ladinoized. On the waiting lists, where names of all cargos are written in Spanish, Alferez Divina Cruz is recorded as Alferez Dios ta čul Cruz.

The names are listed below in the order used in Table 2.

First Level	*Second Level*	*Third & Fourth Levels*
šan čavaščan	šan čavaščan	sčanvaʔal rehirol
sanantonio	santa roša	yošvaʔal rehirol
hč'ulmeʔtik	san hacinto	sča'vaʔal rehirol
santa krus	samporo martil	rehirol mayol
santo rominko	sanantonio	bik'it ʔalkalte
sakramentu	sorirat	muk'ta ʔalkalte
mešon	santorenso	ʔalkalte šuves
martomo rey	šan čavaščan	
č'ulmeʔtik	nativirat	
mayol	rosario	
valalupa	san hose	
mešon	trinirat	
martomo rey	kahvaltik rioš	
pašyon	santo rominko	
kapitan		
mayol		

In keeping with the attempt to make the body of the text straightforward reading for the nonspecialist, I have used more conventional transliterations of Tzotzil proper names there. Thus, Shun in the text would be Šun in the orthography used here.

Bibliography

I. References Cited

ADAMS, RICHARD N., ed.
1957 Political changes in Guatemalan Indian communities: a symposium. New Orleans, Middle American Research Institute, Tulane University.

AIKEN, HOWARD et al.
1955 Tables of the cumulative probability distribution. The Annals of the Computation Laboratory of Harvard University 35.

BARBER, BERNARD
1957 Social stratification. New York, Harcourt Brace.

BORHEGYI, STEPHEN F. DE
1954 The cult of our lord of Esquipulas in Middle America and New Mexico. El Palacio 61:387–401.

BUNNIN, NICOLAS
1963 The flower industry in Zinacantan. Columbia-Cornell-Harvard-Illinois Summer Field Studies Program in Mexico. Mimeo.

CALNEK, EDWARD
1961 Distribution and location of the Tzeltal and Tzotzil pueblos of the highlands of Chiapas from earliest times to the present. University of Chicago. Mimeo.

CANCIAN, FRANCESCA
1960 Functional analysis of change. American Sociological Review 25:818–27.

CANCIAN, FRANK
1963 Informant error and native prestige ranking in Zinacantan. American Anthropologist 65:1068–75.

1964 Some aspects of the social and religious organization of a Maya society. Actas y Memorias, XXXV Congreso Internacional de Americanistas, Mexico, 1962, 1:335–43.

1965 Efectos de los programas económicas del gobierno Mexicano en las tierras altas Mayas de Zinacantan. Estudios de Cultura Maya 5 (in press).

n.d. Political and religious organizations. *In* Handbook of Middle American Indians, Vol. 9, Manning Nash, ed. (in press).

CAREY, SUSAN
1962 Ladino society in Teklum. Columbia-Cornell-Harvard-Illinois Summer Field Studies Program in Mexico. Mimeo.

CARRASCO, PEDRO
1961 The civil-religious hierarchy in Mesoamerican communities: pre-Spanish background and colonial development. American Anthropologist 63:483–97.

EARLY, JOHN D.
1965 The sons of San Lorenzo in Zinacantan. Ph.D. dissertation, Harvard University.

EDEL, MATTHEW D.
1962 Zinacantan's ejido: the effects of Mexican land reform on an Indian community. Columbia-Cornell-Harvard-Illinois Summer Field Studies Program in Mexico. Mimeo.

FALLERS, L. A.
1961 Are African cultivators to be called "peasants"? Current Anthropology 2:108–10.

FOSTER, GEORGE M.
1960 Culture and conquest: America's Spanish heritage. Viking Fund Publication 27.

LEYES
1959 Leyes del estado de Chiapas, primer tomo, texto integrado incluyendo todas las reformas hasta la fecha. Mexico, D. F., Graficos Galeza.

MOSCOSO PASTRANA, PRUDENCIO
1960 El Pinedismo en Chiapas. Mexico, D. F.

NAGEL, ERNEST
1956 A formalization of functionalism. *In his* Logic Without Metaphysics. Glencoe, Ill., Free Press.

NASH, MANNING
1958 Political relations in Guatemala. Social and Economic Studies 7:65–75.
1964 Capital, saving and credit in a Guatemalan and a Mexican Indian peasant society. *In* Capital, Saving and Credit in Peasant Societies, Raymond Firth and B. S. Yamey, eds. Chicago, Aldine.

POZAS, RICARDO
1959 Chamula: un pueblo indio de los altos de Chiapas. Mexico, D.F., Memorias del Instituto Nacional Indigenista 8.

REDFIELD, ROBERT
1941 The folk culture of Yucatan. Chicago, University of Chicago Press.

ROGOFF, NATALIE
1953 Recent trends in occupational mobility. Glencoe, Ill., Free Press.

SIEGEL, SIDNEY
1956 Nonparametric statistics. New York, McGraw-Hill.

SNELL, JOHN E., RICHARD J. ROSENWALD, AND AMES ROBEY
1964 The wifebeater's wife. Archives of General Psychiatry 11: 107–12.

STAUDER, JACK
1961 Zinacantecos in hot country. Columbia-Cornell-Harvard-Illinois Summer Field Studies Program in Mexico. Mimeo.

TAX, SOL
1944 Information about the municipio of Zinacantan, Chiapas. Revista Mexicana de Estudios Antropológicos.
1953 Penny capitalism: a Guatemalan Indian economy. Washington, D.C., Smithsonian Institute of Social Anthropology 16.

VAN DEN BERGHE, PIERRE L., AND BENJAMIN N. COLBY
1961 Ladino-Indian relations in the highlands of Chiapas, Mexico. Social Forces 40:63–71.

VOGT, EVON Z.
1961a Some aspects of Zinacantan settlement patterns and ceremonial organization. Estudios de Cultura Maya 1:131–45.
1961b Chapter on the Navaho. In Perspectives in American Indian culture change, Edward H. Spicer, ed. Chicago, University of Chicago Press.
1964 Some implications of Zinacantan social structure for the study of the ancient Maya. Actas y Memorias, XXXV Congreso Internacional de Americanistas, Mexico, 1962, 1:307–20.
1965 Ceremonial Organization in Zinacantan. Ethnology 4:39–52.

WOLF, ERIC R.
1955 Types of Latin American peasantry: a preliminary discussion. American Anthropologist 57:452–71.
1957 Closed corporate peasant communities in Mesoamerica and Central Java. Southwestern Journal of Anthropology 13:1–18.

YOUNG, ALLEN
1962 Mexico's federal corn warehouses in highland Chiapas. Columbia-Cornell-Harvard-Illinois Summer Field Studies Program in Mexico. Mimeo.

ZABALA CUBILLOS, MANUEL
1961a Sistema económico de Zinacantan: estructura económica de nivelación. Unpublished dissertation, Escuela Nacional de Antropología e Historia, Mexico, D. F.
1961b Instituciones políticas y religiosas de Zinacantan. Estudios de Cultura Maya 1:147–58.

II. *Other Works on Zinacantan*

ACHESON, NICHOLAS H.
1962 The ethnozoology of the Zinacantecan Indians. Mimeo.
BLANCO, MERIDA H. AND NANCY J. CHODOROW
1964 Childrens' work and obedience in Zinacantan. Ditto.
BRICKER, VICTORIA REIFLER
n.d. Zinacanteco patterns of humor. Ph.D. dissertation, Harvard
      University (in preparation).
CANCIAN, FRANCESCA M.
1963 Family interaction in Zinacantan. Ph.D. dissertation, Harvard
      University.
1964 Interaction patterns in Zinacanteco families. American Socio-
      logical Review 29:540–50.
COLBY, BENJAMIN N.
1960 Social relations and directed culture change among the Zina-
      cantan. Practical Anthropology 7:241–50.
1960 Ethnic relations in the highlands of Chiapas, Mexico. Ph.D.
      Dissertation, Harvard University.
1961 Indian attitudes towards education and inter-ethnic contact in
      Mexico. Practical Anthropology 8:77–85.
1964 Elements of a Mesoamerican personality pattern. Actas y Me-
      morias del XXXV Congreso Internacional de Americanistas,
      Mexico, 1962, 1:125–29.
———, AND PIERRE VAN DEN BERGHE
1961 Ethnic relations in southeastern Mexico. American Anthropol-
      ogist 63:772–92.
COLBY, LORE M.
1964 Zinacantan Tsotsil sound and word structure. Ph.D. disserta-
      tion, Harvard University.
COLLIER, GEORGE A.
1963 Zinacantan color categories. A.B. Honors Thesis, Harvard Col-
      lege.
FISHBURNE, JANE
1960 Some aspects of the division of labor in a Zinacantan household.
      Mimeo.
1962 Courtship and marriage in Zinacantan. A.B. Honors Thesis,
      Radcliffe College.
LAUGHLIN, ROBERT M.
1962 El símbolo de la flor en la religión de Zinacantan. Estudios de
      Cultura Maya 2:123–39.
1963 Through the looking glass: reflections on Zinacantan courtship
      and marriage. Ph.D. Dissertation, Harvard University.

n.d. The Tzotzil. *In* Ethnology of Middle America, Vol. 8, Handbook of Middle American Indians, Robert Wauchope, ed. (in press).

n.d. Tzotzil-Spanish Dictionary (in preparation).

SILVER, DANIEL B.

n.d. Shamanism in Zinacantan. Ph.D. dissertation, Harvard University (in preparation).

TAX, SUSAN

1964 Displacement activity in Zinacantan. América Indígena 24: 111–21.

VOGT, EVON Z.

1964 Ancient Maya concepts in contemporary Zinacantan religion. VIᵉ Congres International des Sciences Anthropologiques et Ethnologiques, Paris, 2:497–502.

1964 Ancient Maya and contemporary Tzotzil cosmology: A comment on some methodological problems. American Antiquity 30:192–95.

1965 Zinacanteco "souls." Man 29:33–35.

1965 Structural and conceptual replication in Zinacantan culture. American Anthropologist 67:342–53.

n.d. The Chiapas highlands. *In* Ethnology of Middle America, Vol. 8, Handbook of Middle American Indians, Robert Wauchope, ed. (in press).

n.d. The Maya. *In* Ethnology of Middle America, Vol. 8, Handbook of Middle American Indians, Robert Wauchope, ed. (in press).

n.d. Ancestor worship in Zinacantan. Actas del XXXVI Congreso Internacional de Americanistas, Madrid, 1964, (in press).

n.d. Zinacantan: a Maya community in highland Chiapas (in preparation).

VOGT, EVON Z. (ed.)

n.d. Ensayos sobre Zinacantan. Colección de Antropología Social, Instituto Nacional Indigenista, Mexico (in press).

WARFIELD, JAMES P.

1963 House architecture in Zinacantan. Mimeo.

ZIMBALIST, MICHELLE S.

1963 The corn fields: a study of the social structure of the Grandilla, a Milperia paraje. Mimeo.

Index